Civility in Business and Professional Communication

PETER LANG
New York • Washington, D.C./Baltimore • Bern
Frankfurt am Main • Berlin • Brussels • Vienna • Oxford

Rod L. Troester and Cathy Sargent Mester

Civility in Business and Professional Communication

PETER LANG
New York • Washington, D.C./Baltimore • Bern
Frankfurt am Main • Berlin • Brussels • Vienna • Oxford

Library of Congress Cataloging-in-Publication Data

Troester, Rod L..
Civility in business and professional communication /
Rod L. Troester, Cathy Sargent Mester.
p. cm.
Includes bibliographical references and index.
1. Business communication. 2. Organizational behavior.
3. Communication in management. I. Mester, Cathy Sargent. II. Title.
HF5718.T758   395.5'2—dc22   2006100659
ISBN 978-0-8204-8653-6 (hard cover)
ISBN 978-0-8204-8652-9 (paperback)

Bibliographic information published by **Die Deutsche Bibliothek**.
Die Deutsche Bibliothek lists this publication in the "Deutsche
Nationalbibliografie"; detailed bibliographic data is available
on the Internet at http://dnb.ddb.de/.

Cover design by Lisa Barfield

The paper in this book meets the guidelines for permanence and durability
of the Committee on Production Guidelines for Book Longevity
of the Council of Library Resources.

Acknowledgment

ROD L. TROESTER

In a world that is constantly changing, certain things should and do remain constant. This is not to say that they can be taken for granted. Civility should be one of those enduring values, but one that certainly requires our cultivation and attention. I have been blessed with the support and encouragement of family throughout my career. For 26 years, my wife and children have put up with me and allowed me the time to pursue the profession I love. I am grateful to almost 30 years of students who have taught me as much as I have taught them. A final constant has been the colleagues and friends with whom it has been my pleasure to work and play, especially Cathy Sargent Mester who is the model of the teacher-scholar. Cathy, many thanks.

CATHY SARGENT MESTER   ·

In my professional life, I have been privileged to have had the opportunity to meet three extraordinary individuals who taught me the benefits, the costs, and the necessity of having the courage to speak in ways that promote a more civil and peaceful society. Those three are Mary Lou Kownacki, OSB, Robert E. Alexander, and George Sample. I thank them for the inspiration and model of their own lives in this important work.

In addition, for their patience in bearing with my long hours away from home while working on this project, I thank my husband, son and daughter. Finally, I owe a debt of gratitude to the faculty in Communication and Media Studies at Penn State Behrend, especially my co-author, Rod Troester, who are a constant source of inspiration.

Special thanks to Amanda Kifer for her photographs which add clarity and life to this book.

Table of Contents

PART TWO: APPLICATIONS TO THE CONTEXTS OF
BUSINESS AND PROFESSIONAL COMMUNICATION

Preface

Books are born of a desire to pass important ideas along to others. We believe that through our research in civil communication, we have learned some incredibly important ideas that we now happily share with you. *Civility in Business and Professional Communication* has a reach and a message valuable to anyone who regularly uses communication in the transaction of business. In addition, we offer it as a primary or supplementary text appropriate to introductory courses in business and professional speaking, organizational communication and specialized courses in civil communication.

Why the civility focus? It's really fairly simple—civil communication works! From philosophical, rhetorical and organizational perspectives, there is solid evidence that civil communication leads to greater goal achievement in interpersonal, public and mediated settings. Attitudes of respect and behaviors reflecting them will result in more successful professionals, more pleasant and productive businesses and even a more peaceful and livable society.

This commitment to civility as an important core societal value is based in part on our experience with the Janet Neff Sample Center for Manners and Civility, a teaching and research institute here at Penn State Erie, The Behrend College. Endowed by publisher George Sample, the center's mission to encourage and enhance civility within the college community and beyond. As a successful business professional, Mr. Sample's passion and belief is that civility, respect, and manners separate the ordinary from the extraordinary.

We thank you for your use of this book to carry on that mission.

1

Civility, Communication,

and Commerce

Our society is increasingly lacking in civility! Who hasn't heard that asser-
tion in recent years? From homeowners complaining about litter thrown
into their yards to business leaders upset about employee use of vulgar language to foreign heads of state speaking about American insensitivity to their
cultures—the hue and cry is widespread.

But there are many things our society is lacking—adequate health care,
hurricane protection, homes for stray animals, and so on. Why so much public distress over a lack of civility? The general understanding of the concept
of civility is rather lightweight, after all. Many think of *civility* as just a glo-
rified term for "manners." As such, it has the image of being something nice
to have, but not really a necessity—a little like Grey Poupon mustard.

But, as we use the term here, *civility* encompasses concepts and attitudes
far more significant than the notion of manners. In its broad sense, civility

is most definitely a necessity and its absence a cause for concern.

Civility is the first domino in a chain of events that culminates in business productivity, successful personal relationships, intercultural cooperation, and personal and global peace. By observing more consistent patterns of civility in all relationships, we improve our local and global communities in ways that allow groups to come together to solve the other problems in our society. Civility is the key.

In the chapters that follow, we will explore the nature and scope of civility, both broadly and as it applies to the specific operations of commerce. The beneficial results of civil communication in interpersonal relationships are extensively addressed in books and articles both in the popular and academic press. The economic advantages of civility are less well known, but vital to understand if we are to begin the reversal of incivility in our society. Thus, we will focus on the communication theory in which civility is grounded and apply that theory and philosophy to the specific contexts of business and professional communication. Let's begin with the basics.

Defining *Civility*

Definitions are important starting points for any discussion, but are always troubling to derive. After all, definitions should be definitive, shouldn't they? Ironically, they are not. Instead they always represent a particular writer's value-laden perspective. This is especially true, of course, for the more abstract terms such as *truth, beauty,* and, alas, *civility*. To a great extent it refers to what the speaker or writer wants it to mean. Consequently, we often find ourselves arguing or talking past each other, thinking that we disagree about concepts when actually we are just using the term differently one from another.

Let us then take a look at how the term *civility* is used in everyday parlance and how it has been defined by philosophical, rhetorical, and business scholars. This will lead us to a working definition to be held in mind in considering all its ramifications and implications later in this text.

Popular Parlance

As we hear the term *civility* used by individuals who are not caught up in its finer defining points, it is clear that the term is perceived as both a catch-all label and as a minimum standard of behavior. We say that we admire a particular person because of his "civility," or we angrily accuse another of lacking "civility." The term has even been used to describe automobiles that handle particularly smoothly.[1] It is no wonder that some scholars allege the existence of considerable conceptual confusion about the actual definition of *civility*.[2]

Centuries ago, when philosophers first began to discuss the lack of civility in commerce and public life, they too struggled for an adequate definition. Chapter 3 presents a more detailed explanation of their quandary. But what about the twenty-first century's perspective?

The common usage today implies that *civility* may refer to general standards of etiquette, manners, decorum, or politeness. There are recommendations for following standards of civility on airplanes, in classrooms, in concert halls, on sports teams, and, especially, in workplaces. The apparent meaning intended seems to be a set of basic behaviors that show respect for others sharing our space and provide for smooth accomplishment of whatever goals are applicable in that space.

New employees are often instructed about a company's "civility" standards. For instance, bank tellers are instructed to thank every customer by name at the completion of their transactions; grocery clerks are instructed to show respect when addressing shoppers of diverse ethnic origins; manufacturing supervisors are told they should never use profanities when speaking to their employees. The professional sports team that establishes a dress code for its players is using a "civility" standard.

We are expected to understand the meaning of civility outside the workplace as well. A perfect example exists at Chautauqua Institution, a famous cultural and educational center, which informs its thousands of summer visitors that they are to observe civility standards when attending performances and lectures there. While specific actions are listed as being discouraged according to these standards, the concept of civility itself is not directly explained. As in many other situations, it is assumed that the concept is fundamentally understood.

However, many people use the word *civility* in a less positive light.

There is the sense in some common usage, unfortunately, that the civility standard is an artificially adopted guideline, observed only by sycophants. For instance, we often hear a person arguing with another say in exasperation, "You could at least be civil!" The sense of the term's usage in this case is that civility is a minimum standard of voiced respect to be followed, no matter what a person's actual attitude is. In other words, civility is coating angry or unkind attitudes in respectful language just to get a shared task done.

Congressman Steven Israel, in reestablishing a Congressional Civility Caucus, suggested that the Washington political establishment thinks of civility as not requiring much more than addressing one another as "the honorables . . ."[3] It is this perception of civility as lip service that confuses the concept, at best, and demeans it at worst. The latter is evident in the observation of columnist Eric Alterman that "by insisting on 'keeping things civil' in polite society, repressive powers may suppress ugly truths about their conduct merely because raising them requires bad manners."[4] By this definition, civility should be avoided!

One business consultant takes a middle ground by endorsing the negative definition while encouraging job seekers to practice civility anyway. "Civility means treating each co-worker with respect and compassion, even if the co-worker deserves neither."[5]

A similar perspective is evident in two definitions of *civility* offered by scholars who see civil communication as purely utilitarian and not requiring sincerity. These scholars actually argue *against* promoting civility because of what they see as its artificial nature. Lynne M. Andersson and Christine M. Pearson report that some think of civility as "a source of power; an acceptable ploy for gaining social advantage."[6] While certainly this is a minority view, it is a perspective worth incorporating into any complete definition of the term. Substitute the word *strategy* for the word *ploy* and you have a more objective definition that probably most of us would accept.

The second negative definition of *civility* as it is used in common conversation is offered by Randall Kennedy, who posits in his "Case against Civility" that civility is "a willingness to conduct oneself according to the socially approved rules even when one would like to do otherwise."[7] This definition rightly suggests that civility is about behavior and attitude. All the scholars would agree with that. Where this author differs from the more broadly endorsed perspectives is in his suggestion that one could practice the civil behaviors in the absence of a civil attitude. The relationship between civility as attitude and civility as behavior is an important issue we will explore further later in this chapter.

Finally, we hear the concept of civility referenced in popular parlance by implication as people use the adjective form *civil* to label respect-based actions. Civil court, for instance, hears charges of one person disrespecting the rights or property of another without actually committing a criminal act. *Civil rights* is another phrase couched in an assumption that all persons deserve relatively equal forms of respect—in the workplace, in education, in transportation, in housing, in health care, and especially in the voting booth. It is worth noting that "civil" rights law emerged from the seeds sown by "civil" disobedience. Clearly, disagreement and civility are somehow compatible concepts.

This brings us to a key juncture. *Civility* is used commonly as if everyone understands the same thing by it. Yet there is clear evidence that that is an unfounded assumption. Many have tried to alleviate the conceptual confusion by codifying civility and, thus, defining it.

Codes and Rules

Beginning in the eighteenth century B.C. with Hammurabi, there is extensive evidence of human efforts to define civility by breaking it down into a concrete set of rules. You are identified as civil if you follow the rules or codes. In this instance, we are not talking about actual laws that enforce certain standards of civility, but rather the attempts to define what is expected of civil persons.

Such efforts are manifested in the codes of ethics endorsed by various professional organizations and businesses. Whether your company produces energy, semiconductors, insurance policies, peanut butter, locomotives, herbal supplements, air filters, or cigarette filters, there is a code of conduct governing your behavior on the job. Professionals in banking, training and development, law, medicine, stock trading, education, real estate, and many other fields are guided by their associations' ethical standards. Civil communication is a part of all such codes.

One of the most interesting sets of rules defining civility is the document known as "Washington's School Exercises: Rules of Civility and Decent Behaviour in Company and Conversation."[8] This was a list of

108 standards allegedly written repeatedly by George Washington in a personal effort to make civility a habit. He promised himself and expected of others, for instance, to "sleep not when others speak" and to "be not angry at table, whatever happens." These rules find modern translations in several manners books written for children and teens. The rules are sufficiently extensive to constitute a definition without Washington ever specifically offering one. He clearly believed civility to be an attitude of respect for others and for place that was manifested in specific polite behaviors.

Similarly extensive are the rules of diplomatic protocol codified by departments of state in most "civilized" countries. We expect our national representatives, be they diplomats or high school exchange students, to act in a civil manner when representing the country. To make sure that everyone understands what is meant by a "civil manner," rules are written out. Who stands where in the receiving line, who sits where at the dinner table, how a guest's title is to be used are all decisions that have been reached by government officials and again, collectively, define civility.

Perhaps the ultimate articulator of civility as a set of rules would be Emily Post. In her work, she considers civility to be "a code of behavior, based on kindness and consideration."[9] She proceeds from that definition to lay out an extremely extensive list of the rules making up that code. Often updated, but never fundamentally changed, her etiquette guides are a standard for many individuals and organizations.

The highly formulaic rules known as "Robert's Rules of Order" govern and guide civil behavior in business meetings.[10] Curiously enough, this code, intended to guarantee respectful consideration of diverse positions, was developed for the British Parliament, a body long famous for the outrageously *uncivil* conduct of its members during deliberations. The rules clearly state that a member must be recognized by the chair in order to speak, but that doesn't seem to have stopped some members from actually throwing a chair when their ideas were criticized!

The notion of civility as it relates to a set of rules is embodied in the definition offered by the Drucker Foundation, a nonprofit grant agency supporting civility programs in schools and communities. The foundation's definition reads: "Manners are the rules of social behavior; civility is respect for others."[11] Again we see the idea that civility refers to underlying attitudes which are manifested in observable behaviors.

That dual identity is nicely spelled out in one organization's professional code of conduct. The Financial Executives Association of the Philippines (FINEX) asks its members annually to sign a pledge to operate with "honesty and fairness" and specifically states that this expected civility is defined as "the virtue or trait of not doing anything to intentionally harm or cause harm to a fellow human being—especially in word or deed. Simply put, civility refers to the act of manifesting respect for a fellow human being."[12]

Some definitions of *civility* do tend to focus on attitude more than behavior. Some, however, are quite behavior-specific.

Observable Behaviors

In fact, there are many students of civility who would define the term solely in terms of observable behaviors. This is the "if it walks like a duck and talks like a duck, it is a duck" school of definitions. In fact, the earliest known proponent of civility, Erasmus of Rotterdam, defined *civility* as "outward bodily propriety,"[13] confining his discussion to specific physical behaviors.

In the much-heralded *US News and World Report* story of recent surveys on declines in American civility, the term was defined as the "physical recognition of the dignity of the other."[14] In other words, civility is an action of the body, the face, and gestures that reflects a respectful regard for other persons. This was the definition used by respondents to the magazine's civility survey, which revealed that such physical behaviors were not as common as many would like.

Students recently asked to cite behaviors that conformed to their meaning of *civility* had no trouble generating a long list. Items such as quiet cell phone conversations, leaving generous restaurant tips, unhurried merging behavior on the highways, being on time, and holding doors for persons behind you were typical of the behaviors listed. In their view, persons who regularly exhibited such behaviors were persons they would call "civil." No further definition was needed.

British author Lynn Truss's latest best-seller focuses on the flaws she finds in British conduct. In *Talk to the Hand*, she refers to those civil behaviors so lacking in society as "overt appeasement strategies."[15] That's an interesting take! She seems to align herself with the school of thought that civility is merely a practical necessity, not a desirable virtue. Yet she proceeds to list many specific behaviors that, if adopted by more people, would make British society more civil. So, while her specific definition is a negative attitude, she applies that definition to specific, wished-for behaviors.

Some other writers have simply identified civility as "observing community standards," an apparently observable act. Others see civility as "conveying respect to peers and superiors." The suggestion here is that while civility might involve unseen attitudes, its real nature is evidenced in that which can be seen: observable behaviors.

A more theoretical work, Pat Arneson and Ronald Arnett's *Dialogic Civility in a Cynical Age*, interestingly also defines *civility* in terms of physical action. They identify civility as that "communicative behavior that offers a sense of grace."[16] This is a particularly interesting definition because of the inclusion of the idea of grace, a term with religious associations. If we act in a way that offers "grace," a religious interpretation would suggest that we are treating the other with a degree of honor and a willingness to forgive. That interpretation would be compatible with the general understanding of civility as behaviors grounded in an attitude of respect.

Attitudes

It is that attitude that is key to many others' definitions of *civility*. While there is considerable difference of opinion about what specific observable behaviors ought to constitute civility—do I sit or stand when a lady enters the room?—there is general agreement that the behaviors should be those that most observers would interpret as "respectful."

Whether we are following a set of rules just for appearances' sake, or following the rules from a sense of sincere dedication to their validity, or committing specific civil behaviors, all that we have done that others have labeled "civility" is based in a perceived or actual attitude of respect for others. As such, civility is a communication construct, having to do with the symbols we use to share ideas and opinions with others.

It is interesting that *communication* and *commerce* spring from the same root word referring to working together. It follows that the only way

Table 1.1: Incivility-Civility Continuum of Behavioral Manifestations

←Incivility . . . . .Civility→

Violence against persons	Deliberate damage of others' goods or reputation	Yelling, harassment or intimidation,	Gossip, arrogance, or condescension	Ignoring others	Acknowledging others	Open-minded listening	Using respectful terms of address	Selflessness in everyday encounters	Self-sacrifice for the common good

that either can be done well is if there is mutual realization of the nature of the others and a desire to connect, so to speak, with one another. Many would call such a realization an attitude of respect, or civility. Often, business is described in terms of competitiveness—one company succeeds by beating another in the marketplace. But that is not the foundation of commerce. Its foundation is working *together*—hence the relevance of civility.

Gandhi called it *ahimsa*. A tenet common to several Eastern religions, *ahimsa* is the "eradication of our natural tendency to injure or harm another person."[17] While some practitioners take the meaning in the extreme and become vegetarians to "avoid injury" to any living being, Gandhi focused the definition on a selfless treatment of other people. In referring to our "natural" tendencies to harm others, Gandhi suggests another characteristic important in any definition of *civility*: the characteristic of being a *learned* set of behaviors. In that sense, he shares the perspective discussed earlier that civility is action. Gandhi's addition to that angle is that one can and should learn a set of actions that show an other-centeredness. So, instead of greeting one's guest politely in order to profit personally from the relationship, Gandhi taught followers to greet one's guest politely out of respect for his or her personhood. This is the civil attitude most conducive to productive relationships. If it sounds familiar to you, look back at the code of ethics for the Financial Executives Association of the Philippines.

Many other philosophers and rhetoricians echo Gandhi's sentiment.

Their writings are full of phrases like "unselfishness" and "the common good." This is getting us toward a definition of *civility* that is more aptly described as "multifaceted" rather than "confusing." A continuum of behavior might best clarify those facets.

The respectful attitude underlying behavioral civility is something that some individuals seem to possess from early in life, while others learn it through their life experiences. This book exists because the attitude can and should be learned. Certainly the behaviors manifesting that attitude can also be learned, but are best learned in the context of a respectful attitude. Just playing the civility game for personal gain actually reflects *dis*respect for others. Therefore, that sycophant's view of civility will not be a part of the concept as used in this text.

Summary

From the philosophical to the historical and sociological, civility as a concept has been defined and interpreted in a variety of ways. Many define only what civility is *not*. We have examined those points of view and noted some similarities and common threads, leading us to a working definition that provides a useful framework for our consideration of civility in the business world as discussed in the chapters that follow.

We suggest a simple understanding of civility that involves both attitude and action. We will speak of civility as **the set of verbal and non-verbal behaviors reflecting fundamental respect for others and generating harmonious and productive relationships.** Whether the user labels such behaviors with the word *civility* or not, it is those behaviors that we will mean as we use the word *civility* in this text.

As such, civility is observable, practical, diverse, and virtually a necessity in today's business world.

NOTES

1 David Booth, "Road Test," *Canadian Underwriter*, Summer 2004, 58.

2 Jon Hess and Michelle Kleine, "Popular and Scholarly Conceptions of Civility: A Closer Examination of a Widely Misunderstood Communication Ideal" (paper presented at the annual meeting of the National Communication Association, Boston, 2003), 17.

3 Steve Israel and Timothy V. Johnson, "Plea from within Congress: Let's Be Civil for a Change," *USA Today*, January 10, 2005, 13A.

4 Eric Alterman, "What Would Dewey Do?" *The Nation*, May 23, 2005 (available at: http://www.thenation.com/doc/20050523/alterman).

5 Marilyn Moats Kennedy, "Monitor Your Attitude, Manage Boss' Expectations," *Marketing News*, May 15, 2004, 54.

6 Lynne M. Andersson and Christine M. Pearson, "Tit for Tat? The Spiraling Effect of Incivility in the Workplace," *Academy of Management Review*, Spring 1999, 452–471.

7 Kennedy, op cit.

8 George Washington, "Washington's School Exercises: Rules of Civility and Decent Behaviour in Company and Conversation," *The Papers of George Washington*, 1744 (available at: http://www.virginia.edu/gwpapers/civility/transcript/html).

9 Peggy Post and Peter Post, *The Etiquette Advantage in Business* (New York: HarperCollins, 1999).

10 Henry M. Robert, *Robert's Rules of Order, Revised* (Chicago: Scott Foresman, 1951).

11 Frances Hesselbein, "The Power of Civility," Peter F. Drucker Foundation, Summer 1997 (available at: http://www.drucker.org).

12 Amelia H. C. Ylagan, "Corporate Watch," *BusinessWorld: Manila*, October 4, 2004, 1.

13 Norbert Elias, *The Civilizing Process* (New York: Urizen Books, 1931), 53.

14 Steve Farkas and Jean Johnson, "Land of the Rude: Americans in New Survey Say Lack of Respect Is Getting Worse," Grantee Press Release: Pew Charitable Trusts, April 3, 2002.

15 Lynne Truss, *Talk to the Hand #?*! The Utter Bloody Rudeness of the World Today or Six Good Reasons to Stay Home and Bolt the Door* (New York: Gotham Books, 2005).

16 Pat Arneson and Ronald Arnett, *Dialogic Civility in a Cynical Age: Community, Hope and Interpersonal Relationships* (Albany: State University of New York Press, 1999).

17 Ask Gandhi. 2005. kamat's potpourri. (available at http://www.kamat.com/mmgandhi/ahimsa.html)

2

Communication Theory

and the Civility Connection

If you read the want ads from almost any newspaper in the country and analyze what employers are looking for in their new hires, you will likely find that most listings include some variation of the statement "strong communication skills required." A search of the popular online job search site Careerbuilder.com using the phrase *effective communication skills required* resulted in 160 pages of job listings, or more than 11,000 posted job descriptions, that included these terms—within the past thirty days. Clearly the world of business recognizes, requires, and values "effective communication skills."

There are also volumes of survey and anecdotal evidence suggesting the importance of communication skills in securing jobs, working within organizations, and climbing the corporate ladder. More specifically, the communication skills businesses seem to require are those which promote civil interaction among employees and between employees, clients, and vendors.

If one "Googles" the terms *communication* and *civility*, you would receive in the neighborhood of 2.7 million "hits." Apparently, not only are communication skills important in business and professional settings, but those skills combined with civility are particularly valued.

This chapter will explore what we're talking about when we use the phrase *effective communication skills* in the context of business and professional settings, as well as connect these business-essential skills to the concept of civility. Specifically, this chapter will examine a basic definition of *communication*, the contexts in which communication takes place in business and professional organizations, communication models and the component parts of the communication process, the characteristics of the communication process, the two key message systems used to communicate, the common goals and purposes communication serves in businesses and organizations, and finally an approach to determining the effectiveness or competence of a business and professional communicator. As you will see, civility can and should play an integral role in each of these various aspects of communication.

Defining Communication

As was the case with defining *civility*, precisely defining *communication* can be a challenge. Years ago, scholars like Frank Dance wrestled with the problem and suggested at least fifteen distinct ways that the term could be conceptualized.[1] In every communication textbook, there will likely be a somewhat different definition of the word offered, reflecting the unique perspective being advocated by the authors. While there is considerable diversity in approach and perspective, definitions of *communication* usually focus on several common characteristics, including: the exchange, transfer, and/or negotiation of meaning between people; the use of verbal and nonverbal sign and symbol systems; some sense of purpose, intention, and/or goals to be achieved; the notion of communication being a dynamic process; and some sense or measure of success or effectiveness. A simple working definition of *communication* is: the exchange of verbal and nonverbal messages and the creating, interpreting, and negotiating of meaning from those messages by their users to achieve certain goals in certain situations. Communication, in all of its various forms, is concerned with message-related behavior.[2] For our purposes here, we are also concerned with how this message-related behavior can and should be shaped through an attitude of civility and respect.

Communication Contexts

In order to make studying the broad field of communication more manageable and understandable, communication is normally broken down into the contexts or the situations in which it takes place. This context approach tends to focus our attention on the number of people involved in the communication but should also draw our attention to the differences in the complexity of communication that occur as the number of people involved increases and the situation changes. Keep in mind that each of the communication contexts described here has a unique and extensive body of theory and research associated with it. Depending on your background and whether or not you have taken previous communication coursework, you may already be familiar with some of these contexts, so our treatment here will be brief.

The most basic and fundamental communication context is that of **intrapersonal communication.** While we would likely be suspicious and cautious if we encountered someone literally carrying on a conversation with themselves, intrapersonal communication is something we all do. We all talk to ourselves. Think of all the times you have talked yourself into doing something, silently argued or debated the pros and cons of a particular decision, rehearsed an important presentation before you delivered it, anticipated what you would say in a job interview, or silently strategized before asking your boss for a raise or pitching a new client. In all of these examples, you were communicating intrapersonally.

This internal dialogue or conversation is a prime time to consider the civility connection with communication—as you are planning or preparing to communicate. In addition to thinking about what you are going to say, you should also be thinking about how the message can be shaped and phrased to be clear, effective, and civil—respectful of the other person.

The **interpersonal communication context** is the second and perhaps the most common context in which communication takes place in business and organizational settings. Interpersonal communication usually refers to communication between two people. The term literally means *inter,* or between, persons. Examples of interpersonal communication would include a variety of interview situations, one-on-one meetings with potential clients, casual conversations between coworkers, briefing the boss on the status of a new project, or meeting with a coworker to gather and coordinate needed information for an upcoming presentation.

Normally we distinguish communication contexts based on the number of people involved. However, in the case of the interpersonal communication context, it is both the number of people involved (usually two) and the complexity of the communication that distinguishes this context. There is considerable difference between the interaction that takes place between two close friends and the polite "hello" exchanged with a total stranger or between interviewee and interviewer or superior and subordinate. While the number of people involved in each of these situations remains the same, the nature and complexity of the communication significantly different because the people involved know each other in different ways. The roles people play and the relationships they share help shape the interaction that takes place. The longer the duration and the more developed the relationship, the more personal, unique, and detailed the communication can become. While civility is important with strangers and acquaintances, civility and respect is particularly important for intimate person-to-person, interpersonal relationships.

Expanding to the **small-group context** of communication, the numbers game continues to distinguish the context. Small groups are generally considered to involve between three and twelve individuals. Examples of small groups in businesses and organizations would include staff meetings, committee meetings, project groups, total-continuous quality improvement groups, ad hoc task forces, company sports and recreation teams, as well as the coworkers who regularly meet for lunch.

Even as the number of participants increases from two to three people, the complexity of the interaction increases considerably because the number of two-person relationships that must be taken into account and considered increases. For example, not only does Joe need to account for and consider his relationship with Jan (interpersonal communication), but now there is Harold who must be taken into account. Further, consider what happens if Joe and Jan form a coalition or alliance to exert pressure on Harold? Clearly, the nature and dynamics of the interaction change as the number of people involved increases. A simple equation illustrates the geometrically increasing complexity of small-group communication as the number of people involved grows: the number of relationships = $((N-1)\,2) \div 2$, where N = number of people. As the number of group members increases, the complexity of the communication and the demand for effective communication skills increase. Civil communication skills can help to ease and smooth the interaction that takes place among members in groups and contribute to the success and effectiveness of the group.

Beyond the small-group context is **public or presentational speaking,** one person speaking uninterrupted to many. Thousands of presentations and speeches take place in businesses and organizations every day. Examples of these include new employee orientation sessions, training and development seminars, briefings on current projects and proposals for new projects, sales presentations to clients, representing the company to local civic and community groups, and ceremonial and motivational presentations within the organization. In some cases, these presentations are internal—one member speaking to other members of the organization—and in other cases they are external to the organization—one member acting as a spokesperson for the organization to external audiences.

It would be easy to think of this public context as a one-way form of communication—a speaker talking to an audience—but such an assumption is simplistic and flawed. While it may be true that the speaker is primarily responsible for crafting and sending the message, there is and should be considerable feedback from the audience to the speaker and awareness of this feedback on the part of both speaker and audience in order for effective communication to take place. Additionally, the fact that a person is speaking "in public" places certain societal expectations on the speaker to be civil.

When the one-to-many context of communication becomes mediated **via radio, television, and electronic communication,** additional complexities are created. While there are organizations that use "broadcast" forms of traditional mass communication, the most common mediated form of communication within an organization is computer-based message systems. Computers, email, voicemail, and the Internet are as ubiquitous in the contemporary organization as typewriters, paper memos, and switchboards were years ago.

Examining communication through the contexts in which it takes place provides a convenient means for analyzing and studying communication in business and professional organizations. So when we talk about effective communication skills in organizations, we are talking about communication skills related to intrapersonal, interpersonal, small-group, and speaker-audience contexts. Regardless of the context in which communication takes place, civility can and should play a crucial role in shaping the message-related behavior that takes place. From interviewers representing their company to prospective employees, to salespersons pitching their products and services to clients, to managers supervising a project team, to CEOs motivating employees or facing the media, messages shaped by an attitude of civility and respect ought to be the norm. Not only should communication behavior be civil because it is the right or nice thing to do, but also because an attitude of civility can make the communication process more successful.

Communication Models

So what does the communication process look like exactly? Because communication is a dynamic, not static, reality, the best way to envision it is graphically via a model.

The best models depict communication as a collection of component parts that, when properly arranged, organized, and connected, reveal the dynamics of communication between people. These "arrangement of the component parts" models draw upon a mechanistic comparison suggesting that, like a machine, communication involves individual parts working sequentially together. While somewhat simplistic, these models are illustrative and useful in understanding communication processes. Such models trace their origins to some of the earliest efforts to understand the communication process suggested in the 1940s by Claude Shannon and Warren Weaver, who were primarily interested in understanding communication in the form of telephone connections.[3] The list of component parts used in most of these models includes the following seven components: a sender or source, the message, a channel, a receiver or destination, feedback, noise or interference, and an environment or situation.

The **sender or source** initiates the formulation of a message, which generally has an intended purpose or meaning as well as an intended receiver or audience. The process used to formulate a message can also be referred to as **encoding**—taking an idea and coding it using verbal and nonverbal symbols. Intrapersonal communication as described before certainly helps to shape this coding process. The **message** is composed of words and nonverbal elements that are organized and arranged in such a way as to convey the sender's intended idea.

The **channel** is the connection between the sender and receiver by which the message is conveyed or through which the message travels. When communicating with someone face-to-face, sound waves and light waves, as well as our ability to literally touch the other, "connect" sender and receiver and allow for the sending and receiving of verbal and nonverbal messages. Increasingly, business professionals are using various electronic channels, both the wired and wireless variety, to connect with other people.

The **receiver or destination** is the target audience, the person(s) to whom senders wish to convey their message. It is the receiver's role to select, hear, attend, assign meaning to, and remember—in other words, to listen to—the message. This process is also referred to as **decoding**.

Using just these first four components (sender-message-channel-receiver), in its simplest form, communication has taken place—assuming the sender has "connected" with the receiver through the channel, and each has coded and decoded the message. If only these first four components are included, the model would represent communication as a one-way phenomenon. Adding the **feedback** component or a feedback loop portrays communication as a circular or two-way process. Assuming receivers listen, they are in a position to respond or provide feedback to the sender reflecting their interpretation of and response to the message. This feedback, literally feeding information back to the sender, casts communication as a two-way rather than a one-way phenomenon. As the receiver provides feedback, in effect, the receiver becomes the sender, and the roles of sender and receiver are reversed.

This very traditional approach to the communication model also includes **noise or interference** as an important variable and component part of the process. Noise affects the message, the channel, and/or the senders and receivers. We know that noise in the message—confusing words or grammatical constructions, difficulty hearing or seeing the sender, or the physical environment (uncomfortable chairs or background sound)—can compromise the success and effectiveness of communication by diminishing the fidelity of the channel. We also know that noise *inside* the sender or receiver—preoccupation with other matters, mental fatigue, stress—can compromise the effectiveness of the communication process.

Finally, models typically reflect that communication takes place in a physical, social, and cultural **situation or environment** that shapes how the process can and will take place. For example, communication that takes place inside a classroom is shaped by the arrangement of the chairs in the room, the fact that it is a classroom, and the social relationship created and developed by instructor and student. This last idea, the relationship between the participants, is sometimes referred to as the **communication climate** or the quality of the relationship that exists between sender and receiver.

Likewise, communication that takes place within a business is shaped by the physical features of the organization, the fact that it is a business or professional setting, and the competitive business environment in which the organization exists. Cultural factors also become an important consideration. Not only does the organization create and develop its own unique character and culture, but organizations are becoming more culturally diverse and their members are increasingly required to interact with people from other cultures to compete in a global marketplace.

When assembled, properly arranged, and correctly organized, these seven components or elements can be used to clarify the communication process. See figure 2.1.

Each of these communication components or variables can be examined in terms of civility. An attitude of civility on the part of the sender ought to shape the way messages are crafted and constructed. Both the verbal and nonverbal parts of the message ought to reflect civility and respect for the receiver. Selecting the best channel for sending the message can be shaped by a civil attitude. Ideally, the sender will perceive the receiver with respect and value. The simple act of acknowledging a message by providing feedback is an act of civility. Taking time to consider reducing those noise factors under one's control affects the civility of the communication process. Taking into account the environment and situation in which the communication takes place and the relationships that exist or are being created, and how messages will shape

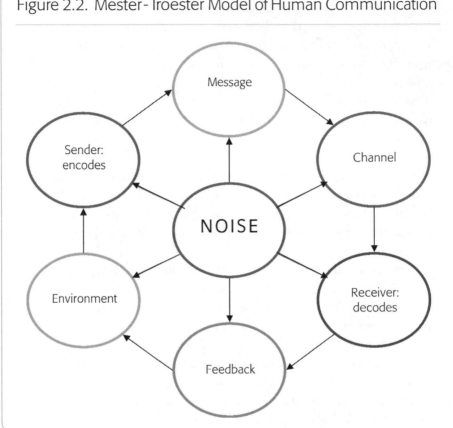

Figure 2.2. Mester-Troester Model of Human Communication

those environments, situations, and relationships ought to be motivated by civility. In short, civility should be considered the eighth component part or variable in the communication process.

Communication Principles

Moving this model from the printed page to depict the dynamics of communication as we actually "talk" to someone requires an understanding of four key principles: (1) communication as process, (2) communication as unavoidable, (3) communication as irreversible, and (4) communication as unrepeatable.

When we say that **communication is a process**, we are referring to the idea that, while the exchange of messages takes place in a specific time and place, that exchange is shaped and influenced by all of the things that precede the current interaction and will shape things that will follow the current interaction. We never start completely from scratch when it comes to communication—there is always a relationship or message that went before, something that we are doing now, and a relationship or result that will follow. Communication is something we do in the here and now, realizing that the here and now is shaped by the past, and that the present will shape the future. For example, the way you greet your friend after class will be influenced by what each of you said during class and will have an impact on how you respond to one another later in the day. When we say communication is a process, we mean that communication is a dynamic, evolving, ever-changing, past-present-future-oriented phenomenon.

Suggesting that **communication is unavoidable** may sound a bit confusing. If I don't say or do anything, how can I be communicating? What if not saying something is perceived by someone as being ignored? Not responding to a smile, a casual greeting, or an email message can, in fact, be interpreted as a message to the sender. While the origin of the phrase is unclear, and grammarians may cringe when they hear it, communication scholars like to suggest that "one cannot, not communicate."[4] Essentially what this principle of communication suggests is that so long as we are in perceptual or sensory contact with another person, we can assign meaning to his or her behavior or lack of behavior regardless of whether it was intended, conscious, or directed at us. Stated a different way, we cannot not behave. Apart from the grammatical awkwardness and interesting philosophical implications of this statement, it is important to remember that while our behavior can be intentional and purposeful as well as unintentional and random, someone can perceive that behavior to be meaningful. Any time we are present in a situation with another person, the potential exists for that person to assign meaning and intention to our behavior.

Anyone who has ever said something in anger or haste can understand the principle that **communication is irreversible.** The criminal defendant who breaks down on the stand and confesses under the prosecutor's intense cross examination cannot later withdraw the impact of that confession. How many times have you wished—sometimes at the moment of expression—that you could retrieve your own words? Once sent, messages cannot be unsent. Communication is an always forward-moving process. In many cases, no amount of explanation or apology can repair the damage the initial message exchange inflicted.

Related to this is the principle that **communication is unrepeatable.** While we can say exactly the same words in the same way to the same person, we never get the opportunity for what a young child might refer to as a communication "do-over." Because communication is a dynamic process, the initial message—rightly or wrongly, for good or for ill—makes an impression on the receiver that cannot be undone. When we are in public, our behavior—civil or otherwise—can and will be perceived by those around us. With thought and care, we can seek to shape that first impression. A civil initial message is much more effective than a civil apology once the damage has been done.

Taken together, these four principles illustrate that communication is a dynamic and future-oriented message-related behavior that can be perceived by those around us regardless of our intention or purpose, and that cannot be undone. We get many chances to behave, and our behavior becomes a part of the ongoing phenomenon that is communication.

Message Systems

There are basically two means by which we can communicate a message. There is a verbal message system comprised of words and all the component parts of language, and there is a nonverbal message system comprised of all the nonword, nonlanguage means by which we communicate.

The verbal message system involves the actual words we use, and the grammatical and syntactic construction and combination of these words to convey our ideas, and the various contextual features allow us to formulate and interpret the meaning or significance of the message. The nonverbal message system involves all of those nonword, nonlanguage means and behaviors that also enable us to convey ideas.

We live in a world of objects and things, a tangible world; we also live in a world of ideas and abstractions, an intangible world. Both of these worlds are made accessible and communicative through the symbols with which we label them. Both things and ideas can become the topics or objects of communication. As senders encode and receivers decode, the verbal and nonverbal message systems serve as the means by which we exchange, transfer, and/or negotiate meaning between and among people.

Key to understanding the nature of symbols is the representational nature of symbols. The easiest way to understand this idea is to think of symbols as *re*-presenting rather than *presenting* ideas. Symbols are at least one step removed from that which they represent. When you ask a coworker to bring you a wrench, you are using the verbal symbol "wrench" to label a three-dimensional object needed to tighten pipe fittings. You use the word as a shortcut, assuming that the other person will interpret it as referring to the exact object you meant. General semanticists (scholars concerned with the study of the relationship between language and behavior) would use the idea of a ladder of abstraction to move from the concrete world of things to the abstract world of ideas. With each step up the ladder, we get farther away from the concrete-tangible world and closer to the abstract-intangible world. Another way to understand the representational nature of symbols is that in the presence of the symbol we tend to think about the object that symbol represents; in the presence of the object, we tend to think of or recall or think of the symbol.

The question of how symbols come to mean or represent is important. Why is it that we associate or connect certain words—symbols—with certain objects or ideas? As we grow up, we seem to have a natural desire to name the things around us. Spend some time with an eighteen- to twenty-four-month-old child and you will find they want to know "What's that?" As they begin to organize and make sense of their world, they are asking what symbol is used to represent a particular thing. Gradually, they move beyond the simple naming of objects to the naming of ideas and feelings. Anyone who has seen the movie or play *The Miracle Worker*, about Helen Keller, knows the importance of these connections between words and things. We all come to associate symbols with things and ideas.

This process of association or connection between symbols and objects was clearly represented years ago by Charles Ogden and I. A. Richards in their "Triangle of Meaning."[5] The three sides and corners of the triangle "connect" a referent, the object; a symbol, the word; and a reference process, our thought process. The thought process is at the top of the triangle; at the bottom are the object and a symbol. Connecting the object and the symbol at the bottom of the triangle is a dotted line representing or "standing for" the idea that the connection between the two is an arbitrary connection made in our minds—and only in our minds. Using Ogden and Richards's triangle and what it represents, there is no inherent or natural connection between the object book (the thing you are reading with covers and pages) and the symbol "book" (four letters arranged in a certain way) that we commonly associate with the object book. In other words, there is an arbitrary connection between the symbol and that which it symbolizes—the object or idea. These thought or referential processes have been under construction and development in each of us literally since we began asking "What's that?"

Then there is the nonverbal message system, which includes all the more physical means of communication at our disposal by which we convey messages. These means would include: appearance (dress and grooming); gestures; facial expressions and eye contact (oculesics); spatial relationships (proxemics); movement and posture (kinesics); tone of voice (vocalics or paralanguage); touch (haptics); and time (chronemics). Suffice it to say that there are multiple and powerful means by which we can communicate messages without—or in addition to—the use of words. Each gesture, glance, or garment is still a symbol representing an idea or attitude—a symbol chosen by the sender and interpreted by the receiver.

The ambiguity of both verbal and nonverbal symbols is particularly pertinent to our goal of communicating with civility. Since words and gestures mean different things depending on the person using them, the person receiving them, and the situation, observing standards of civility is going to be rather challenging. When I look up from my work, does my visitor find that look inviting or intimidating? Will my words be taken as sincere or sarcastic? Such are the concerns of the civil communicator.

The Functions of Communication

Thus far we have suggested a definition for *communication*, presented a model appropriate for examining the process of communication, explained several keys or principles that characterize communication, and introduced the two means or systems by which communication takes place.

Along the way, we have suggested the connection between communication and civility. Before suggesting a model or framework for examining communication effectiveness or competence, it is important to consider what communication does or contributes to businesses and organizations. The functions or goals of communication in the business and professional world can be divided into specific activities that communication allows us to do, and broader, more general ways that communication literally constitutes or constructs organizations.

Patricia Hayes Bradley and John Baird suggest four basic functions of communication in organizations: information exchange, idea and attitude imposition, evaluation and interpretation, and decision-making.[6] Clearly the simple exchange of information between and among members of an organization is important. Members of the organization need to know what is going on in the organization and must **exchange information** to accomplish the work of the organization. **Idea and attitude imposition,** more commonly referred to as persuasion, would be particularly important in fields like advertising, marketing, and sales. Minds must be changed, and persuasive messages are capable of achieving such adjustment and change. Information coming into the organization must also be **interpreted,** evaluated by the members of the organization. Organizations and their members must also learn, grow, and develop based on the processing of information. Finally, communication—the exchange and interpretation of messages—also serves a **decision-making function.** Members of organizations gather and distribute information, persuade and are persuaded by messages, educate and instruct through messages, and use all of these to make informed choices regarding the future of the organization.

In a much broader sense, Bradley and Baird and organizational theorists like Karl Weick argue that, fundamentally, communication behavior creates the organization, that organizations are constituted, constructed, and maintained through communication.[7] Without communication, there would be no organization. It is through the exchange of information, efforts at persuasion, the careful evaluation and analysis of information, and decision-making through communication that organizations are created and exist. All of these essential functions in organizations happen through people communicating.

The story of the origins of Gooseberry Patch, a successful online cooking and country décor business, is an illustrative case in point. Two

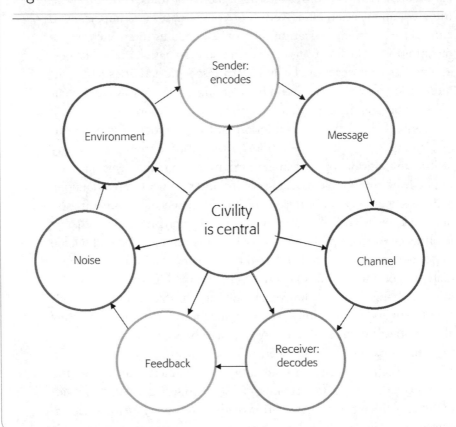

Figure 2.2. The Mester-Troester Model of Civil Communication

women started the business by chatting over their backyard fence. Their conversation gradually grew to include talks with investors, then technology people, artists, and craftspersons. Their whole mode of operation now is based on regular and frequent exchanges of ideas between their staff and their client base. The company truly would not exist without communication.

Communication Competence and Civility

Given the complexity and necessity of the process we have just described, it is obvious that communicators who operate from a civil perspective are going to be more successful than their opposites. Civil communicators are more competent communicators because they are better listeners and craft the verbal and nonverbal components of their messages with special sensitivity to the nature of their fellow communicators. A modified version of our earlier communication model will capture the essence of this perspective.

Civil communication competence begins at the affective level with attitudes of respect, valuing, and a degree of self-sacrifice toward others that begin to shape positive business and organizational environments. If organizational members respect coworkers and value their contributions, the organization is enhanced. Self-sacrifice in this context means that all organizational members should have a healthy respect for other people and realize that they also have needs and goals. Civil communication requires an understanding of and appreciation for the complexity of constructing the right message, verbally and nonverbally, for the right situation, given the nature of the relationship that exists. It is an attitude that recognizes the complex interplay of your needs, the other person's needs, and the needs of the relationship that exists between you. We are arguing here that civility and respect are also important to shaping the competent communicator.

Approaching communication situations in the business and professional world with an attitude of civility is of little use if we don't have cognitive skills to perceive—to see organizational situations and people in organizations with those civil attitudes. Understanding the verbal and nonverbal message systems we use to convey civility in organizations is also essential. Appreciating the importance of listening, responding, and feedback skills should also shape our communication thought processes. Being able to take culture into account, to embrace difference and diversity, and to be open-minded to the opportunity presented by cultural differences should guide our cognitive processes.

Finally, we must use these attitudes and cognitive processes to shape the way we interact in business and professional situations. They should guide the ways in which we construct messages.

Summary

This chapter began by suggesting that communication skills are essential in the business and professional world, from the interview that gets you your first job to climbing the proverbial corporate ladder. We have tried to build a foundation in basic communication theory in this chapter that will be expanded upon and clarified in the remaining chapters. By this point, you should realize that communication involves message-related behavior, takes place in a variety of different contexts within organizations, can be modeled and understood by examining relationships between and among its component parts, is governed by certain principles, requires an understanding of two key message systems, and serves essential functions in business and professional situations. If civility is **the set of verbal and nonverbal behaviors reflecting fundamental respect for others and generating harmonious and productive relationships**, then surely it imbues the best of business and professional communication.

NOTES

1 Frank Dance, "The Concept of Communication," *Journal of Communication* 20 (1970): 201–210.

2 John Reinard, *Introduction to Communication Research*, 3rd ed. (Boston: McGraw-Hill, 2001).

3 Claude Shannon and Warren Weaver, *The Mathematical Model of Communication* (Champaign: University of Illinois Press, 1949).

4 Theodore Clevenger, "Can One Not Communicate? A Conflict of Models," *Communication Studies* 42 (1991): 340–353.

5 Charles Ogden and I. A. Richards, *The Meaning of Meaning* (New York: Harcourt, Brace, and Company, 1946).

6 Patricia Hayes Bradley and John Baird, *Communication for Business and the Professions* (Dubuque, IA: Wm. C. Brown, 1980), 21–23.

7 Karl Weick, *The Social Psychology of Organizing*, 2nd ed. (Reading, MA: Addison-Wesley, 1979).

3

Civility in History

While many bemoan the seeming deterioration of civility currently and yearn for the more mannerly times recalled in our creative memories, the reality of history paints a different picture. Every few years, a new study is done by somebody to explore the popular perception that Americans, in particular, have become more rude. Indeed, the survey results do reveal that the public believes that to be the case. But: More rude than what or whom or when?

A visit to the history books reveals that in actuality there has been not a gradual decline in civility, but rather an ebb and flow in the standards used for civil behavior. A cyclical pattern is evident in which some eras were admittedly more genteel and others more crude than the civility levels so many lament today.

A similar pattern is evident in the level of civility typical within business and industry historically. All one has to do is look at the history of the U.S. labor movement to conclude that worker-friendly business standards have come and gone and come again as executives' apparent respect for their employees' contributions has fallen in and out of vogue. That is just one aspect of civility in the workplace, of course, but it is a revealing one.

We will take a quick trip through "civility-time" in this chapter to create a context for better understanding contemporary behaviors and their likely results. This should also put to rest the notion that our current cultural standards are a step down from those of our forebears.

Ancient Times

Humans were hunter-gatherers by origin. Those who succeeded (and became our ancestors) were those who learned to work cooperatively against common enemies. One caveman on his own did not fare well against a hungry invader, man or beast. But several working strategically in concert had a more satisfying result. So the value of cooperative effort, respecting the special talents of one's co-workers, is innate in our species.

Such cooperation sounds pretty civil. But it is important to keep in mind that this particular cooperative project frequently required the most uncivil act of all—violent execution of one's enemies. Incivility, then, was as much a survival skill as civility was.

Our ancient ancestors also originated the structures of what we now call organized society. Western-style democracy in which we institutionally show respect for everyone was founded in ancient Greece and Rome during the period of roughly 400 B.C. to A.D. 100. Constitutions were written, legislatures formed, and courts established all based on fundamental beliefs in the values of individual freedom and open public communication. Aristotle, Plato, Cicero, and their contemporaries all wrote about civil communication—without using that label, per se—as they addressed the value of understanding one's audience and adapting a message to its sensitivities and expectations.

It should not be surprising that one of the most enduring business practices, the handshake, also had its origins in these early days of human civilization. From the beginning, there was a need for some nonverbal sign of goodwill and trustworthiness among persons engaged in commerce. While an exact date of origin cannot be determined, it is universally acknowledged that the handshake as that symbol began when humans' traditional interactions involved battle.[1] The right hand extended with an open palm verified that the person was being greeted with respect, as the "clean" hand was used and no weapons were visible. Thus, business could be safely transacted.

Ancient times, of course, also marked the founding of the world's major religions. By about A.D. 600, Judaism had been joined by Christianity, Islam, Buddhism, and Hinduism in espousing that persons should live their lives by respecting others and sacrificing their own self-interest. Christians called this tenet the "Golden Rule." In various forms that principle was central to all the major religions and would, today, be called a standard for civility. We must note that, even from those early times, occasional incivility was also common in the name of religion as one group of believers sought to exterminate another, illustrating again the historical fluidity of civility standards.

The Middle Ages

This roughly six-hundred-year period could be fairly labeled a low point in the history of civility. Torture was commonplace; humans were bought and sold as chattel; coarse language was common (read Chaucer!), and public behavior showed little accommodation of the sensitivities of one's fellows.

Public urination and defecation were so much the norm that not even the dinner table was spared the indignity of satisfying one's needs for elimination. Can you imagine the business lunch in 1006? That lunch, by the way, would have been enjoyed by eating most food with one's hands and sharing a beverage via a common cup. The hand would have been wiped on one's sleeve before being proffered to seal the deal discussed over mutton and potatoes.

If you opted for a more cultured business or social outing, you would have taken a guest to the theater, where food also played an important part. Disapproval of any aspect of the production was shown by throwing food onto the stage during the performance.

The explorer Verrazzano noted another particularly uncivil display during his early explorations in the New World. Sailing up the eastern seaboard of what is now New Jersey and New York, his fleet was bade farewell by natives who turned their backs to the passing ships and mooned the crews![2]

The most unsettling display of incivility during this period, however, would have to have been those acts of atrocity committed by so-called

Christians. Chief among the atrocities were the Crusades. Armies of Christian believers of the Golden Rule systematically attempted to wipe out those who subscribed to its Islamic version. Other members of the church commonly demanded payment from sinners who asked for absolution or were dipping into the ecclesiastical till for their personal benefit. Still others were stirring up hatred and fear by burning suspected spiritualists at the stake.

Such abuse and corruption in the church ultimately (and thankfully) led two major contributors to the history of civility to make their mark. That would be Erasmus of Rotterdam and, later, Martin Luther.

Erasmus was actually the first to introduce the specific concept of civility in his writings. He decried the wayward drift of church leaders and pleaded for more peace-seeking behavior, which he emphasized as truer to the original meaning of the scriptures. Considered the "intellectual father of the Reformation," Erasmus was a humanist and superior scholar who abhorred violence and defended the moral freedom of individual human beings. His theoretical explorations of the concept of civility serve as the basis for much of the contemporary study in this field, even though the period in which he personally lived was highly uncivil. His work started the pendulum back up again.

Renaissance, Reformation, and Enlightenment

While historically distinct times, we will consider these three epochs as one due to their singular role in the evolution of civility. Philosophers in this period continued to call for humankind to embrace more con-sistently its respectful side. Thomas Hobbes used the word *manners* quite specifically in *Leviathan* (1651)[3] and joined John Locke in proposing that sacrifice of individual inclinations was sometimes necessary for societal good. Other writers referred to these natural inclinations toward selfish or coarse behavior in suggesting that civility was a means to "gain control" over such instincts. The degree to which such writers were still opposed by the institutional church was nowhere more evident than in the case of Milton, who was excommunicated for despairing over the Fall of Man.

If public opinion surveys had been as common in that time as they are today, surely the results would have vindicated Milton's position. Many both within and outside the church had reached the limits of their toleration of rampant incivility.

The evidence is present both in the development of Puritanism and in the creation of early rules of "courtesy." One approach was that of the government of Oliver Cromwell in England, which enforced a strict (some would say repressive) moral code based on fundamentalist Christianity and included a reformation of manners.[4] A second approach was the delineation of rules for mannerliness when in court—hence the term *courtesy*. The motivation behind these early civility standards, unfortunately, still bore the imprint of attitudes of incivility, for the rules were meant as much for enforcing class distinction as they were for conveying respect.[5] Since only a certain class of people was taught the rules at court, the mannerly were members of the upper class, who could easily identify and look down upon those of lesser station.

One of the interesting developments near the end of this period was the creation of tradecards. We know them today as business cards. As early as 1700 in London, however, they were commonly used prin-cipally as polite forms of advertising one's goods and services.[6] The cards also typically included small maps to the vendor's establishment, provid-ing a much more even-handed kindness than did the formal rules of courtesy.

Finally, the closing decades of this premodern era were notable in civility's history for the emergence of several important documents. The documents known as *Washington's School Exercises* and Lord Chesterfield's letters to his son, though intended personally, had rather significant public impact. In the case of the former, it is reported that George

Washington had such concern for "proper" behavior that he gave himself the assignment of delineating a set of rules, which he wrote repeatedly in order to commit them to memory. It included such admonitions as "When you Sit down, Keep your feet firm and Even, without putting one on another or crossing them." And "Kill no Vermin as Fleas, lice, ticks in the Sight of Others; if you see filth or thick Spittle, put your foot Dexteriously upon it. If it be upon the Clothes of your companions, put it off privately, and if it be upon your Cloths, remove it. Thanks to Him who puts it off."[7] The 110 rules he listed were widely circulated after his rise to fame.

Lord Chesterfield, on the other hand, wrote what has become known as the "turning point in the history of politeness" not for himself, but for his son. In a series of letters, he instructed his son on decorum, basing his instructions on the writings of Cicero. The letters were published posthumously in 1770, taking the form of an etiquette text, allegedly the first of its kind.[8]

The more public documents significant to this era were, of course, the founding documents of our republic. The Declaration of Independence,

Articles of Confederation, and, finally, the United States Constitution all embodied as central themes the rights of individuals, regardless of their diverse natures; the need to subjugate those individual rights when necessary for the greater good of the whole society; and the right of the people to codify standards of conduct related to the exercise of individual liberties. These themes are very consistent with the standards of individual civility as described by Washington and Lord Chesterfield.

It is ironic that while all these philosophers and statesmen were busily defining principles of respectful, civil interaction, there was still an array of highly uncivil acts fully tolerated by the public. Protestants were attacking Catholics and vice versa; slavery was in common practice; women's rights were negligible, and table manners continued to reflect a relatively slovenly style of eating. The table fork was invented sometime in the later part of this era, which undoubtedly made for tidier eating. But it was a slow learning curve.

Society's conflicted attitude toward civility was especially evident in regard to the institution of slavery. In the United States and elsewhere, men, women, and children were being bought and sold via often humiliating public auctions. The slave trade was a business in which profit was the sole motive. Slaves were kept in servitude with no regard for the ties of family and faith, with no hope of an opportunity to act upon their individual gifts and talents. Public debate at the time painted slavery as a civil institution because of how clearly it provided the same kind of class distinctions as the rules of court in Europe. Abolitionists, in fact, were considered *uncivil* for attempting (often via radical means) to eliminate those class distinctions.[9]

Was this the era that survey respondents believed to be more civil than modern society? I doubt it.

The Nineteenth Century

Perhaps some nostalgic lovers of civil behavior are hearkening back to the days of more recent history as described by their grandparents. "When I was a kid, I never spoke to my parents that way!" Indeed there were some remarkable moments of civility in the nineteenth century, but it certainly was still far from ideal.

The distance from the ideal in America was strongly stated by (who else but?) a British writer. In her 1828 *Domestic Manners of the Americans*, intellectual Fanny Trollope castigated Americans for their general level of disrespect and vulgarity.[10] Ironically, the book was written as a travel guide.

Perhaps Trollope had visited Harvard University in her research for the book. It is reported that college students were more than a little rowdy there, often "drowning out tutors' voices in the classroom and drenching people with buckets of ink and water." Not to be outdone, the students at arch-rival Yale University were "wont to express their displeasure with their tutors by stoning their windows and attacking them with clubs."[11] And these were the country's most prestigious universities.

The standard of behavior was not much better in Congress, where shouting down opposing voices was commonplace. One senator, Charles Sumner, was considered to have committed unnamed ethical breaches for which he was caned by his fellow senators on the floor of the Senate itself.[12]

Meanwhile, in England, the debate over standards of civil behavior continued to rage on. The Victorian era brought with it many strict codes of conduct that yielded, as an unintended by-product, increases in the general level of vulgarity. Extreme modesty in female dress and behavior was expected, for example, while prostitution rose dramatically.[13] The most noteworthy proponent of individual liberties, John Stuart Mill, was also a product of this era. His take on civility was that everyone should speak his mind, but in a way that did not offend others by diminishing their civil liberties.[14] This complex perspective touches the heart of the civility-incivility balancing act.

Technology as a medium of communication also made its appearance in the nineteenth century, beginning what would become an endless effort to balance its civil intentions with unintended uncivil side effects. Of course, the beginning of this technological revolution was the telephone. Invented in 1876, the telephone was in many businesses and public places within a few years, and in homes not long after.

The telephone seemed like such a good idea! It was meant to enable long-distance instant communication, saving enormous amounts of time and money. From the beginning, however, its utility and civility were suspect. The key to the public unease with telephones was that they would allow, facilitate even, a greater division in the social classes, since they were too expensive for everyone. Yet, eventually, everyone would need one. The device provided yet another way to silence the underclasses and to challenge authority by creating more open networks of communication.[15] Essentially, it was believed that the telephone would allow any and everyone to come into one another's homes without the obligation to observe the social niceties typical of a guest. You could come unannounced at inconvenient times, speak in any tone you felt like, leave abruptly, interrupt at will—all highly uncivil behaviors. You could even commit all these social sins anonymously. Such civility concerns are an interesting precursor of twenty-first-century communication technology.

The telephone also allowed an increase in uncivil acts that rise to the level of being criminal. As a Scotland Yard inspector warned in 1888, "no other section of the population avail themselves more readily and speedily of the latest triumphs of science than the criminal class."[16] His reference was to the use of the telephone by con artists, such as the one who called a banker allegedly from the banker's home to threaten violence to the family if a certain amount of money were not handed over. Of course, the money was given and the family found safe, there having been no one in the home who had used the telephone.

Simultaneous with the development of technology was a marked change in the nature of the American workforce. The latter part of the century was a time of flourishing immigration as well as the "Great Migration" as freed slaves moved into the northern industrial cities for work. Naturally, these paired events resulted in a greatly diversified workforce—a goal of many seeking workplace civility. Do not assume, however, that the changes were warmly accepted by business. In fact, pay by ethnicity was the norm, with immigrant Irish and Italians and migrating black Americans earning less per hour than other workers.[17] Racial segregation was also typical and affected the operations of schools and businesses alike. Businesses were still relatively small and not yet subject to organizational principles that would later be commonplace.

As you can see, in some respects the nineteenth century saw a "raising of the bar" in terms of civility standards. While individual freedoms were being promoted and expanded, there was a growing awareness that with such freedom come temptations to test its limits. Efforts were well under way, therefore, to clarify the line between civil communication and unacceptably uncivil behavior.

The Modern Era

With the expansion of the world of commerce in the twentieth century, we see increased attention to issues of employee rights and customer awareness that fall within the boundaries of civility. How employees speak to each other and how they are treated by the boss are key elements affecting commercial success, and ideas of the best way to do both were in considerable flux during this modern era.

Frederick Winslow Taylor, the "father of scientific management," was the Peter Drucker of the early part of the century, espousing business theories that others quickly adopted. His perspective was decidedly uncivil in terms of respect shown to employees, perceiving them as equivalent to replaceable parts in the machine of business. He put "little stock into the idea that workers could be motivated through anything but rational economic opportunity. He asserted that given the proper financial incentives, individuals would naturally exhibit appropriate behavior."[18] (If that were the case, today's professional athletes would be the most polite employees in the country.) His theories did not stand the test of time, but did influence the nature of business in that era.

The benefit of treating one's fellows with respect was getting broad treatment in a variety of other venues, however. Across the world, Gandhi had emerged as a spiritual leader teaching principles of nonviolence and mutual respect that impacted governments, businesses, and individuals alike. Deportment was a school subject taught regularly in elementary and secondary schools in many countries of the world. The driving force behind such classes was the Gandhian attitude that all of our fellow travelers through life deserve our respect, and respect is conveyed by a mannerly demeanor.[19] Learn and follow the rules of behavior in public and you will be happier and more successful.

Nowhere was that attitude more fully embodied than in the 1922 publication of Emily Post's first *Etiquette in Society, in Business, in Politics and at Home*.[20] Yes, this is the same book you have seen on the coffeetables of today's executives. It has been regularly revised and updated while still promoting the same philosophy of its origin: people who respect one another act politely and therefore have more successful relationships, both personal and professional. It was the Bible of civility.

By the early 1930s, much of the social divisiveness born from the elitist roots of codes of conduct came to a head. There were large and influential groups of Americans who felt overlooked or diminished in the nation's social contract and began to organize. Chief among these groups were the nation's blue-collar workers who organized themselves into trade unions committed to changing what they perceived to be management's insensitivity to labor.[21] "Business as usual" would be forced to change.

A far less civil group that reorganized during this decade was the Royal Knights of the Ku Klux Klan. Feeling their rights as white citizens to be newly threatened by laws promoting more equal treatment of all citizens,[22] the Klan recast itself into a political and social action group whose existence ultimately had terrible consequences for the civility of their communities.

Soon thereafter, those citizens opposed to the Klan's philosophy and seeking to reinstill more progressive standards for treatment of diverse citizens also began to formalize their organizations. In 1940, the Congress of Racial Equality was founded as the first such organization—a fraternity later joined by the National Association for the Advancement of Colored People, the Southern Christian Leadership Conference, and others.[23]

The civil celebration of diversity in the population was tested by several court cases during this period. The Supreme Court, for instance, was asked in *Chaplinsky v. New Hampshire* to consider whether the public use of obscene and profane words was a protected exercise of individual rights or not. They concluded that, under certain circumstances, such language was dangerously disruptive to public civility and would thus be illegal, subject to arrest and prosecution.[24] The public's right to civility superseded the individual's right to free expression.

Finally, the 1940s was, of course, a decade of war. The preeminence of public civility took a downturn during this period as the nation's security fears dominated. Our nation's lowest point as a bastion of civil liberties was the internment of over 100,000 Japanese Americans shortly after the attack on Pearl Harbor.[25] It is shameful enough that the government took this action. Our national shame, however, should be all the greater for the fact that the internment received virtually no public outcry. As a nation, we assented to the wholesale eradication of the individual rights of one ethnic group.

Similar security fears drove the social phenomenon of the 1950s known as McCarthyism.[26] It was a similarly shameful act for a nation that promotes civility. McCarthyism, after all, was an effort to silence persons having minority views—or even just suspected of having such views.

Business also was impacted by this sense of paranoia, moving during the decade to a more conformity-based set of standards instead of embracing individuality. Some say that an individual's professional success during this period was tied to a willingness to move wherever and whenever required and accept the conformity and homogeneity of corporate life.[27] It was a starched white shirt and necktie world, like it or not.

It is no wonder that the 1960s turned out the way they did. In many arenas, it was a revolutionary time. Civil rights activism was at its highest; the free speech movement launched in Berkeley spread across the country; hate crimes increased; equal opportunity legislation was enacted; and the phenomenon of the suburb became rampant, changing the country's sense of community forever.

Business was also revolutionized by new kinds of managers, who represented more respectful attitudes toward their employees and the customers. A strong example was Kenneth Iverson at Nucor, who instituted an innovative incentive program for workers while minimizing the number of managers. He believed that all employees should be treated equally with no special perks for middle- or upper-level managers. The result was what he called "team-based productivity," giving all employees a degree of ownership in the quality of the work produced.[28] The fact that the company was enormously successful as a result of these changes was not lost on other entrepreneurs and business leaders. This was the kind of civility our parents and grandparents said they wished would return.

But, alas, our national sense of civility standards started downward again due to the highly public ethical breaches of the Nixon administration. Suddenly, *expletive deleted* became a commonplace phrase. The increasing incivility in politics started a trend that we are still suffering from. It is interesting to note the prevalence of articles in business journals lamenting the decline in civil communication in politics—hundreds of mentions each and every year of the decade. Clearly, the nation's overall sense of civility is a concern to the business community.

The period of the late twentieth century is widely believed to have been a less inclusive, more self-indulgent time, contributing to a general reduction in civility. This was the era labeled the "me generation," in which many social programs saw reductions in their federal funding. The civil idea of self-sacrifice for the good of others was not particularly popular.

In reaction to this general attitude shift, many felt that it was time to legislate civility to some extent. The first form of hate-crime legislation, for instance, was suggested by an Anti-Defamation League manual published in 1981.[29] It offered wording that would eventually lead to an avenue for punishment-enhanced prosecution of crimes proven to have been motivated by ethnic- or gender-based hate.

The growing concern that civility seemed to be decreasing was, to a great extent, influenced by the revolution in electronic communication that began in the early 1980s. Two products entered the mass market at that time that have now become so ubiquitous that many believe we must have had them forever—the cell phone and the personal computer.

Recently a little boy asked his mother what kind of computer she had when she was in first grade. She amazed herself by realizing that neither she nor her friends used computers then—and she is only thirty years old!

In truth, IBM entered the personal computer market in 1981, and the World Wide Web came into existence ten years later. With this previously unimagined technology, it became possible to easily communicate with diverse people and information sources in the privacy of your own home. Like the telephone before it, it seemed like such a good idea. Families could keep in touch more regularly; business could be conducted more economically, and research could be updated instantaneously. With such advantages, it would seem that public civility might have been strengthened.

Not so! Research has revealed that while families and friends are able to contact each other more regularly, the civility of their exchanges has diminished.[30] The nature of the technology itself causes the user to be inclined to send off brief notes without much careful writing or proofreading. In addition, messages could easily be sent to multiple addresses simultaneously whether or not the initial writer intended them to. Consequently, a certain brusqueness began to permeate the new electronically connected family.

That is just the negative impact of electronic mail. The World Wide Web itself has also offered painfully extensive opportunities for incivility to become widespread. Any special-interest group can easily create a website. That applies equally to monasteries, small businesses, the American Cancer Society, the USO, and to the Ku Klux Klan. The Web is an equal opportunity playing field. Hundreds of hate groups now have electronic home bases from which they can spread their gross incivility with a click of the mouse.[31]

Just as the Scotland Yard detective noted in 1888, the developments in technology in the 1980s also provided opportunities for the criminal element. The con artist was given a grand new template for his craft. So while the personal computer was generally welcomed by individuals and businesses, on balance it did not benefit public civility.

As for that other revolutionary invention, Motorola introduced the first truly portable cell phone in 1983. But like the introduction of the first telephone a century earlier, it only contributed to existing class distinctions because at a ticket price of $3,000 few could afford the gadget.[32] That changed quickly, as we all know.

The cell phone, in particular, changed standards of civility by blurring the line between public and private space. Personal conversations could now be conducted in virtually any public area. The user could now be in a crowd of people, yet feel as though he or she were within a private bubble of space where only the person on the other end of the phone call could hear the conversation. Communicator anonymity of this sort generated new categories of civility insults.

In the midst of this technology revolution, business was changing as well. Technology changed the whole face of business, eliminating the need for many categories of workers, creating new categories, and giving birth to a truly global marketplace. New leaders emerged to drive this engine and contribute to changing civility in the workplace.

Max DuPree, CEO of Herman Miller, Inc. (a manufacturer of office furniture), was one such luminary in the decade of the 1980s. His philosophy was that all employees should be treated as partners in the corporate endeavor: "It is no mystery that organizations stand a better chance of reaching their potential when we bring the gifts of everyone to bear on reality than when an organization limits itself to the gifts of a few people at the top."[33] As a result of this enlightened philosophy, he saw his business's net worth triple in the decade, while employee absenteeism fell to an industry-leading 1% and employee turnover drop to half the national average. By the way, as of 2006, even though DuPree himself has long retired, Herman Miller continues to be in the top one hundred companies in the country and has now doubled its net worth since DuPree's time.[34]

The business of professional sports provides an opposite example from the late twentieth century, when a startling increase in incivility of the violent sort became commonplace. Fans and athletes alike frequently failed to demonstrate the "restraint of their baser instincts" that defines civility to some. College and professional sporting events, particularly hockey, soccer, football, and basketball, too often dissolved into brawls. Even the levying of significant fines by the sports' governing bodies failed to slow the tendency of fans and athletes to express their frustrations in violent ways.

So much progress happened in technology and industry in this single century that it is impossible to fully capture its essence here. Suffice it to say that there was not comparable progress in the establishment of nor adherence to a clear set of standards of civility. It was truly a century of ups and downs in that regard.

A New Century

With the dawn of the new century, the public's general sense of an absence of civility became headline news. At least two major studies were conducted, one by Pew Charitable Trusts and one by Ipsos Research, to test the degree to which the public felt we had become a rude nation. The conclusions were similar in reflecting the public's perception (rightly or wrongly) that America had become more rude.[35]

Coincidental with this increase in public concern for civility, various legislative and judicial actions were taken that clarified and codified desirable civility standards. The Senate held impeachment hearings for President Clinton because of his apparent sexual misconduct; the Supreme Court issued rulings about school dress codes; the Federal Communications Commission fined networks and individuals who breached the public trust with provocative images; officials of both the National Basketball Association and NASCAR imposed standards for language and dress for their athletes; "bad samaritan" laws were under consideration in several states that would punish passers-by who failed to help a fellow citizen in need; and several major cities attempted to establish civility codes for their business and civic leaders.

Summary

The civility-incivility balancing act rages on. As Lynn Truss says, "Basically, people have been complaining about the state of manners since at least the fifteenth century."[36] We are clearly not as civil as we could be, but, at least in America, we certainly have come an extremely long way from the days of slavery, torture, slovenliness, and predatory business practices. The bar keeps rising, you see, so that the grossest of incivilities are no longer common, making the slightest of incivilities seem more problematic than they would have been in previous generations.

Our concern here is what difference it makes. Business is always affected by the civility in society in general as it responds to market needs. But individual businesses are also even more significantly affected by their internal civility—the type of communication expected between employees, between employees and management, and between the company and its customers and vendors. History has proven that connection. We now need to understand the current level of civility expected generally and, particularly, in the business world as we seek to make the next era better than the past.

NOTES

1 Roman Archbold, "It Matters How You Shake It," 1994 (available at: www.fiveo-clockclub.com/articles/1994/12–94-Handsahake.html).

2 Edward Churchill, *European Settlement of the Mainland: The Story of Maine*. Maine Public Broadcasting Network, 2001 (available at: http://www,mainepbs.org/home-stom/transcript2.html).

3 Thomas Hobbes, *Leviathan or Matter, Form and Power of a Commonwealth Ecclesiastical and Civil* (Chicago: University of Chicago Press, 1952), 69.

4 Peter Gaunt, *Oliver Cromwell* (Washington Square, NY: New York University Press, 2004), 78.

5 *Webster's New Collegiate Dictionary* (Springfield, MA: G & C Merriam, 1961).

6 "Tradecards, 17th Century," *Business Card History* (available at: www.belightsoft.com/products/compuser/historytrade.php).

7 George Washington, "Washington's School Exercises: Rules of Civility and Decent Behaviour in Company and Conversation," *The Papers of George Washington*, 1794 (available at: www.virginia.edu/gwpapers/civility/transcript.html).

8 Jenny Davidson, *Hypocrisy and the Politics of Politeness: Manners and Morals from Locke to Austen* (Cambridge: Cambridge University Press, 2004), 8.

9 Meron Dillon, *The Abolitionists: The Growth of a Dissenting Minority* (DeKalb: Northern Illinois University Press, 1974), 45.

10 J. C. Simmons, *Star-Spangled Eden: 19th Century America through the Eyes of Dickens, Wilde, Frances Trollope, Frank Harris and Other British Travelers* (New York: Carroll and Graf, 2000), 124.

11 S. A. Holton, "After the Eruption: Managing Conflict in the Classroom," *New Directions for Teaching and Learning* 77 (1999): 59–68.

12 "Cheney Helps Drop Congressional Civility," *Erie Times News*, June 26, 2004.

13 G. M. Young, *Victorian England: Portrait of an Age* (London: Oxford University Press, 1957).

14 John Stuart Mill, *On Liberty* (Middlesex: Penguin, 1974).

15 Carolyn Marvin, *When Old Technologies Were New* (Oxford: Oxford University Press, 1988), 92–93.

16 Ibid.

17 W. Lloyd Warner and J. O. Low, *The Social System of the Modern Factory* (New Haven, CT: Yale University Press, 1947), 98.

18 A. J. Mayo and N. Nahria, *In Their Time: The Greatest Business Leaders of the 20th Century* (Boston: Harvard Business School Press, 2005), 35–36.

19 S. Beck, *Gandhi's Nonviolent Revolution* (Goleta, CA: World Peace Communications, 2005).

20 Emily Post, *Emily Post's Etiquette* (New York: HarperCollins, 1997).

21 Mayo and Nahria.

22 Kenneth Jackson, *The Ku Klux Klan in the City, 1915–1930* (New York: Oxford University Press, 1967), xi.

23 Henry L. Gates, Jr., and Cornel West, *The African-American Century: How Black Americans Have Shaped Our Century* (New York: Free Press, 2000), 259.

24 Alpheus T. Mason and William M. Beaney, *American Constitutional Law* (Englewood Cliffs, NJ: Prentice-Hall, 1972), 538.

25 Gregory Robinson, *By Order of the President: FDR and the Internment of Japanese Americans* (Cambridge, MA: Harvard University Press, 2001).

26 Mayo and Nahria, 181–183.

27 Ibid.

28 Ibid., 230–234.

29 Donald Altschiller, *Hate Crimes: A Reference Handbook* (Santa Barbara, CA: ABC-CLIO, 1999), 16.

30 Marina Krakovsky, "Caveat Sender: The Pitfalls of E-Mail," *Psychology Today* 37 (2004): 15–16.

31 David S. Hoffman, *Hate Group Recruitment on the Internet* (New York: Anti-Defamation League, 1995).

32 Edward N. Singer, *20th Century Revolutions in Technology* (Commack, NY: Nova Science Publishers, 1998).

33 Mayo and Naurif, 311.

34 "Herman Miller, Inc., Retains Top Spot in *Fortune's* 'Most Admired,'" February 22, 2006 (available at: http://www.hmhome.com/CDA/SSA/News/Story).

35 "AP/Ipsos Poll: The Decline of American Civilization, or at Least Its Manners," 2005 (available at: http://www.ipsos-na.com/news/pressrelease.cfm?id2827).

36 Lynne Truss, *Talk to the Hand #?*!: The Utter Bloody Rudeness of the World Today or Six Good Reasons to Stay Home and Bolt the Door* (New York: Gotham Books, 2005), 51.

4

Business Communication

Civility and Quality of Life

Now that we have some background about the nature of civility or civil communication, we need to establish its value in the business and professional work worlds. Almost weekly, a new survey is released or opinion glamorized that complains about the apparent lack of civility in the world and, especially, in American business. What's the big deal?

Well, the reason for the concern is that incivility hurts business and civility is beneficial to business. There is a clear relationship. Specifically, we can identify two reasons that more people ought to practice civility more often in the business setting: being civil enhances one's quality of life and being civil enhances the company's bottom line. While these two arguments are interrelated, the reasoning will be clearer if we address them in separate chapters.

Quality of Life: A Working Definition

The phrase *quality of life* is used frequently with reference to health issues, politics, community life, and many other arenas. "Her advancing arthritis is not life-threatening, but does affect her quality of life." "The neighborhood center should improve the community's quality of life." Such applications assume an understanding of the phrase that may not be accurate. So, for our purposes here, as we address *quality of life* in the business world, let's clarify the meaning.

For those individuals participating in the famous Baltimore Civility Survey, the concept was evident in their answers to the question about describing their ideal job. Their responses mentioned jobs that enhanced their feeling of self-worth, giving them a sense that they were personally contributing to their company's success and were appreciated for doing so.[1] That's the quality of life concept.

As we talk with other people in a wide variety of jobs about the nature of communication in the work world and the impact of that which is relatively civil or uncivil, a theme emerges that clarifies *quality of life*. It essentially refers to those aspects of one's job that provide a level of happiness and personal satisfaction quite apart from any financial remuneration. When the boss inquires about how your new car is working out for you, or a friend from another building of the plant stops by to say hello, or an associate thanks you for helping with a project detail, you feel a degree of happiness. We call this an enhancement in your quality of life. By contrast, an argument with a coworker or the discovery of some unkind gossip diminishes your quality of life.

In both cases, the effect has been caused by someone's use of words or behavior that has a decided civility component. Our argument here, then, is that civil communication should be used in the business world because it will benefit the "quality of life" for all the employees involved. Specifically, civil communication provides a quality of life advantage in three respects:

1 Civility is a **character trait** that helps an individual attain personal goals in the professional world.
2 Civility is an **interpersonal style** that makes the workplace more pleasant.

3   Corporate and interpersonal civility is a **behavioral pattern** that provides health benefits, both psychologically and physiologically.

Let us look at each of those advantages in more detail.

Civility as a Character Trait

A good place to begin to see the value of civility to the individual is in the job application process. There are so many strong testimonials to the value of civility in the character of a job applicant that it is hard to know where to start. At every level of the corporate world, it seems that employers are looking to find job candidates whose character fits their corporate needs. Perhaps the words of John D. Rockefeller, an icon of American industry, give an appropriate overview. He is reported to have said, "I will pay more for the ability to get along with people than for any other ability."[2]

Rockefeller is not alone is this view. Nor has his nineteenth-century perspective been contradicted by newer business practices. *Job Outlook 2005*'s summary of surveys of employers seeking to hire college graduates reported that "Employers . . . want new hires who are honest, have good interpersonal and teamwork skills, are motivated and have a strong work ethic. . . . [T]hey complain that new graduates don't know how to dress for work and they don't know how to conduct themselves in the work-place."[3]More briefly, many employers subscribe to the motto "we hire for attitude; we train for skills."[4]

Another job counselor explained the point more completely in an etiquette course offered at the University of New Brunswick: some seemingly qualified applicants are passed over because of the relative incivility with which they conduct themselves in the job interview. "You could be the smartest kid with the best marks, but if you don't present well, you might not get the job."[5] The reverse is often seen; that is, the applicant who dresses well for the interview and speaks confidently and politely is offered a position due to his or her civil demeanor.

One particularly interesting interview technique in this regard was used by a major plastics' manufacturer. The experience, as reported by one of our students, included a problem-solving challenge given to all the applicants interviewing on one particular day. While the candidates worked as a group on the manufacturing problem assigned to them, supervisors formed a circle around the work area to observe the applicants' interpersonal style and communication techniques. They were watching in order to be positioned to make job offers not just to the best problem-solvers among the applicants, but to the best team players among the group. Those with the most civil communication styles were the most likely to be hired.

Other writers have spoken of the job interview as an opportunity to "weed out the uncouth," emphasizing that employers believe that a candidate who behaves politely in the interview is more likely to become an employee who respects supervisors and clients.[6] The recruiters trying to find a job for their clients are, consequently, spending some time training them for the interview itself.

Naturally, the particular interpersonal style for which an employer is looking will vary somewhat from occupation to occupation. But the overall thread running through virtually all employers' perspectives cannot be ignored: civil communication strategies in the initial job interview cause the employer to be more likely to hire you.

You may be wondering about whether such behavior is only an issue in the interview process. The answer is no; your demonstration of civility as a character trait will continue to benefit you in employment because supervisors consider it to be important in their decisions about retention and promotion of employees.

> I previously worked in a department staffed mostly by veteran workers. This experience showed me the importance of civility. My coworkers were constantly working for their own benefit, not the company's, even going so far as to confront me because my tendency to work hard was making the rest of the department look bad. After too many months of hearing coworkers say "I won't do that. It's not in my job description," I moved on, taking a more responsible position in a different firm. My previous coworkers are still there—veterans in the same entry-level positions they were hired into.
>
> *Ryan L. Anthony*
> *Media Specialist, Vocollect*
> *Pittsburgh, PA*

Job counseling specialist Marilyn Moats Kennedy reports that employers are looking for specific attitudes among their employees when deciding, in these challenging economic times, who to let go and who to retain. The attitudes bosses are more likely to reward include: civility, respect for confidentiality, cooperation on group projects, and avoidance of public denigration of bosses or coworkers.[7] Notice that job skills were not included on that list. Instead, retention is all about attitude, because the more civil attitudes there are among the employees, the better every-one's quality of life will be. A landmark study conducted at the University

of North Carolina confirmed this conclusion. Although the researchers specifically sought to understand the effects of workplace *incivil-ity*, the positive effects of relative civility can be extrapolated from their results. So, while they concluded that worker incivility can cost an individual his or her job, it is reasonable to surmise that relative civility will cause an employee to be retained.[8]

The relative role of job skills and inter-personal skills is a topic of frequent conversa-tion among employers and researchers. While job skills are, of course, imperative at every level of any occupational ladder, it is obvious that it is the interpersonal skills that trigger an individual's promotion up that ladder. An engineer who has good design and problem-solving skills is promoted only if those skills are matched with the abil-ity to lead and motivate other engineers. Those are civil character traits.

Civility as an Interpersonal Style

Each of us must deal with the reality of work. For thirty or forty years, we will get up at the crack of dawn, leave the comfort of home and fam-ily, and go to work, where we will spend the next eight to ten hours mingling with other people who have left their comfortable homes to spend the day with us. Ideally, this is a pleasant experience more days than not. Many employees speak of "loving" their job. When asked why, the answer frequently includes mention of the nice people with whom they work.

A job that is anticipated pleasantly and enjoyed is highly treasured. Jobs in which workers' interpersonal style is civil are jobs that meet that standard. Consequently, we can say that the civility thus evidenced yields a generally positive quality of life for the employees.

Partly, such civility happens because of workers observing the so-called rituals of the business world. Business rituals include everything from the standard business-letter format to dress codes, handshakes, and hierarchical privileges. "The rituals and conventions of business . . . help us to project an image of ourselves as smart, traveled, sophisticated and self-assured," say Ted Allen and Scott Omelianuk.[9] In other words, observing the civility standards inherent in business rituals causes us to feel pretty positive about ourselves, making us act generally graciously toward others. Putting on the business suit or uniform, regularly using "sir" and "ma'am," and respecting others' workspace are all rituals that make the day more pleasant for ourselves and others we work with.

In the retail and service sector, that civil interpersonal style also benefits our quality of life by making us better able to deal with "civility-challenged" customers without significant damage to our own self-esteem. We have all observed such customers—the shopper who steps in front of others at the checkout line, the "raging bull" who blames the salesclerk for an item's manufacturing defect, the diner who stiffs the waiter because the steak wasn't cooked well enough. Unfortunately, such examples are far too typical. If they were applying for the jobs of shopper or diner, such individuals surely would have been weeded out in the job interview.

In a complex and rapidly moving industry, timeframes are challenging, deals are highly competitive and the pressure to perform is constant. Frayed nerves and stress come with the business. Behaving in a polite manner in a difficult situation sometimes requires concentrated effort. Sometimes it is the little things. Treat others the way you want to be treated. My experience is the most successful people learn these lessons early and practice them consistently.

Todd V. Irwin
Vice President, Sales, Franklin Interiors
Pittsburgh, PA

Telemarketers are one of the most frequent targets of boorish customer behavior. One recent study reported that call center workers handled an average of five angry calls per day. That's the average—many days were worse.[10]

If we have even one unpleasant encounter such as these, our whole workday suffers because we are made to feel badly about ourselves. But, by practicing a highly civil interpersonal style when responding to such boors, we can improve the situation and our own self-esteem. Yelling at them only makes us feel worse. Speaking kindly, on the assumption the caller has just experienced some unspeakable tragedy, will boost our own sense of worth. The result, obviously, is better quality of life.

A generally civil interpersonal style practiced by supervisors also creates more loyal and team-oriented employees. The story is told of one aspiring chef who moved from one restaurant to another working under temperamental chefs who screamed and swore like stevedores. Realizing the personal stress she felt in such environments and noting the high employee turnover rate in such restaurants, Chef Kelli Klingbeil promised herself that life would be different when she had a restaurant of her own. And so it is. Now the chef and co-owner of a major restaurant, she runs a kitchen where "manners count." The result is employees who are hard-working and loyal.[11] We find ourselves actually *wanting* to work overtime when the boss shows sincere gratitude for our effort. Quality of life, thus, is measured not in hours worked but in satisfaction gained.

> It is important to me to create an atmosphere for my direct reports where they feel comfortable expressing their opinions and always feel that their ideas are value-added. I have found over the years that this is one of the best ways to build confidence in my staff and for my staff to have confidence in their own work. We all know that we do better work when we are confident that our contributions are valued and taken seriously.
>
> Risa Glick
> Quality Assurance Test Manager
> Northrop Grumman Corporation
> Sterling, VA

In the business called church, there are many examples of the benefits of civil leadership. Although one might assume that most church leaders are automatically civil to their staff and congregations, that assumption would be wrong. Those who do practice a highly civil interpersonal style are those whose churches grow and who never face a shortage of volunteers. The pastor who remembers everybody's name, asks about ailing family members, and shows up with a bucket when the youth group starts its car wash is the pastor whose church members keep coming back—they are loyal.

Recently, a friend told the story of a pastor asking him to take on a particular project by saying something to the effect of "You have just the talent we need for this job." How could he say no? He took on the project, the pastor helped to get other people involved, and the task was done well—that's teamwork. It is also a good business model for the attitude that yields satisfied, happy employees.

Satisfaction has a psychological component that should not be over-looked in our study of workers' quality of life. The famous "Hawthorne studies" conducted by the Harvard Business School in 1927 drew con-clusions that are still relevant today: workers' psychological needs must be met if they are to be motivated to work well.[12] In other words, civil interaction in the workplace is more psychologically satisfying than uncivil interaction and because of that, satisfied employees will work harder and not gripe about it. A supervisor who speaks with respect and helps to create a supportive work environment has addressed the individual employee's needs for physical comfort and social stimulation, allowing a degree of ego gratification that we call quality of life factors. This leads us to the third area in which workplace civility contributes to quality of life—the health area.

Civility as a Healthy Behavioral Pattern

In this era of rising health care costs and the emergent popularity of preventative medicine, it is incumbent on all of us to understand those controllable factors in our lives that contribute to our relative health, both physical and psychological. Stress is at the top of that list. Clearly, if we can either limit the stress in our lives or develop healthy ways to respond to stress, we will be healthier. Yet many employees have been unable to achieve that goal.

The business setting seems to be a stressful place due to time pres-sures, close working conditions, personality clashes, and regulatory paper-work overload, among other things. The result is employees who are unable to cope and, therefore, unable to work as productively as they could or should. One workplace survey, for instance, found that employees were bothered by their coworkers' failure to be polite, failure to express gratitude, failure to use consistently good personal hygiene, and failure to speak quietly in shared workspaces. These "overloaded" employees said that, as a result, their own productivity was diminished and that they seri-ously consider looking for a different workplace as a result.[13] Notice that all of the complaints listed above are typically labeled as incivility.

Several studies in the field of occupational health come to consis-tent conclusions about workplace stress. Their overriding conclusions are that "as encounters with uncivil behavior rose, so did symptoms of anxiety and depression; and that incidents of rude behavior were tied to less job satisfaction."[14] So, here again, we are seeing a link between on-the-job civility and perceived quality of life.

A particularly insidious form of workplace incivility that has an observable and significant effect on workers' mental and physical health is the case of the workplace bully. There is a certain glorification of the bully due to the popularity of professional wrestling, tabloid coverage of entertainers running amok, and reality TV's amusing portrayal of uncivil business moguls. To watch all of that on television or in the news, one would think such behavior has no negative impact. That would be wrong!

Being bullied contributes to hypertension, increased cholesterol, smoking, alcohol consumption, decreased physical activity, and job strain.[15] On the other hand, workplaces characterized by cooperative, respectful supervisor-employee relationships find themselves with healthier employees.[16] One classic example was the experience of a young woman working for an urban planning firm in Michigan who characterized her boss as "brilliant" but a bully. Her experience was not unique, as one in fourteen people in Michigan report having similar bosses. She was too stressed to take it for long and left to work for another disheartened employee who had started his own competing firm. They have been sufficiently successful that they have driven the bully's firm out of business.[17] Now guess who is stressed!

The bully's tendency to yell at and demean subordinates is an uncivil communication pattern that makes those employees who choose to stay literally ill. Sometimes the behavior isn't the loud aggressive type, but a more subtle form of attack known as patronizing. We may have seen or experienced such a boss who seems to give praise, yet follows through with nothing—no tangible rewards. A recent study found that the patronizing style was especially used by male bosses with regard to female subordinates, contributing to a cycle of actionable discrimination.[18] The important consequence here is that the employee is made to feel undervalued, a blow to the quality of life.

One final and tremendously telling blow from workplace incivility is the toll it takes on our physical health. As mentioned earlier, bullies cause hypertension and related coronary diseases. But the incivility doesn't even have to rise to the level of bullying for those impacts to be felt. Simple acts of injustice put a strain on our health, particularly our heart health.

Some even consider job stress to be sufficiently dangerous to qualify as a disease. A Japanese study determined that the body's natural reaction to office clashes is similar to that which occurs when an impending wound is sensed: the blood prepares itself for clotting as it would after a physical blow. The study noted that it should not be a surprise that managers suffer heart attacks at twice the average rate during two periods: the week immediately after giving a subordinate a dismissal notice and the week of a daunting deadline.[19]

British researchers found that employees who reported experiencing a relatively just workplace had a statistically significant lower risk of coronary heart disease than those who described their workplaces has having low or only moderate levels of justice.[20] Another study conducted by the same team, but with different employees, found that workplace stress resulted in a doubled rate of hypertension and other cardiovascular problems.[21] Given that heart disease remains the number-one killer of adults, an increased risk of that dimension is extremely important to address.

There are health risks that each of us bears through no fault of our own. One person is prone to arthritis due to an injury in youth; another is susceptible to skin disease due to a lack of melanin, and another suffers from knee problems just because she is female. But some health problems are within our conscious control, such as lung disease linked to smoking and orthopedic injuries caused by participation in high-risk sports. We would add to that list, stress-related illnesses caused by workplace incivility. It does not have to happen! By conducting ourselves with civility and responding to others' incivility in more respectful ways, we will be healthier.

There have been at least eight different bills introduced in state legislatures designed to protect employees from the negative health impact of abusive employers. The so-called Healthy Workplace bills note that abusive work environments cause employees distress in the form of such things as anxiety, depression, reduced immunity to infection, sleep disorders, and hypertension. They further posit that, under existing law, employees cannot seek any redress for such abuse unless it seems grounded in ethnic, racial, or gender discrimination. So the bills propose to change that by giving aggrieved employees a right to sue for as much as $25,000 as compensation for their pain and suffering at the hands of uncivil supervisors.[22] To date, none of these bills has succeeded in becoming law.

But just the fact that legislators have been trying to change workplace environments by force of law is significant. It is recognition that everyone deserves a certain quality of life and that it is being denied by some employers who practice abusive or uncivil styles of communication.

Summary

We started this chapter by asserting that people working in business and the professions should learn to communicate with civility because it will make a positive difference in their quality of life. In short, you will be happier, more satisfied, and more relaxed if civility is your normal mode of interaction.

There are numerous research studies that have explored that question and come to the same answer. But, just for a moment, consider the lessons learned from your own experiences. Have you ever worked for a boss who bullied you? Have you ever worked in an environment where whining dominated employee conversations? Have you ever worked for a boss who treated you with genuine respect? Have you ever had a job you looked forward to going to each day? Answer those questions and then correlate your answers with a recollection of when you were happiest and less stressed. You will see the connection: civil communication on the job increases your quality of life.

A researcher for *Fortune* magazine had an interesting revelation on this point when "going undercover" to find out what life was like for employees of some of the magazines "Top 100" companies to work for. After playing roles as a bellman, a retail clerk, an oil field worker, and a driver for a package delivery company, he said he was amazed that other companies do not offer the same quality of life to their employees as these award-winning companies do. He noted that "it's not rocket science"; it is the simple things that make employees happy, loyal, and less stressed.[23] He is right; it is the simple things—simple civility.

NOTES

1 Civility Works, Baltimore Workplace Civility Study, 2001 (available at: http://www.civilityworks.com/resources.html).

2 John D. Rockefeller, cited in Sue Fox, *Business Etiquette for Dummies* (New York: Wiley, 2001), 12.

3 "Good News for College Graduates: Employers Want You!" *Job Outlook 2005* (available at: http://www.jobweb.com/joboutlook/2005utlook).

4 Danielle Herman (senior communication consultant, Erie Insurance Group), personal correspondence with the author.

5 Shawna Richer, "Little Fork for Salad; Don't Order Spaghetti," *Globe and Mail*, March 5, 2003.

6 Rachel Konrad, "Tight Job Market Turns Tables on Interview Process," 2002 (available at: http://news.com.com/2102–1017).

7 Marilyn M. Kennedy, "Monitor Your Attitude, Manage Boss' Expectations," *Marketing News* 38 (2004): 54.

8 Lynn Andersson and Christine Pearson, "Tit for Tat? The Spiraling Effect of Incivility in the Workplace," *Academy of Management Review* 24 (1999): 452–471.

9 Ted Allen and Scott Omelianuk, *Esquire's Things a Man Should Know about Handshakes, White Lies and Which Fork Goes Where: Easy Business Etiquette for Complicated Times* (New York: Hearst, 2001), 2.

10 Paul Blaum, "Researchers Study the Effects of High Stress on Service Industry Employees," *Penn State Intercom*, October 2004.

11 Maureen Wallenfang, "Minding Your P's and Q's Makes Workplace Better for Everyone," *Knight-Ridder Business News*, February 13, 2005.

12 "What Leaders Should Know about Basic Human Behaviors at Work" (available at: http://www.leadershipadvantage.com/basic Human Behaviors at Work.html).

13 Nancy Feig, "Mind Your Manners: Etiquette in the Workplace," *Community Banker* 14 (2005): 50–51.

14 Lila Cortina, "Incivility in the Workplace: Incidence and Impact," *Journal of Occupational Health Psychology* 6 (2001): 64–80.

15 Mica Kivimaki, "Justice at Work and Reduced Risk of Coronary Heart Disease among Government Workers: The Whitehall II Study," Workplace Bullying and Trauma Institute, 2005 (available at: http://www.bullyinginstitute.org/res/justiceheart.html).

16 Sharon Nelton, "Face to Face," *The Nation's Business* 83 (November 1995): 18–25.

17 Maragarita Bauza, "Fire Your Boss: What to Do about That Bully at Work," *Erie Times-News*, May 25, 2005.

18 "Patronizing Behavior Can Negatively Affect Women Employees' Performance," 2005 (available at: http://live.psu.edu/index.php?sec).

19 P. R. Johnson and J. Indvik, "Workplace Stress," *Public Personnel Management* 30 (2001): 457–466.

20 Kivimaki, op cit.

21 Amanda Gardner, "Bullying, Heart Disease, Injustice at Work," *HealthDay News*, October 24, 2005.

22 David C. Yamada, "A Model Act to Provide Legal Redress for Targets of Workplace Bullying, Abuse and Harassment, without Regard to Protected Class Status," *Georgetown Law Journal* 88 (2000): 475–536.

23 Daniel Roth, "Trading Places," *Fortune*, January 9, 2006 (available at: http://www.money.cnn.com/2006/01/news/companies/bestcos_undercover/index/htm).

5

Business Communication

Civility and Profits

Be civil because it will make you happier and healthier. That sounds like a good plan, doesn't it? It may also sound a little unrealistic. After all, business tycoons historically did not become tycoons by being nice. Many, in fact, had reputations as tyrants whose highest priority was protecting and advancing their own profit motives. If you are a business owner, you should rightly ask, "What good is civil communication going to do my company?" We will argue in this chapter that civil communication will make your company profitable. The cost-benefit analysis is generally positive. As implied earlier in our discussion of employee quality of life, happy employees are productive employees. But there is more to it than that. Let's look at the bad news first.

Financial Costs of *Incivility*

When employees are unhappy in their work environment due to abusive bosses or stressful relationships with coworkers, they are not very motivated to work hard. That translates into lost productivity, which can be financially measured. Just picture the slouching, slow-moving behavior of a child walking to the school bus stop, and you will get the right image of the behavioral results of a lack of motivation.

In fact, in one study by DuPont Corporation, more than one fifth of employees reported they were inclined to turn down company requests for overtime or assignments that were somewhat more stressful than normal.[1] They were not motivated to put forth the extra effort that might have been profitable for the company but costly for them in terms of personal stress.

Negative attitudes about work were also the focus of two other significant surveys. The Baltimore Civility Study concluded that there are several troubling facets of employee unhappiness. Perhaps the most worrisome is that a significant number of bored and blasé employees just stay on the job for lack of something better to do. That cadre of "dead wood" workers is costing the company money in terms of diminished productivity and, potentially, infecting other workers around them, thus spreading their costly disease.[2] The Pew Charitable Trusts study as reported in *U.S. News and World Report*, broke down employee response to incivility on the job as follows: 37 percent believed that their commitment to the organization declined, 22 percent acknowledged decreasing their effort at work, and 10 percent

When the Erie Regional Chamber for Growth and Development issued a call for businesses and community organizations to pledge themselves to civility, more than 220 responded, representing over 17,500 people working in the area. Clearly, business and industry in our region believe that civility and its impact on our economic future is much more than a publicity stunt.

As a community, it is important that individuals and businesses recognize that the "pledge to Community Civility" is not about pointing fingers or placing blame. And signing the pledge does not mean that you are uncivil. The pledge is about standing together to create a climate of respect for reasonable public debate. The pledge is a rallying cry for all of us to take responsibility for the atmosphere we create for economic growth.

Rebecca Martin
Vice President, Erie Regional Chamber
for Growth and Development
Erie, Pennsylvania

decreased the amount of time they spent at work.[3] It is difficult to put a specific dollar figure on this motivational illness.

Real illnesses, on the other hand, are part of a package of readily measurable costs of employee malaise. These are the lost time costs. While some employees keep coming to work even though they are experiencing some degree of stress or unhappiness, others just don't come at all. They are absent due to real work-related illness or injury or to take time for some form of decompression.

The most recent cost survey regarding unscheduled work absences determined that each day of missed work costs the company (on average) $660 in direct payroll costs.[4] That is per employee, per day. The annual costs to a large corporation can easily rise to seven figures. If these costs were incurred purely due to flu outbreaks, age-related illnesses, or seasonal sinus problems, employers would rightly feel inclined to accept and tolerate the costs. But only 35 percent of the absences recorded in this study were due to actual physical illness; 26 percent were due either directly or indirectly to job-related stress.[5] In other words, a lack of civility contributes to lost time costs in the hundreds of thousands of dollars. The civility link is particularly evident in the report's conclusion that the absences from stress and "entitlement mentality" were twice as high in companies with poor or fair morale (as determined by another survey) as opposed to those companies having good or very good morale.[6]

Absenteeism will, of course, frequently result in an employee's departure from the company, either willingly or unwillingly. Turnover rate in a company carries its own additional cost. Since many firings and voluntary separations are the result of employee dissatisfaction, the related costs need to be added to our calculation of the financial impact of incivility.

Experts say that overall cost, per employee, will average $150 of salary because of the cost of paying a temporary worker, the cost of low productivity of the exiting employee, the cost of conducting an exit interview, the cost of losing the company's training investment made in the exiting employee, the cost of managerial time in reassigning that employee's work, the cost of the severance and benefits package, the cost of unemployment insurance premiums, the cost of lost contacts, the cost of advertising and recruiting for a full-time replacement, the cost of the new hire, the cost of training that person and the potential cost in lost business if the exiting employee takes any contracts or customers with him or her out the door.[7] Clearly, most businesses could not afford to experience much turnover at all. If some of those departing workers choose to leave because they have been treated uncivilly by management, the maxim of "shooting oneself in the foot" comes to mind. A disheartened $50,000 employee, under this formula, would cost a company $75,000 in the final salary year. What business could afford that cost of incivility?

A recent departure at prestigious Morgan Stanley cost the company considerably more. For over eighteen years, they were led by the powerful but "feisty" Phillip Purcell. He was reported to be "ruthless, autocratic and remote," demanding, rather than encouraging, employee loyalty.[8] After years of bearing up under this atmosphere, employees at every level began to rebel, leaving at alarming rates and causing the company's overall worth to decrease dramatically. According to one analyst, this was a classic example of the need for modern chief executives to be more "inclusive, open and transparent" or bear the huge cost of employee turnover caused by their own incivility.[9]

Even if employees don't slack off or absent themselves from work, their health-related costs due to workplace stress constitute another significant financial liability to the company. Health care costs are, of course, a significant corporate responsibility, no matter what the nature of the employees' health problem is. Our own employer offers several different health plans whose cost to the university runs between $250 and $550 per employee per month. Those costs, like everyone's, have been on a steady upward swing.

According to a recent American Psychological Association study, employers should be very concerned about the impact of mental illness charges on the increasing cost of health insurance. By their tally, mental illnesses cost society about $129 billion annually, half of which is attributable to lost productivity in the workplace.[10] And that figure was from fifteen years ago; more recent data paint a picture that should be of even greater concern to American business. The 2001 data reported in the *Wall Street Journal* suggest that depression alone costs businesses, directly and directly, about $70 billion per year.[11] Estimates vary, but it seems that the number of employees who seek treatment for work-related stress, anxiety, and depression could be 10 to 20 percent of the workforce. That includes on-the-job injuries resulting from an inability to handle stress.[12] As you can see, corporate America has had to invest a considerable amount of money in insuring and caring for those workers who are the targets of workplace incivility and must deal with the resultant stress.

Perhaps the height of workplace incivility is the legally actionable harassment that happens on occasion. It is also the height of the financial burden of incivility that an employer may face. In our currently litigious society, people who feel victimized are likely to fight back by suing not just an individual, but also the company that individual works for. The costs a company might face include direct claims won by the plaintiff as well as attorneys' fees and expenses, adding up, potentially, to several million total dollars in cost for even one suit. Recent verdicts have awarded millions to individual plaintiffs who have sued their employers for harassment or discrimination.[13] Even legal firms are not immune from suit. The Boston Bar Association's Task Force on Civility report cautions members that any "inappropriate" behavior on their part (for example, yelling, hostility, dismissiveness) would exacerbate adversarial proceedings and incur additional legal fees.[14]

A couple of case studies will illustrate the potential cost of litigating incivility. In Vallejo, California, a high school teacher sued her district officials as well as the state administrator, alleging that their demands that she teach outside of her certification area constituted bullying. In a three-and-a-half-year legal battle, she sought compensation for emotional distress, punitive damages, and civil penalties for harassment, discrimination, and retaliation. The total cost to the school district when the court supported her allegations came to over $500,000, and that's not even counting the indirect cost of lost time for those employees called to testify or prepare documents for the case.[15] As they say on the news, "that's your money," and it was a cost incurred as a direct result of employer incivility in handling a disagreement with an employee.

Unfortunately for employers concerned about profits, the school district's case is mirrored in those of many corporations. Among the cases and awards were suits against Babies R Us resulting in a $205,000 settlement for the plaintiff, a $1.9 million settlement against a Minnesota meatpacking plant, and a $500,000 settlement won by one hundred employees of a chain of auto dealerships in Colorado.[16]

These are just a few examples of the financial costs of workplace incivility. Add that to the previously listed costs of employee time, absenteeism, turnover, and health care and you get a pretty discouraging picture of the financial plight faced by businesses that tolerate a climate of incivility in their workplace.

A final story will add a unique twist to the picture of the financial cost of incivility. So far, we have focused on acts of incivility committed by management, with employees as the victims. The W. T. Grant story illustrates how management and the public, too, can be victimized, leaving the corporation to foot the bill. Many readers may not remember the retail giant W. T. Grant, but for nearly half a century it was the place folks went to buy everything from ant traps to zippers to everything in between. In a misguided effort to hitch its wagon to the growing credit industry in the 1970s, the company issued its own store credit card along with a massive incentive program for store managers to sign people up. Managers who didn't get enough credit applications were subject to humiliating punishments like pushing peanuts across the floor with their noses. Naturally, managers worked hard to avoid humiliation and signed up droves of new credit card holders. Within a few years, it became clear that a mistake had been made. Too many of the new cards were being used joyfully by people who actually lacked the means to pay. By 1974, the company had to write off $10 million in bad debt and by 1976 it had to declare bankruptcy.[17] That's why you haven't heard of W. T. Grant. Thanks to an effort to manage by incivility, upper-level management committed financial homicide and left 980 communities without the stores they had come to depend upon.

You get the picture. When businesses tolerate incivility in any aspect of their operation, they put themselves at financial risk. Logicians tell us that proof that one thing does not work should not lead us to conclude that its opposite does work. We need to specifically explore the financial effect of corporate policies opposite of those just described—in other words, policies that encourage civil communication by managers and employees.

Financial Benefits of Civility

In our cost-benefit analysis, we have so far established that being uncivil can cost a company millions. Fortunately, there are many companies that have had the happy and opposite experience of reaping financial rewards by practicing and promoting more civility between management and employees, within employee groups, and between the company and its clients. Their experiences are quite telling. From small, family-owned companies to major international corporations, the evidence of the financial benefit of civil communication expectations and practices is solid.

A 2003 study of workplace civility that examined numerous companies over a five-year period focused on the all-important shareholder return. The conclusion was that workers' strong positive emotions correlated reliably with corporate financial success.[18] Those "strong positive emotions" could be defined as happiness, job satisfaction, or a sense of being treated with respect—civility.

If it sounds like we are saying that "nice guys finish first," it's true. This is not to suggest that only companies practicing civil communication can be financially successful; we are merely pointing out that civility as a corporate standard does not threaten the bottom line and may, in fact, increase it.

In the retail sector, several well-known and highly successful companies are qualified to serve as "poster children" for corporate civility. They would include Costco, Starbucks, IKEA, and the Container Store. Their corporate belief is that treating employees well is good business.[19] They have significant annual profits, pay valued quarterly dividends, show monthly sales increases, and do it all while paying good wages and benefits. Because of those compensation packages, their workforce is loyal, which means that the company is less likely to incur the significant costs of turnover addressed earlier.[20]

Costco, for instance, is the national leader in the warehouse club busi-

> Because my company has taken the time to focus on communication in the workplace, it has been financially successful. Ranked in the top 25 of *Fortune*'s "100 Best Companies to Work For" every year since the list's inception, Smucker's understands that by using civility in the workplace, they will flourish. New employees are given a laminated copy of a letter originally published in the 1980's by then CEO Paul Smucker that highlights the four ideas he expected employees to observe in their daily interactions: thanking employees for a job well done; listening with full attention; looking for the good in others; and having a sense of humor. He believed that mutual respect within the plant leads to success on the store shelves. He has been proven right.
>
> Julie Hale Abbott
> Sales and Marketing Systems
> Coordinator, J. M. Smucker Co.
> Cleveland, OH

ness. Its CFO, Richard Galanti, stresses that the company got that way by following four central principles: obey the law, take care of your customers, take care of your employees, and respect your vendors. By endorsing such civil policies, Costco stores do an average of $120 million in annual business, compared to the $60 million of their largest competitor.[21] So we are back to the important business principle that satisfied employees are productive employees and productive employees make money for the company.

> All employees in my company are required to complete annual training focusing on standards of business conduct, workplace violence, harassment and diversity in the workplace. The result is enhanced teamwork, open communication and respect for others that translates into delivery of quality products delivered on time to the customer—contributing to the company's financial success.
>
> Such training is rapidly becoming the industry standard.
>
> Risa Glick
> Quality Assurance Test Manager
> Northrop Grumman Corporation
> Sterling, VA

A second factor that makes civility a profitable business practice is its impact on the return customer demographic. Whether a company is selling matches, cars, or matchbox cars, return customers are keys to its sales volume and profit. Return customers tend to buy more than first-time buyers, and they are an unpaid army of spokespersons for the quality of the goods purchased, thus generating new customers for the store or manufacturer. A maxim in automobile dealerships, for instance, is that the sales department sells the first car, but the service department sells the second. Put simply, we come back to a place that treats us well.

That even includes electronic places. Reporters for *Entrepreneur*, a magazine for e-tailing, recently investigated the sales practices of several online businesses and found that they were universal in endorsing the importance of good customer service as the best way to get the highly profitable return customers.[22] Various specific practices were described, highlighted by the practice of sending handwritten notes to customers of PearlParadise, a seller of gems. They describe the value of the notes this way: "the goodwill that comes of this is tremendous."[23] Of course, goodwill becomes good buying!

An organization coordinating the work of landlords even came up with a little mantra about the value of happy customers, emphasizing their role as return customers:

Happy customers will come back meaning less work and worry for you.
Happy customers do not complain or present problems.
Happy customers will sell your property to other potential customers.[24]

This is all about making rental housing a money maker, not a money pit, and clearly civil customer service is central to that end.

Even the legal profession agrees that its members need to practice civil communication with clients and colleagues in order to get the repeat business that spells profit. At least thirty-six state bar associations and sixty-nine local associations have adopted civility codes in some form.[25] This has happened because of a recognition that any uncivil behavior on the part of an individual lawyer hurts not just that lawyer's chances for repeat business, but the whole profession as well.

Recently, our own community has engaged in an aggressive effort to promote civil standards in the conduct of business and politics. Like other municipalities, ours has leaders who recognize the connections between doing business civilly and doing business profitably. In laying out their plan for mass endorsement of its Pledge to Civility, the Erie Regional Chamber and Growth Partnership emphasized that constructive public discussions of community issues will translate into economic success because civility encourages growth.[26] At this writing, it is too soon to tell if that expectation has come to fruition. But the experience of other business and industries certainly bodes well for the Erie initiative, since it is banking on service and entertainment industries wherein the return customer is critical.

A third and final element of corporate profits directly linked to the company's endorsement of civility standards is in the area of image. Of course, a company's image influences repeat customers and the overall productivity of employees discussed earlier. But it also includes factors somewhat separate from those two elements.

There is, for instance, how a company's image will influence a first-time customer or client to visit and buy. This is a very complicated issue in the business world. A company tries to create an image that will attract customers who are a good match for the services or goods produced. So a toy store wants to appear family-friendly and affordable; a locomotive manufacturer wants to appear powerful and reliable over time. A business that creates the right image attracts customers, and that makes money. To a great extent, however, the best image is generally one that conveys trustworthiness, regardless of the industry.

If executed well, image-driven campaigns can pay back in profits. In the world of sports, for instance, Sammy Sosa served as spokesperson for Habitat for Humanity projects in his native Dominican Republic. This was during the height of his home-run record chase in which he established himself not only as a slugger, but also as a genuine and civil individual. The spot cost about $300,000 to produce but generated an estimated $8.3 million in media value.[27] That is a handsome return on the investment. On the other hand, spokespersons such as Kobe Bryant and rapper Ludacris have lost contracts because stains on their public images were hurting the products they were attempting to promote. The endorser with a trustworthy image transfers that image to the product and, in turn, increases the product's profit.

Another field in which creation of image is important separate from the issue of generating repeat customers is the field of real estate. Attracting customers initially in that business is often a matter of creating an image of trustworthiness and a reputation for respectful customer service. A home is such a personal thing to be buying and selling that customers are looking for the company that shows respect for their personal values.

As a result, the National Association of Realtors has created a code of ethics that commits realtors and realtor associates to behaving civilly toward clients, colleagues, and competitors. The code recognizes that professional cooperation is profitable for all parties concerned.[28] In the code, you will find admonitions to be fair, honest, respectful, and objective. These standards are proposed by the profession as a means to the dual purpose of profit and customer service. These two masters, unlike others, can be simultaneously served.

Image is about perceived character, and image sells. An example of that connection to civility can be found in the sports-business world. As you may have heard in following the build-up to the 2006 Super Bowl, the Pittsburgh Steelers have a very loyal fan base. It is clear to those of us who live near Pittsburgh that the existence of such loyalty is not an accident. Rather, it is the result of careful attention to the team's image as being "family-friendly." By carefully working to create and preserve that image, the Steelers sell lots of tickets regardless of their won-lost record. The positive, civil public image contributes to the team's profitability.

Summary

The old saw "Nice guys finish last" has been around so long that most people utter it every now and then without pausing to consider its truth. An Internet search of that phrase, in fact, generates a list of over a million articles. A scan of those articles reveals a very important point that should make us a little more cautious in assuming the value of the saying: while being "nice" will indeed doom you to last place in rugby and mud wrestling, it actually will be an advantage on the playing fields of the business world.

Customs of encouraging or tolerating uncivil behavior and communication are very costly to employers in legal settlements, health care payouts, and low employee productivity—making incivility a financial liability. Habits of encouraging, or even requiring, civil communication by employees generates the triple financial benefits of higher productivity, generous return business, and positive product image.

If you are looking at the attitude and behavior we call civility purely from a cost-benefit angle, there is no question that it generates far more income than it loses. Promoting civil communication at all levels in your workplace will contribute to business success.

The modern domestic manufacturing arena is one fraught with the tension that accompanies a struggle for survival. Fierce global competition, skyrocketing material and energy costs, un-tethered health care premiums and uncompromising price and delivery expectations by customers have stress at critical levels. Constant pressure to work more efficiently, reduce overhead costs and streamline processes often places employees at odds with one another and frequently relegates our basic concern for each other to an afterthought at best.

One of founder George DeArment's fundamental principles was the insistence that people count more than machines. In today's climate of rapid machining advances and clamoring to automate processes in the interest of competitive survival, his founding tenet has been more than a good idea in theory. Our company has proven that it is possible to be committed to progressive manufacturing and still be committed to your employees. We are able to do this by bringing civility and a basic concern for each other out of the mothballs and back into the spotlight.

Randy Ferguson
Director of Communication
Channellock Corporation
Meadville, Pennsylvania

NOTES

1 P. R. Johnson and J. Indvik, "Workplace Stress," *Public Personnel Management* 30, no. 4 (2001): 457–466.

2 Lilia Cortina et al., "Incivility in the Workplace: Incidence and Impact," *Journal of Occupational Health Psychology* 6, no. 1 (2001): 64–80.

3 S. Farkas and J. Johnson, "Land of the Rude: Americans in New Survey Say Lack of Respect Is Getting Worse," Grantee Press Release, April 3, 2002.

4 "Costly Problem of Unscheduled Absenteeism Continues to Perplex Employers," CCH Internet Research Network, October 12, 2005 (available at: http://hr.ccd.com/press/releases/absenteeism/default.asp).

5 Ibid.

6 Ibid.

7 William G. Bliss, "Cost of Employee Turnover," *The Advisor* (available at: http://www.isquare.com/turnover.cfm).

8 Joseph Nocera, "The Legacy of Purcell: Tough Guys Finish Last," *International Herald Tribune*, June 18, 2005 (available at: http://www.iht.com/bin/print_ipub.php?file=/articles/2005/06/17/yourmoney).

9 Andrea Redmond, 2005. Quoted in Nocera.

10 "Mental Health Benefit Is Cost Effective," APA Online, 1993 (available at: http://www.apa.org/practice/costeffe.html).

11 Elyse Tanouye, "Mental Illness: A Rising Workplace Cost," *Wall Street Journal*, June 13, 2001.

12 Johnson and Indvik, op cit.

13 Ibid.

14 Task Force on Civility in the Legal Profession, Boston Bar Association, May 23, 2002.

15 Sarah Rohrs and Kenneth Brooks, "Teacher Settles Lawsuit with VCUSD for $225,000," *Vallejo Times-Herald*, February 13, 2006.

16 Stephanie Armour, "More Men Say They Are Sexually Harassed at Work," *USA Today*, September 17, 2004.

17 Adam Horowitz, *The Dumbest Moments in Business History* (New York: Penguin, 2004).

18 Towers Perrin, "Working Today: Exploring Employees' Emotional Connection to Their Jobs," 2003 (available at: http://www.civilityworks.com/resources.html).

19 Susan Reda, "Nice Guys Finish First: How to Succeed in Business by Doing the Right Thing," *National Retail Federation Stores Magazine*, 2004 (available at: http://www.stores.org/archives/2004/06/cover.asp).

20 Ibid.

21 Susan Reda, "Costco Wholesale Club: A Big Box with a Big Heart," *National Retail Federation Stores Magazine*, 2004 (available at: http://www.stores.org/archives/2004).

22 Melissa Campbell, "Happy Returns," *Entrepreneur Magazine*, January 2004 (available at: http://www.entrepreneur.com).

23 Ibid.

24 Jan VanVoorhis and Pat VanVoorhis, "Turn Your Customers into Happy Customers," *Owner News*, January 2003 (available at: http://www.rentors.org/newletterarticle).

25 Task Force on Civility in the Legal Profession, op cit.

26 "Erie Regional Chamber Members Pledge to Civility," *Erie* 1, no. 1 (2005): 10–13.

27 Sabrina Jones, "In Public Service Ads, Celebrities Can Drum up Fame or Shame," *Washington Post*, August 18, 2003.

28 "Code of Ethics and Standards of Practice of the National Association of Realtors," January 1, 2006.

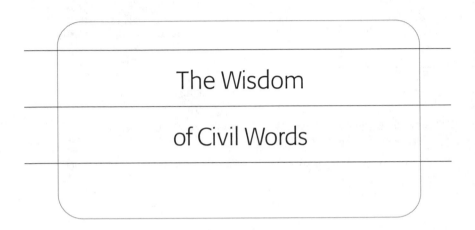

6

The Wisdom

of Civil Words

Ever found yourself wondering how your friend could possibly have misinterpreted you as he or she did? You are certain that you said to meet under the Boston Store clock and there you were standing and waiting for what seemed like an hour, only to discover that your friend was under the outdoor clock while you were under the indoor one. Your words were perfectly clear— or so you thought!

We have discussed communication theory and the special value of civil communication in the business setting. Understanding those concepts is one thing and applying them is another. That is why we turn now to the vital issue of concretely applying the principles of civil communication in the business setting. We will first consider several overarching guidelines for productive workplace communication and then turn our attention to specific recommendations for each of the major contexts in which business communication takes place.

Words, Attitudes, and Behavior

Our first overall guideline is about words, those tricky things that we rely on so heavily and use so cavalierly. They are powerful but complicated tools. This is nowhere more true than in the workplace, where time is of the essence. Always in a hurry, we often fail to take time to think carefully about our word choice. Generally, that works out alright, but too often it leads to confusion, conflict, and lost productivity. To minimize those potential negative consequences, we will explore the critical principle that **reliance on relatively civil word choice is smart business strategy.**

Recall the earlier discussion of human reliance on two symbol systems for conveying messages—the verbal (words) and the nonverbal (expressions, gestures, and appearance). In both cases, the medium is a symbol, carrying as much connotative meaning as denotative. So, even simple words like *clock* might be interpreted differently by two individuals whose frames of reference are slightly different one from another. It is the implications of those different meanings that are important.

In my family, I am frequently described as "short." Although average by the standards of clothing manufacturers, I am four inches shorter than the average height of all the other women in the family and twelve inches shorter than the average height of all the men. Except for the indignity of having to stand on telephone books for the family picture, being labeled "short" has not really caused any problems for me because the varying interpretations of that word are not important in my lifestyle. NFL quarterback Doug Flutie, by contrast, nearly lost his chance for a great career because some considered him too "short" for his chosen career. The scouts and owners used *short* as a pejorative term in their analyses, whereas Flutie considered the label to be of no more consequence than other labels like "left-handed" or "bald." It was a factor that might call for some adaptation but was hardly crippling. He adapted well, becoming a likely Hall-of-Famer. Others have not so easily overcome the negativity of the words with which they are labeled. The word is a symbol that is given power and meaning by the user and by the receiver. As such, it is a strategic communication tool.

In the business world, power has been ascribed to an interesting assortment of words and metaphorical symbols used to describe various management styles. Aggressive managers are called "cutthroat" or are said to have a "take-no-prisoners style" in which they don't hesitate to "step on toes" or "walk over anybody else" to get to the top. If a major mistake is made, these managers threaten that "heads will roll" and remind their staffs that this is a "dog-eat-dog" industry. Look at that list of metaphors again. Sense any civil attitudes there? Such word symbols wrongly suggest that successful management results from incivility. We need to change that image, and, because of the power of words, we can do it by changing the verbal symbols on which we rely in the workplace.

The change needs to be made because poor word choices are costly to a company's quality of life and bottom line. We have already discussed both of those goals in some detail. But let's be specific about verbal incivilities at this point. One management consultant puts the cost of "toxic talk" in the multimillions of dollars, pointing to the case of *Harris v. Forklift Systems*, in which an offended employee was awarded over $1 million in damages due to enduring a pattern of crude and demeaning language from her supervisor.[1] It is worth noting that the Supreme Court upheld that claim, noting that actual psychological damage from incivility did not have to be proven in order for harassment charges to be affirmed. Writing for the Court, Justice O'Connor pointed out that "a discriminatorily abusive work environment, even one that does not seriously affect employees' psychological well being, can and often will detract from employees' job performance."[2] Words have that power, and uncivil words in the workplace are too dangerous to be tolerated.

How has the standard of acceptable workplace language changed, and what can be done to raise the bar back up so that employees feel comfortable enough to work at the highest levels of productivity?

Slippery Slope of Declines in Verbal Civility

For a variety of reasons, the standards for business-appropriate word choice have been in gradual decline. This is not surprising, as recent decades have seen a general move toward informality in the workplace and the embracing of a very broad interpretation of citizens' rights to free speech. Ever since the "free speech" movement of the 1960s, standards of acceptable speech in any public forum have become quite liberal. The Supreme Court, in introducing the principle of "community standards" for evaluation of obscenity charges, essentially ruled that there is no national standard of proper language. Even the most famous case challenging those standards, George Carlin's 1978 "Seven Dirty Words" monologue, became a legal matter only because of the complaint of one listener. All the other thousands of listeners who heard Carlin speak the words "you're not allowed to say on television" simply took it in stride.[3] America had become a very language-tolerant society.

This tolerance was also present in the workplace. Casual dress codes replaced the "business suit" standard, it became acceptable to address supervisors by their first names, and on-the-job swearing was not regularly penalized. One business writer called this a tendency to "chumminess" that blurred the linguistic line between casualness and rudeness.[4]

During this era, the public became accustomed to many negative role models regarding civil language. The public laughed and laughed when Archie Bunker called his son-in-law "Meathead" and his wife "Dingbat." Little did we know that this *All in the Family* dialogue was simply the forerunner of amazingly uncivil speech in the entertainment business and elsewhere.

Rappers sang lyrics sprinkled with expletives and obscenities and still were granted plenty of airtime and sold millions of records. Athlete interviews were not edited for civility; television became more and more "blue," and politicians freely engaged in profane disagreements with one another in public legislative sessions.

Even business leaders had the reputation of using inappropriate language. "There is a gigantic disconnect between real authentic conversations and the artificial voice of business executives and managers. When your audience hears 'bull,' they make negative assumptions about the person or company that spews it."[5] This is not to say that all business executives spoke disrespectfully, simply that there were many who did so, serving as negative role models for aspiring executives.

What makes the low standards for civil word choice more dangerous is that those persons who objected to them were reluctant to speak up. It is the adult form of peer pressure. Nobody wants to be the first one to express offense and look like an "outsider" in the network. Etiquette expert Judith Martin explains that even though people were alarmed at the increasing use of profanity, it was socially necessary to pretend they weren't shocked.[6] People perceived a tolerance of incivility to be necessary to get along with friends and coworkers.

The Pendulum Swings Back

In recent years, however, we have seen an increasing willingness of people offended by crude, offensive, vulgar, and profane language to complain publicly. It seems that our capacity for tolerance has been tested too much, and more, and more people are insisting that words used in any public setting should be civil. While many are ordinary citizens trying to bring about change in their own homes or workplaces, others are people in positions of authority who are able to create penalties and sanctions mandating more civil word use.

In several well-publicized cases, professional athletes have been fined by their sport's governing body for use of vulgar or obscene words in media interviews. For instance, Dale Earnhardt, Jr., used the "s" word when asked about the significance of his victory in a Nextel Cup race in 2004. It was used in the most casual context, just as you hear it often in conversations among friends on the sidewalk or coworkers chatting over lunch. But NASCAR did not take it lightly. As an organization, it has been trying to create a strong, family-friendly image and its management believes that drivers who swear conflict with that effort. They had fined and penalized drivers before and didn't hesitate to do it again, even though the driver was Earnhardt. He was fined $10,000 and docked twenty-five points in the Nextel Cup standings.[7] In doing so, the NASCAR executives were signaling to the drivers that their words affect NASCAR's business and that they are subject to civility standards set by the organization.

In another case of public profanity, a Michigan canoer who instinctively uttered an expletive when he swamped his canoe in a state park faced stiff fines for public vulgarity. The issue was, in the view of the court, that the park had the right to control speech when doing so would enhance the park's business. Although later overruled by the Michigan Court of Appeals on the grounds of vagueness, the principle behind the law was not challenged.[8]

Congress has attempted to join the battle for civility by increasing fines for indecency on the airwaves. The FCC has the right to penalize broadcast license-holders as well as program producers if inappropriate language occurs on air, particularly during the hours that impressionable children might be in the audience.

In some cases, the trend toward controlling uncivil word choice has been manifested by industry self-censorship, thus foregoing any actual legal repercussions. Just as the NFL instituted tape delays for the Super Bowl entertainment following the Janet Jackson fiasco, some corporations simply make clear to their employees that profanity and vulgarity are not to be used in their companies. New York restaurateur Rhoda Steffel, famous for the quality and longevity of her staff, credits her new employee training for the civility that typifies her restaurant. "The 'f' word isn't a word we care for. I tell them right off the bat we don't swear."9 There is no need to prosecute anyone when it is established at the outset that one's job responsibilities include speaking in a way that would not offend your grandmother.

The court of public opinion has been heard on this matter as well. Several prominent politicians have been caught using vulgar language during public moments, and their support in the polls has dropped. Vice President Dick Cheney famously used an expletive in a nasty exchange with Senator Patrick Leahy on the Senate floor a few years ago, for example. I wrote to him to complain, as did many other citizens. While miffed by the unapologetic, formulaic response I received from the vice president's office, I was pleased to see that his popularity with the voters began a decline at that point from which he would never recover. Even more pointed evidence of public distaste for incivility among its leaders was the 2006 midterm election in Pennsylvania in which several prominent political leaders were voted out of office. Several of those voted out had been engaged in bitter name-calling battles with their political opponents for some time.10 While their words were not legally actionable, these politicians have paid a price for vulgarity in other ways.

In addition to issuing penalties, some businesses and industries have created very specific speech "codes" that their employees are expected to observe if they wish to keep their jobs. Generally speaking, speech codes are unenforceable in the general population. Some colleges and universities, for instance, have attempted to establish codes for student language use only to have them all struck down by courts seeking to preserve free speech in the public arena. But businesses are different. There is an understanding that he who pays the bills makes the rules in the private relationship between employer and employee.11

Referred to generally as "anti-cussing" policies, corporate speech codes have been put in place in businesses as diverse as supermarkets, construction companies, and automobile manufacturers. As one employer explains it, they are not trying to restrict anybody's rights, but simply to create a less chilling business climate—and it has worked.[12] Businesses that observe civil codes of word use tend to be successful businesses.

Public schools enjoy a similar right to regulate their employees' and students' language. Most school districts have some sort of policy on acceptable language. But recently, so many students have "pushed the envelope" that some schools are beginning to think that they must act like businesses and put some muscle behind those policies. Some, like the Conneaut schools in Ohio, have proposed a framework of fines, including a $300-per-indecency assessment.[13]

> While there are no specific guidelines on worker use of words in our company, courteous and professional behavior is expected. This is called out in our employee handbook as a prohibition of "foul and abusive language" while on the job.
>
> Todd Irwin
> Vice President, Sales
> Franklin Interiors
> Pittsburgh, PA

Want to keep your home cuss-free? Buy the *TV Guardian* that edits the language of television programs automatically. Want your workplace cuss-free? You can impose rules and penalties, as some of those companies described have done. A better solution, however, is to practice civil choice of language as a matter of routine yourself and, thus, become a role model in your own work world. Let's get specific.

Five Lessons for Productive Civil Language at Work

Did you have one of those mothers who used to say to you, "If you don't have anything nice to say, don't say anything at all?" If so, we hope you are still living by that little maxim, for the first lesson about talking is actually about *not* talking.

Lesson One: The best words to choose when caught in an unexpected, emotionally charged situation are no words at all.

Everyone agrees that the words we should avoid in a positive business environment are usually the ones that fall out of our mouths "accidentally." You find out that the printer has run out of paper right in the middle of printing your report that is due in an hour. "Oh, s . . . !" You fall when hurrying up the stairs to catch a colleague before he leaves for Denver. "D . . ." You confront a subordinate leaving the building with unauthorized files. "You . . . Stop right there!" In each instance, the tongue has started before the brain was fully engaged or when the brain was overridden by emotions.

Clearly, being silent when upset or angry is very difficult. But didn't your mother also tell you to count to ten? Just step out of the situation long enough to process what is going on, allowing yourself the necessary, but usually brief, time to choose words that will contribute to a resolution of the situation rather than further inflame everyone's emotions. Being at work, in the presence of other persons with whom you need to maintain a professional relationship, requires that you use a different vocabulary than the one you use while repairing your car or playing a pick-up game of basketball in the neighborhood. There truly is no place in the business setting for swearing. Taking a mental pause will allow you to shift to that more professional vocabulary.

You are now in gear. You have recognized the value of controlling your vocabulary for the business environment. Now, which words will be strategically best? As you speak, the best, most civil words are identifiable, in part, by their appropriateness to the specific circumstances. Just as you would tell your parents about your car accident by emphasizing that the damage is "minor" and you are "alright," you should choose your words in any business exchange by considering who your listener is.

Lesson Two: Use words respectful of the specific listener to whom they are addressed.

Is the listener a customer or client? Is the listener a new coworker? Is the listener a project team member? Is the listener your supervisor or your subordinate? Is the listener someone who is similar to you in background or significantly different from you? Is the listener meaningfully or only casually involved in this business process? It all makes a difference.

When we take such factors into account, we are more likely to choose words that respect the individual's role and perspective, thus becoming more likely to have a productive communication exchange.

Consider the restaurant business, for example. Hosts and waitstaff have to use some word to address the customers who are strangers to them. Do they say "folks"? Do they say "sir" or "ma'am"? Do they say "honey" or "dear"? Do they say "you guys"? All of the above can be heard in just about any restaurant on any given day, although "honey" and "dear" seem to be reserved for older customers. But which words the waitstaff chooses does make a business difference. First, it will affect their tip. Second, the choice will also affect the restaurant in the long term because of the customers' decision to return to this place or not. Why? Because the customer interprets the words as symbols reflecting the staff's attitude, and that interpreted attitude affects their assessment of the restaurant. The older man addressed as "honey" may feel demeaned and insulted, and the professionals addressed as "you guys" may feel devalued. "Sir" and "ma'am" carry much less symbolic baggage and convey the customer respect that will keep them coming back.

Likewise, terms of respect should also be chosen for conversations among colleagues within any office. Pseudo terms of endearment and nicknames are rarely appropriate forms of address, and diminutives such as "Billy," "Suzie," or "kid" should be avoided as well. They are not respectful of the professionalism of the person addressed. Consequently, not only are the terms uncivil, but they create a distraction that diminishes the chances of successful communication.

One small landscaping firm in our area is known for the staff's ability to remember the names of the customers and address them respectfully on each visit. Greeting a customer with "Good morning, Mr. Johnson" is a wise and civil verbal choice. With just those four words in the opening of the employee-customer communication, respect has been established, and respect translates to return business.

Choosing words for their appropriateness to the listeners is not limited to terms of address. Rather, that criterion should affect your choices about nearly all the words spoken. For instance, casual wording is fine for casual conversations in the corridor, but more formal wording should be used in official meetings.

Use of jargon is another issue impacted by consideration of the listeners. In every work setting, there are terms used that are peculiar to that industry or to that particular company. Such terms are called jargon and serve the purpose, generally, of facilitating communication within that setting. In the construction industry, for example, employees can refer to "two-by-twelve's" and be assured that everyone around them knows the particular type of wood being referenced, and those working in the locomotive industry know that a "truck" does not run on roads, but on rails.

While jargon promotes clarity within the group of people familiar with the terms, it creates confusion for neophytes or outsiders. The confusion is made worse by the fact that not only are such listeners left in the dark about what those words mean, but they are also made to feel disrespected for their lack of knowledge. You know the look you can get when somebody says to you, "You mean you never heard of . . . ?" The feeling of being perceived as either stupid or not important enough to be in the know is very disheartening. That is exactly the reaction of listeners when we speak to them using jargon with which they are not familiar. It is simply uncivil to choose jargon under those circumstances.

Consideration of listeners and choosing words accordingly suggests a third lesson about the most strategic choice of words in the business arena. It has to do with clarity and precision. Often the most civil words, those most appropriate to the listeners, are so because they are also the clearest among the possible choices.

> There is a difference in how we communicate internally on the team and how we communicate with clients. Our internal communication is certainly less formal and more driven by urgency and stress. The same message may be communicated to a client and to a coworker in very different ways. Communicating with clients is often more about asking questions, gaining commitment and managing expectations. Try reaching those critical objectives without consideration of the client's exact nature and choosing words accordingly!
>
> Todd Irwin
> Vice President, Sales
> Franklin Interiors
> Pittsburgh, PA

Lesson Three: Respect the reality of the situation by choosing temperate and accurate, not inflammatory, words when describing or commenting on ideas, issues, or persons.

Naturally, it is always wise to use terms at the lower levels of the abstraction ladder whenever possible. After all, *Holstein* is much clearer than *livestock*. Even though both terms are accurate labels for a specific cow, the less abstract term will be more useful in accomplishing a clear exchange of information about the animal. That's the problem with inflammatory language—it is too abstract, causing confusion and/or unintended consequences.

By inflammatory language, we mean words that are exaggerations of truth, having a more dramatic effect than is needed or useful. The team member who says your ideas are "the stupidest he has ever heard" is clearly exaggerating. (If not, this person has not listened to many politicians!) The boss who warns that your report better be on time or your promotion will "go up in flames" is also exaggerating. The colleague who says that his new concept for an ad campaign is "the most amazing thing ever" has evidently not heard about sliced bread! In each instance, words were chosen for dramatic effect, not for clarity.

Unfortunately, the effects sometimes go beyond confusion, to insult and injury. Such exaggerated descriptors, when negative, damage the self-esteem of the person whose ideas were critiqued. In addition, the image of the person using the exaggerated words is diminished as other listeners dismiss the judgment for its ridiculousness. These negative consequences reflect that inflammatory language is not only inaccurate, it is also uncivil.

Instead, choose words to describe your reactions accurately, tempering your judgment in relativity. Ask questions to make sure you understand what it is that you will comment on. State any negative impressions with objectivity and without personalizing the judgment. So, a bad idea is "unworkable," or "impractical," instead of the "stupidest you ever heard." State your positive impressions with equal objectivity, grounded in reality. The great idea can then be described as "insightful," "worth pursuing," or "creative" instead of rising to the incredible level of the "most amazing ever." Now, you will be understood without having insulted anybody or damaged others' perceptions of your own insight.

Speaking of insults, don't! One of the tricky facets of words is their ability to carry or be perceived to carry discriminatory insults. These are often referred to as a litany of "ists": language perceived to be racist, sexist, ageist, elitist, and so on. Obviously, any intended or unintended discrimination in workplace language is an unwise strategy.

One nursing home administrator recounts the story of language that was misunderstood as insulting, illustrating the importance of choosing appropriate words for the audience. She said that in looking over a night nurse's charts, she found the notation that one patient was "s.o.b." Appalled at the nurse's use of such a derogatory term for one of their patients, she held a meeting about proper language to use when a patient was difficult. Later the nurse quietly educated the administrator that, in medical shorthand, "s.o.b." means "short of breath." Thinking that the chart would be read only by medical professionals, the nurse inadvertently used language that others would certainly find highly uncivil.

Lesson Four: Use objective, nondiscriminatory language that respects the uniqueness of all individuals.

Some uses of discriminatory language are so egregious that the user is cited for violation of the Equal Employment Opportunity Act. The specific nature of those transgressions is, or should be, quite obvious. The more subtle forms of discriminatory, uncivil language are what concern us here.

Lawyers working together on a suit to be filed on behalf of female Medicare recipients may, for instance, refer conversationally to the clients as "blue-hairs." The label does not deny any rights to those women or cause them psychological or financial damage. However, it does create a single-faceted image of them as persons. It stereotypes them, and in so doing causes the lawyers to think of them only as old and female instead of old, female, accomplished, talented, intelligent, powerful . . . the list could go on forever. *Blue-hairs* is a subtly disrespectful term that has counterparts in the labels used for persons of different races or ethnicities or classes than the speaker. No such language is acceptable in the business setting, in formal or informal exchanges. As the editors of *Esquire* point out, discriminatory language "demonstrates an unfair and unwarranted lack of respect for whole groups of people."[14] That makes it bad for business, whether the victims of the labels are being directly addressed or not.

In our example, the older clients were not present to hear the term *blue-hairs*." The effect is indirect, in that the users of the word may tend to act with less civility toward the clients in subsequent face-to-face meetings because of having casually referred to them disrespectfully out of their presence. It is a matter of the language influencing the mindset of those who use the words and those who tolerate them. As we have repeatedly noted, attitude is key to civility in behavior, so positive attitudes should be reflected even when the persons described are not within earshot.

The final lesson for civil word use may be more controversial. Virtually everyone agrees that we should always strive to hold our tongues when angry, to use language appropriate to the listener, to use precise terminology, and to avoid racist and sexist language. But now we enter the ambiguous world of "dirty" language.

Lesson Five: Respect your listeners by using clean language all the time on the job.

The admonition is controversial in part because there are such varied definitions or interpretations of what is "clean" and what is "dirty." It's like what people say about art, "we can't define what we like, but know what's good when we see it." The television, music, and movie ratings may be helpful; their systems distinguish between the dirty and the clean by weighing the presence of gratuitous sex, violence, and/or profanity. Those ratings assist us in the context of entertainment, but not in the context of business. You may be saying, "Surely none of that behavior happens in businesses!" It may not happen, but language describing it may certainly be heard in just about any workplace.

The most frequent occurrence may be in office humor. "Dirty" jokes shared among coworkers are as common as pennies in your pocket. Told to members of the opposite sex, they may actually constitute sexual harassment. Told to a same-sex audience, they are simply unprofessional in their implied disrespect for the opposite sex and the privacy of intimate encounters. When a setting tolerates such jokes over time, a chilling climate is created that tends to limit the productivity of whatever group is the target of the jokes.

Clean language also means that the four-letter words heard so often in casual conversations should be avoided in the workplace. Students on their way to management class recently were complaining about the formal nature of an upcoming assignment for which they had to wear "suits and s. . . ." Can you picture it? Not only is the wording inaccurate, but the image is vile. If they speak that way on the job, they will discourage the kind of team-building conversation that is necessary in today's workplaces. Given the extensive drilling in vocabulary that we have all endured, we surely have a sufficient number of words in our brains to cover just about any circumstance without having to resort to the language of the gutter.

Why else is this lesson so controversial? The answer is that many people consider swearing to be a normal part of adult behavior and any attempts to limit it to be unfair constraints on their linguistic freedom. In taking that position, they are assuming that unclean language is harmless. Unfortunately, there is no evidence to support that position. It's about image, after all. If you want to be perceived as intelligent, competent, and professional, you will not use offensive language, including vulgarities, profanities, and obscenities. "Practicing civility means using language that empowers rather than disparages, builds trust rather than deceives and helps others rather than hurts them."[15] By its very nature, swearing is an implied attempt to use words as weapons. Thus, swear words are hurtful by definition. Their too-frequent use contributes to an atmosphere of disrespect that hurts businessb as well as individuals.

Summary

It would be nice to think that everyone with whom we work is intelligent and sophisticated enough to not be offended by off-color jokes or vocabulary or by exaggerated ravings or discriminatory or disrespectful phrasing. That would make life easier, as we would not need to filter our talk or have different vocabularies for the different settings of our lives. But that's totally unrealistic. The real world, especially the world of business, puts great stock in our ability to use words well. We must choose the words that put ourselves and our company in the best light, creating a positive work environment in which workers are always motivated to work at their highest level of productivity.

By adopting the five basic lessons for civil language and encouraging the same in our coworkers, we can stimulate positive change in the business environment. We will raise the bar linguistically, and add to the company's success economically. A "civil tongue" is smart business strategy.

NOTES

1 Ted Pincus, "Toxic Talk in Workplace Costly to Employers," *Chicago Sun-Times*, September 13, 2005.

2 *Harris v. Forklift Systems*, Supreme Court Collection, Cornell Law School, 1993 (available at: http://supct.law.cornell.edu/supct/htmn/92–1168.ZO.html).

3 Faith Sparr, "From Carlin's Seven Dirty Words to Bono's One Dirty Word: A Look at the FCC's Ever-Expanding Indecency Enforcement Role" (paper presented at the National Communication Association Convention, Boston, MA, November 2005).

4 Robert Z. Nemeth, "A Little Civility Goes a Long Way," *Worcester Telegram and Gazette*, August 22, 2004.

5 Brian Fugere et al., *Why Business People Speak like Idiots* (New York: Free Press, 2005), 19.

6 "Who Gives a @#$% about Profanity," CNN.com, 2006 (available at: http://cnn.world-news.com/pt/cpt).

7 "Earnhardt Docked Points for Vulgarity," *Erie Times-News*, October 6, 2004.

8 "Cussing Canoeist's Conviction Thrown out, along with 105-Year-Old Law," Freedom Forum.org, 2002 (available at: http://www.freedomforum.org/templates/document.asp?documentID=15992).

9 Maureen Wallenfang, "Minding Your P's and Q's Makes Workplace Better for Everyone," *Knight Ridder Tribune Business News*, February 13, 2005.

10 "Tensions over Gaming Bill Flare with Senate Slur," *Erie Times-News*, October 8, 2004.

11 Rachel E. Silverman, "On-the-Job Cursing: Obscene Talk Is Latest Target of Workplace Ban," *Wall Street Journal*, May 8, 2001.

12 Ibid.

13 John Bartlett, "Potty Mouth? Keep It out of School," *Erie Times-News*, December 15, 2005.

14 Ted Allen and Scott Omelianuk, *Esquire's Things a Man Should Know about Handshakes, White Lies and Which Fork Goes Where: Easy Business Etiquette for Complicated Times* (New York: Hearst, 2001),159.

15 Bethami A. Dobkin and Roger Pace, *Communication in a Changing World* (New York: McGraw-Hill, 2002), 144.

7

Nonverbal Civility

An organization that provides job training to unemployed individuals reports the sad experience of learning that one of their graduates has lost his job again. Why? They soon learn it is due not to the client's lack of job skills but to his inability to look at coworkers and customers on the job. It is his nonverbal behavior that has gotten in the way of his career.

We are brought up being told that our actions speak louder than our words. There is considerable truth to this saying when you consider some of the early research done on nonverbal communication. Years ago, researchers studying the impact of messages discovered that the language and words we use carry 7 percent of a communicator's attitudes, the voice 36 percent, and other nonverbal channels of communication the remaining 55 percent.[1] Other research found that 35 percent of the social meaning of a message is conveyed verbally, while the nonverbal factors carried the remaining 65 percent of the social meaning of the message.[2] Clearly the nonverbal message system is an essential element to effective communication in general and civil communication in particular.

If you need further convincing as to the importance of nonverbal communication, recall the frustration of carrying on an important phone conversation and wishing you could see your conversational partner to gauge his or her interest or response. Try carrying on a conversation with someone wearing dark glasses and try to determine if they are maintaining eye contact with you—which is an indication of involvement. Imagine the best romance novel, spy thriller, or page-turning murder mystery with all except for the direct dialogue between characters removed—absent all the descriptions of the people, places, and action. You'll likely have a boring book. In each of these examples, the key missing elements that would complement and complete the verbal parts of a message are the nonverbal ones.

In this chapter we'll examine in more detail what we mean by nonverbal communication, explore some of the special considerations that must be taken into account as nonverbal messages are interpreted, explain how we use various types of nonverbal behavior to communication in business and professional settings, and suggest some guidelines for the civil use of the nonverbal message system.

Defining the Nonverbal Message System

Definitions of **nonverbal communication** are as varied and diverse as those for civility and communication. If we look simply at the term *nonverbal*, we are literally concerned with all the nonverbal or nonword/language means by which we exchange messages. Ronald Adler and Jeanne Elmhorst give a succinct working definition of *nonverbal communication* as "those messages expressed by other than linguistic means."[3] Clearly this definition and the field of nonverbal communication cover considerable message territory, including: appearance, bodily movement, posture, gestures, facial expressions, spatial relations, the voice, touch, and time. How these diverse messages are interpreted becomes an important consideration to understand before sharpening your skills at using these messages in a civil fashion.

Interpreting the Nonverbal Message System

Our thought processes connect an object or idea to the word or symbol used to represent the object or idea. Assigning meaning to the verbal part of the message requires an understanding of how this referential process works. Interpreting and assigning meaning to nonverbal messages requires an equally sophisticated background in the nature of nonverbal messages and the factors that must be taken into account in their interpretation. If the verbal message system requires us to take into account the vocabulary—the individual words, grammar, and syntax (the arrangement of words to convey ideas), and context (the setting in which the words are used)—much the same is true of the nonverbal message system.

The vocabulary of the nonverbal message system is composed of all the different types of nonverbal messages. Like words, each type of nonverbal message can be examined individually, in isolation from each other, but doing so often complicates and compromises the accurate interpretation of the complete message. In normal interaction, several types of nonverbal behavior are combined and work together to form a message in concert with the verbal aspects. These combinations form the grammar and syntax of nonverbal communication.  We combine a certain tone of voice, facial expression, and gesture along with the words we are using to convey an idea to another person. Take three simple words like "You are fired!" and see how many different meanings you can convey by changing your tone of voice, level of eye contact, and facial expression. The meaning changes. How we place all these nonverbal factors together into a certain context or situation also becomes important. Those three little words in the context of a friendship rather than work take on clearly different meanings. As we craft and construct messages using nonverbal behaviors in terms of the nonverbal vocabulary, grammar and syntax, and context elements, we also need to keep in mind three important principles that govern how we interpret nonverbal behavior.

First, nonverbal messages should be interpreted collectively, not independently. Early in the study of nonverbal communication, popular books suggested that by understanding nonverbal communication you could "read a person like a book"—specific behaviors were words to which individual meanings could be assigned.[4] The assumption was that by examining individual behaviors—a look, another's bodily posture, a particular gesture, or a certain facial expression—we could interpret the message. We now know that all the various types of nonverbal behavior need to be combined and considered collectively in order to assign meaning to the message accurately. In much the same way that words, combined through grammar and syntax, function to convey ideas, the elements of the nonverbal "vocabulary" when combined and arranged also function together to help convey ideas. The head nodding in agreement, the positive facial expression, and the forward-leaning bodily posture taken together might well indicate that the interviewer is truly interested in your response. In isolation, however, each of these behaviors is ambiguous.

Second, nonverbal behavior is both conscious and intentional and unconscious and unintentional. Unlike words, which are almost always used with intention, much of the time we simply behave without conscious thought or intention of the potential communicative impact of our behavior. How often have you consciously thought about the expression on your face, the posture you assume, or the gestures you use? The maxim "We cannot not communicate" is especially true of nonverbal communication— we cannot not behave. So long as we are in sensory contact with another person, it is possible and likely that both parties will assign meaning to the verbal and nonverbal behavior of the other regardless of conscious intent. Does the yawn we notice during an important presentation indicate boredom with our presentation—or a late night with a sick child? Does the lack of eye contact indicate a lack of interest or preoccupation with an important decision? It is possible to read too much or too little intention into the nonverbal behavior of others; caution must be exercised when assigning such intention.

Third, nonverbal communication is regulated by the society and culture in which it occurs. We all learned the grammar and syntactic rules for using the verbal message system way back in elementary school—or at least we should have learned these rules. But how did we learn to use our eyes, face, gestures, posture, space, touch, and voice appropriately? It was the society and culture in which we were raised that schooled us in the proper use of these symbols. Children are told not to stare at others or to "wipe that smile off your face." We learn that certain gestures are offensive while others complement a good speech. We learn over time how close or far away we should stand from others depending on how well we know them. We learn who we can touch, where, how often, and in what way touch is appropriate. We learned verbal grammar and syntax in the classroom; we learned and continue to learn the nonverbal grammar and syntax out in the world of experience.

The culture in which we learned the rules shapes the rules we learned. One of the most important factors to keep in mind when interpreting nonverbal behavior is that its interpretation is governed by both the society and the culture in which it occurs. The same gesture, spatial relationship, or touch in a different culture can have a significantly different meaning.

Classifying Nonverbal Civility

There are seven different types of nonverbal message behavior that can be used to convey messages. While we'll examine them separately, keep in mind that they are used in combination with each other and to complement and complete verbal messages.

Appearance

Before we have an opportunity to verbally say anything, the way we choose to dress and groom has communicated an impression to those around us. Notice the intentional use of the word *choose*. As is the case with many types of nonverbal messages, we can exercise choice and control over how we present ourselves if we approach nonverbal communication strategically. A T-shirt with offensive language or graphics, rightly or wrongly, sends a message to those who see it about the person wearing it. The amount of skin one wishes to display and any body art that skin may contain conveys a message about the person—rightly or wrongly.

You never get a second chance to make a first impression. Clothes make the man or woman. These maxims may be trite, but they also contain valuable and enduring truths. The first thing we tend to notice about the people around us is their appearance. Our choice of hair style, facial hair (or lack thereof), makeup, and jewelry all potentially convey messages.

There are small libraries of books and dozens of Internet sites offering advice for those who want to dress for success in the business and professional world. Sorting through all of this sometimes conflicting information without the assistance of increasingly popular image consultants becomes a daunting and confusing task, especially in the professional world. We can offer some basic advice.

The businesses and organizations we associate with, implicitly or explicitly, come to influence the clothing and grooming choices we make. For example, nowhere is dress and grooming more important in the business and professional world than in the interview situation. A recent survey by the National Association of Colleges and Employers found that nearly three quarters of the respondents said a candidate's grooming had a strong influence on their opinion of the candidate.[5] Recognizing this, the savvy and aspiring newcomer to an organization will do some research on the dress and grooming standards appropriate to that organization. Sales of business attire likely increase in the spring as a new crop of college graduate prepares to enter the workplace.

In many ways, all business and professional organizations—formally or informally—have some type of a uniform or, at the very least, a dress code. McDonald's requires a uniform; Home Depot encourages collared shirts and clean jeans; American Express Financial expects shirts and ties. By joining the organization, we tacitly agree to abide by that uniform or code. There will always be a degree of tension felt between the need or desire to conform to organizational expectations and the desire to maintain our individuality within the organization. Different organizations are more or less tolerant of deviations from the accepted uniform or dress code.

Uniforms and dress codes serve several essential functions within organizations. First, they simply identify who is and who is not a member of the organization. Recall a time when you mistakenly asked a fellow customer for assistance in a retail store—mistaking her or him for an employee. Uniforms and dress codes also convey an image of the organization to the public. Many organizations have quite detailed guidelines employees are expected to follow. How employees dress and groom conveys an image, a message to the public about the organization. Even the National Basketball Association (NBA) has imposed a business casual dress code on players when they are acting in an official team or league capacity or conducting NBA business.[6] The NBA officially recognizes that appearance conveys an important message about the organization as a whole. Because players become role models, the NBA wants to convey a professional image to the public and youth. While this decision was met with some resistance, it is a position that reflects reasonable concern about the impact of nonverbal symbols.

Generally speaking, most organizations are fairly conservative in terms of dress and grooming expectations. Suits and jackets, collared shirts, and ties are generally the norm for men. The era when women were expected to wear dresses and suits has given way to the acceptance of slacks and pants. This being said, the arrival of "casual days" in organizations caused considerable confusion given these traditional norms. How casual could one be without being too casual? There is even some evidence to suggest that in creating a more relaxed atmosphere, casual days have led to a decrease in productivity, manners, and punctuality,[7] indicating a connection between nonverbal choices and civil attitudes toward work.

Good grooming complements professional appearance

Every spring, an interesting transformation takes place among seniors on college and university campuses anticipating job interviews and graduation. Long hair and scraggly beards give way to neat haircuts and clean-shaven faces; various kinds of body art—tattoos, piercings, and unique hair coloring and styles—give way to more conservative and concealing business suits and modest grooming. These predictable transformations are all in an effort to adapt and conform to professional expectations in terms of grooming. How we choose to adorn our bodies as we interact in the business and professional world is important and should be approached strategically.

Bodily Movement, Position, and Gestures

How we move, position our body with respect to others, and gesture to others can be powerful nonverbal means of communication that all fall under the study of kinesics. Generally we speak with others in a face-to-face orientation. Imagine a small group of friends or colleagues standing in a circle as you approach. If one of your colleagues notices you and fails to move to include you in the group of friends, you will likely feel unwelcome and excluded. The opposite is true if your colleagues welcome you into the conversation by simply expanding the circle to include you. Giving someone "the cold shoulder" demonstrates the use of bodily movement and position as a means of communicating civility or incivility, inclusion or exclusion.

The posture we assume can convey the interest we have in the speaker, the speaker's topic, and the situation. When people are interested in a speaker's topic, they generally "sit up" and "pay attention" by way of the posture they assume. A slouched posture tends to convey the opposite message, a lack of interest and attention. The caveat to these generalizations, as you read earlier, would be that too much or too little can be read into another's nonverbal behavior. One interesting feature of movement and posture is that we tend to mimic or echo the behavior of our partner(s) in interaction, something referred to as response matching.[8] If you observe a conversation, try watching how the participants mimic, match, or echo each others' movement and posture.

While we normally think of gestures as being most important in a speaker-audience situation, think about all of the ways that the hands and arms can be used to convey messages. In a public-speaking situation, we typically use gestures to help illustrate (convey size, shape, location, and movement) and reinforce (through pointing, fist-shaking, or podium-pounding) the ideas we are trying to convey. Gestures can also be used as emblems or substitutions for words. For example, in a manufacturing setting, the hand drawn across the neck always means "shut down the machine." The "okay" gesture created by touching the thumb and index finger together and extending the remaining fingers signals something is alright, almost physically forming the letters "o" and "k." Pointing one's thumb up or down conveys agreement or disagreement—unless you're in the Roman arena, where it conveyed life or death. The list of such emblems can be quite long.

Facial Expressions and Eye Contact

Perhaps the most noticed bodily means of nonverbal communication would be the face. We know that the face is capable of communicating interest, boredom, excitement, shock—literally hundreds of feelings and emotions. While there are several fairly universal facial expressions, including fear, anger, shock or surprise, happiness, disgust, and sadness, all facial expressions are critically important in communicating emotions.

Not only are the eyes essential to receiving messages, they are a powerful means of reaching out, connecting with another person, and sending messages. Edward Jones Investments, one of the *Fortune* "100 Best Companies to Work For," reports that the company's success is due in large part to its reliance on face-to-face communication with clients. They perceive eye contact as a valuable contributor to the business relationship.[9]

Oculesics is the formal study of eye behavior. By making eye contact with another person, you create a bond and begin to establish a relationship with that person. Likewise, failing to establish eye contact or ignoring the gaze of another fails to connect or acknowledge a relationship—except in the negative sense. It is not uncommon to use eye contact or the lack thereof in a strategic manner. Students walking across campus refuse to make eye contact with the professor whose class they just skipped. Coworkers refuse to make eye contact with the supervisor who is waiting for an important report. The eyes then are both the receivers of messages and a powerful means for sending messages in interaction.

Spatial Relationships

The study of proxemics, or how we use space and territory, has been an important area in nonverbal communication dating to the early work of scholars like Edward T. Hall in the 1950s.[10] Much of what such early scholars discovered still holds true today; we are essentially territorial creatures. We stake our territory, we mark our territory, and—when necessary—we defend our territory from invasion and contamination. Students routinely "stake out" a seat in a classroom regardless of whether they are assigned to a particular seat or not. They tend to notice and react when another student sits in "their seat." Coworkers often exhibit the same behavior and come to expect a certain seating arrangement in meeting and conference rooms. Perhaps these territory-staking behaviors are a result of assigned-seating at the dinner table during childhood, where traditionally the head of the household assumes the position at the head of the table with remaining family members assuming seats according to age and thereby relative status. It is curious to note that children often tend to continue to assume these seating arrangements even after leaving home.

Riders on mass transit systems often will mark their seat by placing personal items on the seat beside them, in effect claiming the whole seat as theirs. When asked to move these personal belongings by another rider who wishes to use the seat, they sometimes convey their dismay—nonverbally through facial expression or a sigh of annoyance. Office workers feel a sense of violation if their personal space is violated by coworkers taking liberties by moving or rearranging office furniture or disturbing personal items on a desk.

As a means of formalizing the study of spatial relationships, Hall suggests that there are four zones of space in which we all operate and in which we feel comfortable carrying on certain types of interactions. These include: intimate distance extending from our body to roughly eighteen inches, casual-personal distance from eighteen inches to four feet, social-consultative distance from four to twelve feet, and public distance beyond twelve feet.[11] Given these zones, we tend to become uncomfortable when strangers get too close—encroach on our territory. However, interacting with friends and close acquaintances in the same close proximity is acceptable. At the other extreme, it would be awkward to carry on a romantic conversation with twelve feet separating us from our partner. Over time, we have come to know and use these various zones of space for different types of communication. Most business would be transacted in the social-consultative and public zone depending on the situation and nature of the interaction. In addition to recognizing and using these zones, we also learn other lessons—for example, that those who are older and/or of higher status generally exert more control over space and the use of space, especially in the business and professional world.

Office space, the assignment and use of company-supplied and -owned space, becomes an important concern. The size, location, number of windows (or lack of windows), as well as the size and quality of office furnishings can become contentious issues in organizations. Because space is valued and valuable, those who have and control space tend to be those with the most power and influence in the organization. Corner offices and those located in close proximity to the boss's tend to be the most valued.

The appearance of the now-ubiquitous cubicle in organizations has changed the use of space in organizations, along with the popular Dilbert comic dedicated to those occupying cubicles. Envisioned by its creator, the now-deceased fine arts professor Robert Propst, as a mean for improving productivity in the late 1960s, the cubicle revolutionized the use of space in organizations.[12] While the final verdict may not be in on the positive or negative influence the cubicle has had on organizations and people in organizations, the fact that offices became more open and people more accessible and exposed has changed the use of space. With cubicles, floor-to-ceiling walls that had provided quiet and a degree of privacy to workers in organizations disappeared, replaced by partition-like walls that in theory could facilitate interaction among members of organizations. While organizations reportedly spend $3 billion per year on cubicles—the largest share of office furniture sales[13]—the human costs and their impact on civility in organizations have not been calcu-

lated. Among these less tangible costs would be: noise levels increase, personal privacy decreases, confidentiality while communicating in person or on the phone is compromised, individuality in office décor and personal artifacts and decoration tend to be more regulated.

Along with the use of space is the arrangement of the physical environment. It is instructive to spend some time simply observing how people arrange the physical space under their control. By visiting several offices, you can get a sense for how welcoming the office might be. Desks and tables, for example, can be used as a physical barrier to separate people in conversation, while the lack of such physical separation creates a different environment for interaction. Think about how mem-

bers of the clergy can create a different environment with a congrega-
tion or audience simply by using or not using a podium or dais. Not
using the podium tends to increase attention and decrease napping and
daydreaming.

The Voice

If you remember the advice that "it's not what you say but how you
say it," you are well on your way to understanding the role of the voice
in cultivating civility in business and professional settings. The boss
who shouts critical comments gets an entirely different level of employee
loyalty than the one who speaks in a conversational tone. Vocalics or
paralanguage, the study of the voice as a means of communication,
involves vocal features like tone, rate, volume, pitch, intensity, and the
use of pauses. Stated differently, vocalics involves everything we do with
our voice other than pronounce the words. One easy way to understand
the importance of vocalics is to consider the voice to be a musical instru-
ment and the verbal message to be the notes to be played. It is our voice
that brings the words to life, gives them color, shapes their intent, and
crafts their character and meaning. Without the voice, the verbal message is neutral; with the voice, the meaning of the verbal message
becomes richer and clearer.

Touch

Our ability to touch, what is also referred to as haptics, is one of the
most unique and intimate forms of communication because it involves
actual physical contact between people. We have all experienced touch
as a powerful means of communication since birth—it is perhaps the first
type of communication we experience. The key considerations for touch
as a means of nonverbal communication are who touches whom, how
and where they touch, and how frequently they touch. The relationship
that exists between communicators is perhaps the most important medi-
ating factor in each of these considerations. The more familiar and intimate the relationship, the more touch is appropriate; the more distant
and professional the relationship, the more touch would be inappropriate.

Yet, strangely enough, handshakes and pats on the back are common
occurrences in the business and professional world. A handshake is

probably the most common form of greeting in American culture. However, even the simple handshake is subject to many different considerations—how firm should the grasp be, how many times should we "pump" the other's hand, what is the proper duration of the grasp? Some suggest that the best handshake involves two firm quick and confident pumps followed by the release of the other's hand.[14] While such forms of touch are common in the business and professional setting, caution should be taken especially regarding touch between members of the opposite sex because of the potential for misinterpretation.

Time

Since we cannot taste, touch, hear, see, or feel time, we generally structure our perception and understanding of time metaphorically by comparing time to money, a commodity that can be spent, saved, invested, or wasted. The formal study of time is referred to as chronemics, but, in a way, we have all studied and learned about time all of our lives. Research suggests that as a society we are becoming more impatient, whether we are waiting in the grocery checkout line or being placed on hold by a customer service representative.[15] We also know that there are significant cultural differences in perceptions and uses of time.

Especially in the business and professional world, time is a valuable commodity. We are paid for our time; employers expect to make money from their investment in our time, and we will likely lose our job if we waste too much time. Customers and clients expect organizations to value their time and will likely cease to be customers or clients if too much of their time is wasted by an organization. Customers and clients should not be kept waiting not only because it is rude to do so but also because it is bad business.

One particularly interesting feature of time in an organizational setting is that, like space, members of differing status levels are allowed to use time in different ways. For example, students at colleges and universities come to believe that there are a set number of minutes that they must allow for the tardy arrival of a professor. The higher the rank of the professor, the longer they think they are supposed to wait. Rarely are such guidelines committed to policy. The business equivalent of this situation would be that the boss is allowed to be late, wasting the time of subordinates, but subordinates are not allowed to waste the time of their boss.

Guidelines for Civil Nonverbal Communication

Given the complexity of nonverbal communication and the multiple ways in which we communicate nonverbally, arriving at specific guidelines or suggestions for the civil use of nonverbal communication becomes difficult. If we were to attempt to suggest a firm set of rules for the use of nonverbal behavior, there would likely be at least one exception or caveat for each rule. Instead, we will suggest six guidelines that can be followed for the civil use of nonverbal communication in business and professional settings.

Since we usually use both verbal and nonverbal elements to convey a message, the first guideline is to *make sure the verbal and nonverbal messages complement each other*. Research suggests that if we perceive a contradiction between the verbal and nonverbal parts of a message, the nonverbal part of the message will be most influential in shaping the meaning we assign.[16] At the simplest level, if the words we are using are meant to convey excitement and enthusiasm, we should also be nonverbally excited and enthusiastic in our tone of voice, facial expression, and gestures. The opposite is also true: if we are verbally serious, we should be nonverbally serious. If we are making an important presentation, we want to convey the gravity of the situation in the way we choose to dress and comport ourselves. There should be a degree of consistency between the verbal and nonverbal parts of the message.

For example, a relatively new police officer had been told that his sergeant would be available if needed, but that the department's expectation was that he would handle his new responsibilities competently and professionally. On one of his first days on the job, the young officer responded to a call about a dangerous dog. As he was taking the witness's statement, he saw another patrol car approaching down the street and assumed that another officer had been sent to help him. But the car stopped a block away. After completing his conversation with the witness, the young officer walked to his own car and, looking down the street, saw his sergeant, leaning on a fence next to his own car, just watching. The sergeant's actions spoke loudly to confirm the earlier words that he would be available to, but trusting of, the young officer.

Nonverbal communication should be appropriate to the people and the situation. One size does not fit all; we should not approach a world requiring a tailored approach to communication with an off-the-rack attitude. This is especially true in terms of dress and grooming. That baseball cap you have been wearing all through college will not cut it in the office or boardroom. If the situation is formal, the dress and attire should also be formal. Then there are the exceptions. If an executive wanted to connect with workers on the shop floor, perhaps dressing down might be appropriate and more effective. A new client who arrives at the organization on casual Friday might be less inclined to do business with the organization. It is not the client who is dressed inappropriately, it is the representative of the organization. Adapting to the situation and the demands of the situation and relationship are important.

We can and should all become more aware of our use of nonverbal communication. Since we have been communicating nonverbally since birth, certain nonverbal behaviors have become so habitual that we may have become desensitized to the importance of our own and others' nonverbal behavior. Watching people in a busy downtown business district can be a rich source of insight. You will discover that there are patterns and similarities as well as random and unique features to non-verbal behavior. Watch people coming and going at a busy building entrance. Those entering double doors are likely using the door on their right while those exiting should also be using the door on their right to ensure the smooth flow of traffic. Observe those who hold doors for others—a simple civil act, as is thanking the person holding the door regardless of gender. It is useful to watch those who seem to be following the "rule" as well as those violating the rules—and how people react and respond to the rule breakers. Studying the layout of offices and the layout of individual offices can also be instructive. Is the spatial arrangement of the office and furniture inviting, or does the open door really not invite one into the space? Becoming more aware of our own and others' nonverbal behavior is useful so long as we keep in mind that nonverbal behavior is both conscious and unconscious, intentional and unintentional.

Being aware of others' space is also important to civility. Especially in the era of the cubicle, something as simple as managing the volume of conversation becomes important. With the proliferation of cell phones, we have all inadvertently learned more about the personal lives of total strangers as well as coworkers than we care to know. It is almost as though all the space that used to be for public interaction has become private, and all those interactions that used to be conducted in private have become public. Civility requires that we be respectful of both the public and private space around us, keeping in mind that we share that space with others.

We should also be sensitive as to how our nonverbal behavior will be perceived by others. Becoming more aware will help us to develop this sensitivity, which is especially important in the areas of space, tone of voice, and touch. If we stand too close to a coworker, we create tension—their space is being violated. Standing too far away can perhaps convey a stand-offish attitude.

Consciously being sensitive to how our tone of voice and all vocal features might be perceived will result in more civil interactions. It is possible and desirable to deal with difficult and potentially conflict-producing situations with a calm and civil tongue. The outcome of doing so will likely be better for the immediate situation and the longer-term relationship.

Because touch is such an intimate form of nonverbal communication and its use so relationally determined, people in the business and professional world must be sensitive to how touch will be perceived. Handshakes are normal and expected; hugs and more intimate types of touch may be perceived as inappropriate at best and harassing at worst.

We should be careful and cautious as we interpret the nonverbal behavior of others. We can miss certain nonverbal behaviors—literally not see or perceive the behavior of others; we can also misinterpret the behavior of others. As we have suggested, nonverbal behavior must be perceived holistically. Various specific behaviors work together to convey a particular message and meaning. The civil communicator is both self and other-oriented; considering both how their behavior will be interpreted as well as how they should interpret the other's behavior. They manage their own behavior as they try not to miss important behaviors from others or misinterpret important behaviors.

Finally, we should attempt strategically to use and manage nonverbal communication to convey civility and accomplish our goals. Just as we can make conscious choices about the words we use to convey our ideas, we can make conscious and strategic decisions about how we dress and groom, use our voice, face, and eyes, manage spatial relationships, and move and gesture.

Strategically, by adhering to the implicit or explicit uniform or dress code, we lend respect to the organization and the image the organization wishes to convey. Practically, organizational dress codes and/or uniforms identify for customers and clients who is a member of the organization. Personally, how we choose to dress and groom allows us to shape the perceptions and impressions others will form of us. Through our management of our attire, we can manage—at least to a certain extent—how we present ourselves to those around us. What is appropriate to this situation, given the professional relationship that exists—or is being created—and the goals being pursued by the parties involved? Answering this question can help to determine the civil use of dress and grooming.

The simple wave of the hand exchanged by friends or acquaintances is a clear gesture and message of civility and acknowledgment that can also be a deliberate strategy to initiate communication. Clearly there are more uncivil gestures; most notably, the extended middle finger commonly known as "the bird" is a more profane substitution for the "f" word. In a slightly different way, nodding one's head in agreement or shaking one's head in disagreement substitute for the actual use of words. All of these emblems have communicative value in their ability to convey ideas and can be used to civilly or uncivilly communicate a message.

Even a smile can be strategic. The simple and civil act of putting a smile on your face will likely change your mood and will quite possibly elicit a smile from those you encounter. Try intentionally smiling at the next ten people you encounter in class, at work, or at home. Chances are that your smile will be reciprocated. It almost seems to be a societal or cultural rule that smiles or casual greetings are returned in kind. So is smiling important? Only to the extent that it might create a more pleasant climate among the people with whom you associate.

Eye contact can be used in a civil way to establish and create connections between people, or uncivilly to ignore or exclude people. The eyes can also strategically be used uncivilly to violate that societal rule learned in childhood about staring at another person. Such use would constitute a violation of the space of another person using the eyes rather than the body. The reminder here is that many types of nonverbal behavior can be under our conscious and strategic control.

Respecting and strategically using time also becomes a means of conveying civility in the business and professional world. While there may be a relationship between time and status in organizations, time and the use of time as a nonverbal message ought to be used to convey messages of respect—valuing the time of colleagues and coworkers—rather than as a symbol used to arbitrarily reinforce status difference in organizations. Not only because it is the right thing to do, but also because it is bad business to waste anyone's time.

Summary

To be civil in our nonverbal behavior requires us to strive for the verbal and nonverbal messages we send to complement each other. Civil communication should be appropriate to the situation and relationship at hand. The more aware of and sensitive to nonverbal behavior we become, the more likely our messages will acknowledge others and convey civility. If we are careful not to miss cues and misinterpret the behavior of others, the chances for civil communication are increased. Finally, civil communication requires us to manage and behave strategically in ways that are appropriate to the situation, respectful of the people and relationships involved, and responsive to the unique demands of the situation.

As we have described nonverbal civility, it involves respectful decisions about what to wear in the business setting; how to use gestures, movement, and facial expression; where to sit or stand in relation to others; and how to use your voice expressively and temperately. Following these guidelines will help you to get a job and keep it, even getting promoted along the way. You don't want to make the mistake of one forsaken salesman we encountered whose ill-fitting suit, white socks, and shifty eyes cost him any chance of achieving the credibility he needed to sell one of our student organizations on the value of his company's products. Look credible, act trustworthy, and the business success will follow.

NOTES

1. Albert Mehrabian, "Communication without Words," *Psychology Today* 2 (1968): 53–55.

2. Raymond Birdwhistell, *Kinesics and Context* (Philadelphia: University of Pennsylvania Press, 1970).

3. Ronald Adler and Jeanne Elmhorst, *Communicating at Work: Principles and Practices for Business and the Professions* (Boston: McGraw-Hill, 2005).

4. See, for example, Julius Fast, *Body Language* (New York: Pocket Books, 1971).

5. Survey available at: http://www.naceweb.org/press/display.asp?year=&prid=236; accessed June 1, 2006.

6. "Explaining the NBA Dress Code," *Washington Post*, October 20, 2005, E3 (accessed online October 20, 2005).

7. "New Wrinkles in Casual Dress Codes," *Kiplinger's Personal Finance Magazine*, November 1999.

8. Phillip Emmert and William Donaghy, *Human Communication: Elements and Contexts* (Reading, MA: Addison-Wesley, 1981), 81.

9 Mark Modlo, Edward Jones Investments, personal interview, July 2006.

10 Edward Hall, *The Silent Language* (New York: Fawcett Premier Books, 1959).

11 Edward Hall, *The Hidden Dimension* (New York: Anchor Books, 1969).

12 Julie Schlosser, "Cubicles: The Great Mistake," *Fortune*, March 22, 2006 (available at: http://money.cnn.com/2006/03/09/magazines/fortune/cubicle_howiwork_fortune/index.html); and Yvonne Abraham, "The Man behind the Cubicle," *Metropolis*, November 1998 (available at: http://www.metropolismag.com/htnl/content_1198/n098man.html).

13 Schlosser, op cit.

14 Ted Allen and Scott Omelianuk, *Esquire's Things a Man Should Know about Handshakes, White Lies and Which Fork Goes Where: Easy Business Etiquette for Complicated Times* (New York: Hearst, 2001), 6.

15 Calvin Woodward, "AP Poll Finds Americans in a Hurry," *Star Tribune*, May 28, 2006 (available at: http://www.startribune.com/484/story/459861.html).

16 James Stiff, Jerold Hale, Rick Garlick, and Randall Rogan, "Effect of Cue Congruence and Social Normative Influences on Individual Judgments of Honesty and Deceit," *Southern Speech Communication Journal* 55 (1990): 206–229.

8

Culture, Civility,

and Communication

The United Nations once dealt only with governments. By now, we know that peace and prosperity cannot be achieved without partnerships involving governments, international organizations, the business community and civil society. In today's world, we depend on each other.
—*Kofi Annan, United Nations Secretary General*

Civility is not only an issue in the United States; civility has become an issue of concern throughout the world, especially in the context of business and organizations. For example, in 2004 the Financial Executives Association of the Philippines (FINEX) called on members to renew their pledge of support for the organization's code of ethics. It is the obligation of members to report violations of the rules of proper conduct and "non-observance of civility by a member or members of FINEX," because "civility strengthens the foundations of ethical behavior."[1] In Tokyo, a special government panel invited citizens to submit examples of rude public behavior and has started a public information campaign featuring Big Bird and Elmo cautioning and reminding people to behave in public. A government official leading Tokyo's response to bad manners stated that "civil liberties should always be subjected to the wider needs and expectations of the community."[2] Also in Asia, the Chinese government has formed the Communist Party's Spiritual Civilization Steering Committee in recognition of the fact that rude behavior can potentially damage China's reputation in the world as preparations are made to host the 2008 Olympic Games.[3] On the Continent, some French employers, seeking a competitive edge, are offering international etiquette training classes.[4] Similar offerings are available in Germany, where "Employers fear rude behaviour can harm productivity at home as well as cause embarrassment abroad," with one workplace campaign using the slogan "Things Go Better When You're Nice."[5] Similar efforts are underway across the channel in England.[6] Closer to home, Canadians are reportedly experiencing the same concerns about civility as is evident in the United States.[7] What all of these examples suggest is not only a concern and need for civility worldwide, but the need for an international and intercultural background to the issue of civility in business across different cultures.

Culture is a key variable in any consideration of effective communication and is especially important in the development of civil communication skills. If there is one variable that shapes every aspect of our communication attitudes, thoughts, and behaviors, it is culture. Culture shapes factors including our fundamental values and beliefs, social customs, religious and ethnic traditions, history and folklore, and myths and legends.

It is important to remember that we are born into a culture, not born with a culture. The culture into which we are born and raised determines the language we learn. The language we learn influences the ways we think about the world around us. The language we learn and the way it influences our perceptions of the world shape our communication behavior. Assuming that we share a common cultural and language community, communication is *relatively* easy. If, however, we're trying to interact with someone from a different cultural background and language community, communication becomes much more complicated. Literally, not only are different people communicating but they are communicating through different cultures.

As we suggested earlier, there are good reasons for incorporating civility into our business and professional communication. Civility makes for a more pleasant work environment, healthier relationships, and a more successful organizational bottom line. Much the same is true with respect to intercultural communication. Intercultural civility can contribute to a more pleasant work environment, build healthier and more productive relationships, and improve the organizational bottom line. If people from different cultural backgrounds wish to communicate civilly, there are challenges to be overcome. In this chapter we'll address these challenges by explaining what intercultural communication is and why it is important in the business and professional world. The important cultural differences that influence the way we communicate will be examined especially as they relate to civility. While the concept of civility is common across cultures, the means used for expressing civility and respect can differ significantly. Understanding these differences will be important to your success. Finally, you'll find suggestions and recommendations for improving civil communication in intercultural situations.

The Importance of Intercultural Communication

Intercultural communication is communication that occurs between individuals and groups from different cultural backgrounds. As we explained, communication takes place in a variety of contexts, usually focused on the number of people involved. Following this context approach, intercultural communication can involve two people, a small group, or a speaker-audience situation. The key distinguishing feature that sets intercultural communication apart from other communication contexts is that the interactants involved do not share a common cultural background or, in many cases, a common language. In order to be effective and civil, communicators must adapt to the key **differences that make a difference interculturally** and that influence communication success and effectiveness. These differences are grounded in relatively uncivil attitudes that can be summarized as: an **ignorance** of the other person's language and culture, an attitude or degree of **arrogance** in thinking that one culture is better than or superior to another, and perhaps a measure of **laziness** in thinking that these differences don't matter. Before exploring these barriers in more detail, it is important to realize why a basic background in intercultural communication is useful in the business and professional world.

Organizations and the people who make up organizations are becoming increasingly more culturally diverse, primarily because of changing national demographic patterns. According to figures from the 2000 U.S. census, Hispanics are now the largest minority group in the country, comprising 13 percent of the U.S. population, followed by blacks at 12.7 percent, with whites and other smaller minority groups making up the rest of the population. In twenty short years, the percentage of whites in the U.S. population decreased from nearly 80 percent in 1980 to just fewer than 70 percent in 2000.[8] These demographic changes are even more pronounced in certain cities and regions like the Miami and Los Angeles areas.

The changing demographic and cultural face of United States is reflected in the racial, ethnic, and cultural makeup of U.S. organiza-

tions. Even classrooms are becoming increasingly diverse. A recent basic public-speaking class was made up of half traditional eighteen- to twenty-four-year-old college students, two international students, several returning adult students, and six recently laid-off former factory workers returning to continue their educations, including one sixty-year-old who had last been in a classroom forty years earlier. This diversity enhanced everyone's learning experience. It also required everyone—instructor and students—to think in new and different ways.

Adapting to and accommodating these demographic and cultural changes will require new skills on the part of all organizational members. Therefore, one reason a basic background in intercultural communication is important is that interacting in and managing twenty-first-century organizations demand such an understanding. A second compelling reason for intercultural training can be found in the increasingly global and interconnected world economy.

In recent years, the world has become a smaller place. International trade and commerce have expanded. Technology has made communicating as accessible and instantaneous as picking up the phone or typing a few keystrokes. In order to not only survive but thrive in this new economy, U.S. organizations are learning to do business in a globalized economy. One of the most important skills to be learned is how to communicate effectively with customers and clients from different countries and cultural backgrounds. From a purely pragmatic perspective, an intercultural communication background has become an essential skill for doing business. If communication skills are essential for success in the business and professional world in general, a background in intercultural communication is essential for success in the global business world in particular.

As the United States and U.S. organizations become more diverse and compete in an increasingly global economy, it is important to examine the cultural differences that influence the way we communicate, especially as they relate to civility. P. M. Forni, of the Johns Hopkins University Civility Project, summed up the situation well: "No workplace in the world is as diverse as the American one. Fostering a workplace culture of civil openness and inclusion is clearly in the interests of most American organizations today. This is the culture of the future, which will allow organizations to do well in the global civilization of the new millennium."[9]

Cultural Differences That Make a Difference

Speaking the same language and having some background in cultures other than our own is obviously a prerequisite for effective communication in a diverse workforce and global marketplace. While English may be a dominant language in the business world, ignorance of other languages and cultures could be perceived in the business and professional world as cultural arrogance. Such arrogance might reflect the attitude that one language and culture is superior to another. This attitude is called ethnocentrism.[10] If we are ethnocentric and believe our culture is superior, this tends to imply that other cultures are inferior. Such an attitude is not conducive to effective communication and is especially detrimental to civil communication.

Ignorance and arrogance can lead to laziness on our part; the assumption that the rest of the world ought to be more like us, like me, like my company, and like my country. Realistically, the chances of foreign organizations, countries, or the world in general changing to assimilate U.S. culture and values are not good. Successful members of 21st century organizations will need to accommodate and adapt to cultural differences. If differences are embraced, accommodated, and even celebrated, civil communication can be enhanced.

The starting point to such accommodation is to understand the key cultural differences that will influence intercultural civility in general and communication behavior in particular. We have selected an even dozen of these differences for your consideration—realizing your own experience and research may suggest many more. The first six differences focus on general ways of thinking that require understanding and accommodation while the final six are factors specific to different types of nonverbal communication.

Language and Perception

Not only is language an essential means for conveying and sharing messages, the language we use also fundamentally influences the ways we think and even what we think about. For example, living in the Great Lakes region, we have several different terms for snow—lake effect, granular, corn, sleet, powder, etc., while someone living in the south— who might never have seen or experienced snow, just sees frozen white powdery stuff on the ground or in a picture. The frozen white powdery "stuff" has not changed, but our perception of it is sharper and more discriminating because of the language we use. Imagine a language like that of the Native American Hopi which literally has no equivalent word for time. For the Hopi, imagining the future is difficult and linguistically impossible. [11]

Consider how we think about an argument or a disagreement through the metaphor of war and battles—"attacking" the positions of others while we strengthen and "defend" our own position. Such metaphorical understandings may not make much sense in cultures that see conflict in less militaristic terms and strive for harmony and are uncomfortable with disagreement and conflict like many in Asia. The literal or figurative nature of a language, its formality or informality, the prevalence of jargon, and the use of idioms and colloquialisms can influence the ways in which we think—which may be different from other cultures. These linguistic differences can cause misunderstanding between cultures.

When interacting interculturally, it is important to at least make the effort to learn some of the language. Even learning some basic greetings and a few important phrases of those from different cultures will contribute to civil communication and more positive initial relationships.

Individual versus Collective Orientation

An important characteristic of any culture is how it values the efforts of individuals and groups. In the United States, there is a long history and tradition of an individualistic orientation—phrases like "rugged individualism," "looking out for number one," and "what's in it for me" characterize this orientation. Other cultures, particularly many Asian cultures, place more importance and value on the good of the group one belongs to than the efforts of single individuals.

These two fundamental orientations influence the way people communicate. People from individualistic cultures tend to be more direct, seek and take individual credit for success, and assign blame individually; people from collectivist cultures tend to communicate more indirectly, ambiguously, and share credit and blame.[12] These fundamental orientations also influence how members of the culture approach conflict. Members of individualistic cultures tend to approach conflict with a more direct communication style, while members of collectivist cultures approach conflict with a more indirect, avoidance, and mutually face-saving style.[13] Asian business executives may not explicitly say no, when in fact they are saying no in a way that saves their Western counterpart the embarrassment of having a proposal rejected. The civil intercultural communicator will accommodate and adapt to these differing cultural orientations by knowing when to be direct and indirect, how to assess and assign credit and blame, and how to approach conflict more effectively.

Perceptions of Gender

Perceptions of the role of women differ widely across cultures, from equality to servitude and everywhere in between. Rightly or wrongly, much of the world did not, has not, and likely will not experience the type of women's movement the United States experienced in the 1960s and '70s. In fact, it is entirely possible that a highly successful female executive from a U.S. company would need to employ a male subordinate as a surrogate in order to conduct business in some countries. While this may be galling, it may be culturally necessary.

In certain conservative Muslim countries, the role of women is severely limited, to the point that it is rude even to inquire as to the welfare of a Muslim businessman's wife and family—it is just not appropriate. Knowing something of these cultural customs, not necessarily agreeing with such customs, can facilitate civil communication between such diverse cultures. This is not to suggest that things don't change; witness the fact that two recent U.S. secretaries of state have been women—the highest diplomatic office in the country. Accommodating differing cultural perceptions of the role of women is simply a means of facilitating global business relationships.

Perceptions of Time

In the United States and many northern European countries, we have what is termed a monochronic perception of time. We perceive and understand time as a valuable commodity to be wisely spent, carefully invested, and certainly not wasted. Monochronic cultures value being on time to appointments and spending time in meetings and at the office productively, and feel slighted and offended if others don't share the same perceptions. Other cultures, for example those of southern Europe, the Middle East, and parts of Latin America, have what is termed a polychronic perception of time. Such a view places more importance on people than productivity, or maybe more accurately, investing time in people and relationships in order to achieve productivity, and the ability to accomplish several tasks at the same time. In a polychronic perception of time, being on time is more relative or flexible—the appointment or meeting starts when everyone arrives. Taking time to build relationships before and during the meeting is more important than arbitrarily finishing a meeting on time. Time spent communicating helps build positive relationships that facilitate the conduct of business in such cultures.

The clash of different time orientations can be a source of considerable misunderstanding and perceived incivility depending on one's cultural perception of time. Is the Arab uncivil for keeping the American waiting, wasting her time, or is the American uncivil for not being patient and taking time to build a relationship? Flexibility and a willingness to accommodate such difference require knowing these differences and a civil and respectful attitude willing to adapt to such differences.

Perceptions of Conflict

Different cultures also perceive conflict in different ways, from valuing and embracing a good argument or discussion to extremes of politeness and even a refusal to say "no" for fear of offending. American and many western European cultures value a straightforward, direct approach to conflict, telling the other party in the conflict exactly where we stand. Such directness would be perceived as rude and uncivil in Asian cultures like Korea and Japan, which value harmony over conflict. In these cultures, it is rude to openly express conflict and disagreement, almost to the point of not being able to say "no" when in fact "no" is exactly what is meant. Saving face and enabling your business partner to save face are valued over "knowing where you stand" with your partner in the conflict or disagreement. You can imagine the frustration and perceived incivility both parties might experience if they are unaware of the other's differing perception of conflict versus harmony.

High- and Low-Context Cultures

We know that both the verbal and nonverbal parts of a message are important in conveying the meaning of the message. We also know that some cultures depend more on the verbal while others place more emphasis on the nonverbal aspects of messages. High-context cultures attend more to the nonverbal nuances and subtleties implicit in messages, while low-context cultures focus more attention on the direct, straightforward, more explicit verbal messages.[14] Asian, Middle Eastern, and South American counties would be in the high-context category, while the United States and many European countries would fall into the low-context category.[15] When people from these different cultural backgrounds interact, each should be aware of and sensitive to the other. While we in the

United States may value and expect direct, honest, and straightforward discussion, we need to be aware that people from high-context cultures will be attending more to the nonverbal implicit messages we are sending. Specifically, "individuals in a low-context culture might appear rude or abrupt to someone in a high-context culture. Likewise, someone in a high-context culture might seem shady or distrustful to an individual in a low-context culture."[16] Given the likelihood for misunderstanding, civil communication would advise care and caution in order to accommodate this fundamental difference.

Civility in intercultural exchanges begins by knowing something of the language and perceptual difference that will be encountered. It requires an understanding of the value placed on the individual versus the group or collective. Acknowledging that different cultures perceive gender, time, and conflict in fundamentally different ways is essential. Recognizing that different cultures depend more or less on the verbal and nonverbal aspects of messages as they are received and interpreted is important background knowledge to keep in mind. Knowing that cultures can differ significantly in how business relationships are initiated and cultivated could make or break such relationships. The skilled civil communicator is willing to accommodate these differences, and takes the time and effort to take these differences that make a difference into account before engaging with individuals from other cultures. In addition to these general cultural differences, there are several specific differences in nonverbal behavior to which the civil business and professional communicator must attend when encountering a new culture.

Greeting Customs

In the United States we prefer to move relationships along a trajectory toward informality almost to the point where we want to be a friend to everyone we meet. We shake hands, exchange names—preferably first names, and engage in a bit of small talk as we get to know a new acquaintance—skills that generally serve us well. Intercultural civility requires that we be prepared not only to exchange handshakes, but bows (of differing degrees), hugs (of differing intensity), and perhaps even kisses (on one or both cheeks) as we greet someone from a different culture. Hesitating or demonstrating a reluctance to exchange such greetings can be perceived as rude and uncivil. Knowing how to shake hands (we prefer a firm handshake, Asians less firm), how low to bow (in some cultures there are classes to master the complexity of bowing), how firmly to hug, and whether to kiss one or both cheeks requires knowledge of the culture on the part of the civil communicator. Knowing something of these details may seem unimportant, perhaps even trivial, but knowing the proper way to greet someone from another culture paves the way for building personal and business relationships.

The exchange and presentation of business cards may also be a part of the greeting ritual. If such an exchange takes place between U.S. business executives, the business card is likely viewed functionally—it provides necessary contact information for the new acquaintance. The same exchange of business cards between a U.S. and a Japanese executive should take on much more symbolic importance. The U.S. executive should realize that to his or her Japanese counterpart, for example, the business card should be treated with the same degree of respect you have for the presenter. Business cards should be taken in both hands, carefully read and examined, and certainly not simply shoved into a pocket or, worse yet, deposited in one's wallet to be sat upon. Those routinely doing business interculturally are also well advised to carry bilingual business cards, with one side printed in English and the other side in the language of the other country.

The exchange of small gifts is also appropriate in certain cultures. Knowing the types of gifts that are appropriate is yet another mark of the civil intercultural communicator seeking to build respectful relationships.

Following culturally appropriate greeting behavior and rituals, knowing how to address someone from a different culture presents the next challenge. In the United States we generally desire to know everyone on a first-name basis rather than honoring and respecting formal titles and status relationships. The only formal titles that we commonly pay much attention to would include those used for doctors, clergy, elected officials, and, in colleges and universities, professors (sometimes). This trajectory toward informality has the potential to be perceived as rude and inappropriate with people from more formal cultures, and even with older members of our own culture. Honoring and respecting titles is a means of conveying respect for another's position and standing within an organization and culture and respecting his or her cultural traditions. Referring to persons from a different cultural background using their full name and title (Mr., Mrs., Ms., Professor, Doctor, Reverend/Father/ Rabbi/Imam, or their equivalents) until invited to use more informal and familiar forms of address is important—realizing that such an invitation to informality may not occur.

Knowing something of the language and social customs of a different culture is obviously important to knowing which title to use, and whether formality or informality is appropriate. The situation requires even more cultural research and knowledge if titles of royalty or elected government officials might be involved. Even within the United States, showing deference and "respecting our elders" is another mark of civility. Using "Mr. and Mrs." or "Sir and Madam" in addressing older customers and clients is appropriate until invited to use more informal means of address.

Clothing and Attire

We know that the impression we create is in large part shaped by the way we choose to dress. Decisions we make regarding clothing and attire, especially in intercultural situations, should be made carefully and conservatively. If civility in part means conveying respect, it is important to respect the cultural traditions and norms of the different culture. The usual conservative business suit for both men and women is generally acceptable. The key is to be modest and conservative rather than stylish and trendy. In Middle Eastern countries that follow strict Muslim traditions, women must be especially careful and modest. What may be fashionable in a Western setting may be perceived as rude, offensive, and even illegal in certain Middle Eastern countries. In extreme cases, failing to honor and respect cultural and religious customs has had tragic consequences. Witness the killing of two Iraqi tennis players and a coach by Islamic extremists who accused the players of offending Allah by wearing shorts.[17] While an extreme example, it illustrates the importance of respecting cultural and religious traditions. Dressing for success interculturally means adapting and accommodating to the customs of other cultures. Civil communicators will respect the traditions and customs of the other culture even when doing so may violate their personal beliefs and preferences.

Spatial Relationships and Position

While the tendency for people to be territorial creatures may be a universal cultural factor, cultures differ significantly in terms of how much space or territory they find comfortable for different types of interactions. Sensitivity to these differences is required to facilitate civil and effective communication. The four different zones of space related to different types of communication transactions still exist interculturally, but each culture may have differing perceptions of the size of these zones and different perceptions of the types of interactions that can be conducted in the various zones.

Adapting to and accommodating these differences can be difficult and even a bit uncomfortable. For example, generally people from the Middle East, southern Europe, and Latin America tend to prefer less space (smaller zones)—closer face-to-face conversation—than many of us would find comfortable, in some cases preferring to be close enough to smell and/or feel the breath of the person to whom they are talking.[18] Image this scene: an Arab businessman unknowingly violates the proxemic comfort zone of the Western businessman, who steps back to increase his or her comfort zone, which prompts the Arab to step forward, as the Westerner continues to step back. Chances are that both are offended by and perceive the other to be rude. Civility requires an understanding and accommodation to such differences.

Tactile Relationships

Some cultures are more tactilely oriented than others. Generally, touching or contact cultures would include Arab, Jewish, eastern European, and Mediterranean cultures, while western European (Germany, England) and North American would be less tactilely or contact oriented.[19] The key word here is *generally*, because even within cultures there are differences.

In the United States, touch is heavily regulated by societal norms in terms of when, where, how, and who may touch whom. When visiting another country, we may think it odd to see two men or two women walking arm-in-arm or with their arms around each other. We may feel uncomfortable exchanging kisses of greeting when meeting people from other cultures. It is important to remember that our cultural norms and perhaps even "taboos" might not be practiced in other cultures, and, in fact, such casual touching is normal, acceptable, and expected. It is also important to remember that touch and space are very much related—cultures that prefer more or less space also tend to prefer less or more physical contact. Knowing and anticipating these types of differences makes it easier to avoid responding negatively and risking offending someone in her or his cultural surroundings and being perceived as uncivil.

Gestures

Perhaps no other type of nonverbal behavior has the same potential to interculturally offend and communicate incivility than gestures, specifically the type of gestures referred to as emblems. These are gestures used as a substitute for words or ideas. Because emblematic gestures are used in place of a word or idea, they tend to have rather precise meanings, and, in some cases, profane, obscene, and sexually explicit meanings. In terms of intercultural civility, it is important not to inadvertently "swear" with our gestures. For example, the thumbs-up and okay gestures of approval are extremely offensive and rude in Brazil, Australia, Spain, and many Middle Eastern countries. A bit of your own research on the Internet will reveal the meanings or referents of these gestures. Just as the language we use can be rude and offensive because of the associations we have between words and the objects to which they refer, so too can gestures have offensive referents. Civil intercultural communicators do their homework not only on the spoken language of the culture, but also on the language of gestures appropriate to a particular country and culture.

Eye Contact

Many of us were brought up to look a person in the eyes, to think the eyes are the windows to the soul and that those who refuse to make eye contact are likely hiding something. We may have been taught not to stare or maintain intense eye contact. There are numerous culturally specific norms related to the "proper" and appropriate use of the eyes. The important thing to realize and remember is that these norms are culturally specific. In some Latin American countries, establishing and maintaining direct and prolonged eye contact can be a sign of disrespect. Realize that a lack of direct eye contact can be a sign of deference and respect—depending on the culture and the gender of the participants. Keep in mind that there is a natural relationship among eye contact, facial expression, and spatial relationships—further complicating civil intercultural communication. Knowing how to use the eyes appropriately in different cultures requires care, research, and sensitivity to differences.

Suggestions for Developing Civil Intercultural Communication Skills

There is no way any book chapter can hope to incorporate all the intercultural background information necessary for the successful and civil conduct of communication within diverse contemporary organizations or in the global marketplace. We have briefly outlined twelve important differences that make a difference in order to introduce you to the complexities of communication in intercultural situations. Along the way, we have suggested how these differences relate to establishing and building civil communication relationships.

It is important to keep in mind that cultural diversity exists within the organization as well as between organizations and global business partners. As demographic trends suggest, the internal cultural dynamics of the contemporary organization are becoming as complex as the external organizational dynamics. The coworkers we encounter may likely require the same cultural accommodation and adaptation as the potential client or customer in the global marketplace.

We have been careful to use the terms *accommodation* and *adaptation* rather than *assimilation* in discussing how cultural difference should be approached. By definition, when we accommodate we are adapting to something new, we are willing to change, we are trying to be helpful. We have purposefully not used the term *assimilate* in referring to cultural differences because it suggests that the different culture be absorbed into the familiar culture, that the minority culture be absorbed into the dominant culture. Perhaps the most difficult question in this regard is: Who should accommodate and adapt to whom? Ideally, each culture should accommodate, adapt, and learn from the other. Practically, the best advice may be captured in the old adage "When in Rome, do as the

Romans do." In other words, when visiting and experiencing a new culture, do your best to accommodate, adapt, and learn about that culture and communicate in a civil and respectful manner. Unfortunately, there is no guarantee that this accommodation, adaptation, and willingness to learn will be reciprocated when businesspeople from other cultures experience the United States. These are important issues and questions to consider and remember as we offer three basic suggestions for developing civil intercultural communication focused on a developing a positive attitude, increasing our cultural knowledge base, and actively practicing new skills.

Open-Mindedness versus Ethnocentrism: Attitude Is Key

An open mind to the changes that are occurring within U.S. organizations and the growing importance of the global marketplace is perhaps the most critical quality a business professional can have in the early years of the twenty-first century. The trends toward increased cultural diversity within domestic organizations and increased activity in global marketplaces show no signs of leveling off, let alone slowing down. Being open to these opportunities, possibilities, and challenges will be an essential characteristic for the people who will manage and work in contemporary organizations and compete in the global marketplace.

A basic understanding of the complexities of intercultural communication will help to meet the challenges and turn them into opportunities and possibilities. Knowing, accepting, and accommodating the fact that coworkers from different cultural backgrounds not only come from different language communities, but may have fundamentally different orientations in terms of the importance of individuals versus groups, gender, time, and conflict will enable professionals to communicate more successfully. However, simply "communicating our point" is not enough; intercultural interactions within and outside organizations can and should be marked by civility. Respecting coworkers and the cultural backgrounds of coworkers by accommodating differing means of civil interaction will enrich the workplace and the relationships among people in organizations.

Much the same is true of communication in the global marketplace. Simply communicating or conveying a message will not be enough. It may accomplish the immediate goal but will not build the kinds of positive relationships that are marked by acceptance, understanding, and a respect for different cultural backgrounds and traditions. Only by infusing intercultural interactions with an understanding of differing customs, norms, and traditions of civility will we build the mutual respect needed for successful long-term international business relationships. The "good (or bad) old days" of arrogant and ethnocentric attitudes expressed by expecting the rest of the world to be, believe, and act more like us will not well serve successful twenty-first-century organizations. An open mind should seek new information, the only cure for intercultural ignorance.

Do Your Homework, Cure Your Intercultural Ignorance

This chapter has provided a background in some of the differences that make a difference when people from diverse cultures interact. In the course of your career, you will likely experience what many refer to as culture shock, defined as "the transition period and the accompanying feelings of stress and anxiety a person experiences during the early period upon entering a new culture."[20] One way to ease or cure culture shock is to arm yourself with good information about the new culture. This requires homework and research on your part. One consistent recommendation cited in the intercultural communication literature is to learn and know as much as you can about different cultures.[21] Fortunately, there are a variety of readily available resources at your disposal to aid in this learning process. The Internet is one valuable source of such information. "Googling" the terms *international business practices* resulted in an astonishing 345 million hits. Given the sheer volume of information you'll find as you mine this resource, be sure to evaluate carefully the quality of the information you find. Obviously any good library will provide general intercultural information as well as country-specific information. At the end of this chapter, we have included a small sampling of the available resources to get you started. A willing and open mind will seek the information and background needed to overcome the cultural shock and difference we are likely to encounter on the job as well as in the global marketplace—and prepare us to be more civil and successful in both.

Practice, Explore, Celebrate

A positive attitude and new knowledge are of little value if you don't put them to use. Realize that exercising new attitudes and under-standings will likely be awkward and uncomfortable. After all, it has taken us years to learn the cultural customs, rules, and norms with which we are familiar. Realize that the same level of awkwardness and discom-fort may also be true for your counterpart in an intercultural encounter. Recognizing and talking about differences in a civil and respectful man-ner important. Such conversations are useful learning experiences for both parties—each learns about the other's cultural background, traditions, and customs. In the process, relationships are established and can be cultivated if we civilly accommodate the differences we will encounter.

Traveling is another way to expand our cultural knowledge and experience, so long as part of our travel preparations is to investigate the culture of our destination. The old stereotype of the "ugly Americans" trampling on the customs, values, and norms of their destination will do little to enhance civility. One of the most transforming and valuable expe-riences a college student can have is to study abroad. Many universities offer a variety of these types of experiences, some short term, some for an entire semester or year. Living and studying abroad allows for the development of conversational language skills beyond what students normally learn in the classroom. Such language skills become valuable assets in the job market. This type of longer-term travel and living expe-rience increases intercultural understanding and might later give grad-uates an edge in the job market as companies seek culturally experienced employees.

Summary

Organizations and workers should find ways to celebrate and embrace diversity as an opportunity to be exploited (in the positive sense of the term) rather than a problem to be solved. Civil verbal and nonverbal communication skills, coupled with an understanding of important cultural differences, increase the chances of cultural diversity positively rather than negatively influencing twenty-first-century organizations. If like-minded people tend to think alike, different-minded people—those from differing cultural backgrounds—will likely think differently about decisions, problems, and possibilities. Cultural diversity brings new ideas, insights, and perspectives to the organization that can strengthen the organization—assuming its members have effective and civil communication skills. Organization members who are open-minded and willing, knowledgeable, and informed, and skilled at practicing civil communication, can make cultural diversity a valuable organizational asset rather than an organizational liability.

Additional Resources

R. E. Axtell. *Gestures: The Do's and Taboos of Body Language around the World.* (New York: Wiley, 1998).

Axtell has written several books on the dynamics of intercultural business.

Carley Dodd. *Dynamics of Intercultural Communication*, 3rd ed. (Dubuque, IA: William C. Brown, 1991).

Textbook that provides good background information and research on intercultural communication written from a communication perspective.

Norine Dresser. *Multicultural Manners: New Rules of Etiquette for a Changing Society.* (New York: Wiley, 1996).

Dresser wrote a column for the *Los Angeles Times* called "Multicultural Manners" and taught at various colleges in the Los Angeles area. According to the author, the book is designed for "ordinary Americans coping on an everyday basis with people unlike themselves." It is a good resource for changing workplaces, schools, and social situations.

Philip Harris, Robert Moran, and Sarah Moran. *Managing Cultural Differences: Global Leadership Strategies for the 21st century*, 6th ed. (Amsterdam: Elsevier Butterworth Heinemann, 2004).

Textbook that approaches intercultural communication from a businessmanagement perspective.

Peggy Kenna and Sondra Lacy. *Business France: A Practical Guide to Understanding French Business Culture.* (Lincolnwood, IL: Passport Books, 1994).

This is part of a series of pocket-size books covering business etiquette, communication style, problem solving and decision-making, and meetings and presentation styles for the following countries: China, Germany, Italy, Japan, Korea, Mexico, Spain, and Taiwan.

Judith Martin and Thomas Nakayama. *Intercultural Communication in Contexts*, 3rd ed. (Boston: McGraw-Hill, 2004).

Recent intercultural communication textbook that provides broad background information and research on intercultural communication.

Terri Morrison, Wayne Conaway, and George Borden. *Kiss, Bow, or Shake Hands:How to Do Business in Sixty Countries* (Avon, MA: Adams Media, 1994).

As the title suggests, the authors profile sixty countries, including: background on the country; cultural orientation (cognitive style, negotiation strategies, and values systems); common business practices; and advice on protocol.

Carol Turkington. *The Complete Idiot's Guide to Cultural Etiquette*. (Indianapolis, IN: Alpha Books, 1991).

Provides an overview and background on international etiquette followed by no-nonsense and humorously presented advice for North and South American countries, eastern and western European countries, Asia and the Pacific Rim, an the Middle East—twenty-six countries in all.

http://www.awesomelibrary.org/Classroom/Social_Studies/Multicultural/Intercultural_Com munication.html

This site lists many intercultural and multicultural resources and provides links to even more.

www.crossculturalnonverbals.com

This website provides information and additional links in five areas: physical appearance, gestures and greetings, gift-giving and manners, proxemics and hap- tics, chronemics.

http://www.culturegrams.com/

"Culture Grams" are concise four-page descriptions of 190 countries published by ProQuest Information and Learning. You can purchase the complete set or indi- vidual country profiles.

http://www.executiveplanet.com/

Executive Planet describes itself as providing "valuable tips on business etiquette, customs and protocol for doing business worldwide. Our guides are co-authored by experts in international business etiquette, who are available to answer your questions on the discussion board."

http://www.getcustoms.com/2004GTC/index.html

This site is associated with Terri Morrison and the book *Kiss, Bow or Shake Hands* listed above and describes online commercial resources for global business travelers.

http://www.state.gov/travelandbusiness/

The website for the U.S. Department of State provides a wealth of information on international travel and business. Consular information sheets provide detailed information on hundreds of countries profiling history, customs, travel tips, crime, and so on.

http://www.un.org/

The website for the United Nations contains information on 190-plus member states.

NOTES

1 Amelia Ylagan, "Corporate Watch," *Business World: Manila*, October 4, 2004, 1 (available at: http://proquest.umi.com/pqdweb?did=706810661&sid=1&fmt= 3&clientld=9874&rqt=309&vname=pqd).

2 Martin Bashir, "Elmo, Big Bird Enlisted to Patrol Manners in Japan: Nation Built on Ancient Rituals Confronts Shifting Manners," ABC News Report, February 3, 2006 (available at: http://abcnews.go.com/2020/print?id=1577018).

3 Jocelyn Ford, "Chinese Working on Their Manners," American Public Radio Marketplace Segment, August 17, 2006 (available at: http://marketplace. publicradio.org/shows/2006/08/17/AM200608176.html).

4 "Global HR Round-up: French Seek Competitive Edge through Etiquette Classes," *Personnel Today*, March 14, 2006 (available at : http://www.personneltoday.com/ Articles/Article.aspx?liArticleID=34360&PrinterFriendly=true; accessed June 29, 2006).

5 "Germans Mind Their Manners to Boost Productivity," *Personnel Today*, February 22, 2005 (available at: http://www.personneltoday.com/Articles/Article.aspx?li ArticleID=28086&PrinterFriendly=true; accessed June 29, 2006).

6 Jennifer Harper, "Manners a Top Priority at Work," *Washington Times*, March 15, 2006. (available at: http://www.washingtontimes.com/national/20060314– 104502–6470r.htm; accessed June 29, 2006).

7 Charlie Gillis, "Socially Unacceptable: A Whole New Genre of Rudeness," *Macleans.C*, April 5, 2004 (available at: http://www.macleans.ca/topstories/life/ article.jsp?content=20040405_78050_78050; accessed June 29, 2006).

8 "Hispanics Now Outnumber Blacks as Largest U.S. Minority Group," Associated Press story in *Erie Times News*, January 22, 2003. Also see CensusScope.org at: http://www.censusscope.org/us/print_chart_race.html.

9 P. M. Forni, *Choosing Civility: The Twenty-Five Rules of Considerate Conduct* (New York: St. Martin's, 2002), 56–57.

10 Carley Dodd, *Dynamics of Intercultural Communication*, 3rd ed. (Dubuque, IA: William C. Brown, 1991), 51.

11 Edward Hall, *The Hidden Dimension* (New York: Doubleday Anchor, 1966), 92.

APPLICATIONS TO THE

CONTEXTS OF BUSINESS

AND PROFESSIONAL COMMUNICATION

Civility in the

Interpersonal Context

You pull into the parking lot at the beginning of the day. Walking into your office, you chat with several coworkers, commenting on the weather and the heavy traffic. As you approach your office, you greet colleagues and remind them of the staff meeting scheduled for later in the morning. Your administrative assistant has arrived early, and asks how your son's soccer game went and reminds you of an important client meeting in the afternoon. After updating each other on family, friends, and your busy days, you log on and open your email and pick up the phone to answer your calls. Another day on the job has begun, and, like on all other days, interpersonal communication will be a dominant part of your day.

The most common type or context of communication in the business and professional world is interpersonal communication—interactions that generally involve two people. These two-person personal and professional relationships are at the foundation of any organization. The communication that takes place through these relationships is both business-related (getting the work of the organization done through meetings and client reminders) and simple social interaction among coworkers (talking about the weather, family, and friends). Both types of interaction are important to the success of the organization. Some estimates suggest that our social interactions consume much more time (up to 90 percent) than our task-oriented and business-related interactions on the job.[1] This is not to suggest that people on the job are simply wasting time talking to their colleagues. As social creatures, we know that these interactions are vital to shaping the social environment of the organization and are an important reason why we go to work.

Given that the average person can anticipate spending roughly a third of their working and waking life in some type of organizational setting, careful consideration of the quality of the environment where you will spend this part of your life is essential. Since the quality of the work environment is largely shaped by the quality of the communication that takes place in that environment, focusing on making interpersonal communication in organizations as civil and respectful as possible is impor-

tant for the organization's success. Civil interpersonal communication in the workplace is also in your best interests both professionally and personally.

To establish and cultivate civil interpersonal relationships on the job, there are several key considerations on which to focus. First, a positive and civil communication climate must be established in the organization by the members of the organization. Second, the status hierarchy within the organization needs to be acknowledged but not overemphasized. Third, the verbal and nonverbal communication strategies we have explained need to be practiced along with a participatory attitude that makes all organizational members responsible for cultivating a civil environment. Fourth, effective listening skills must be developed and practiced to ensure that ideas and the people expressing them are valued and appreciated. Finally, organizational members must remember that small acts of civility and respect can make big differences in shaping the organization's climate and positive personal relationships.

Cultivating a Positive and Civil Communication Climate

We know that all communication takes place in a physical, social, and cultural environment. It is the social environment rather than the physical and cultural that most closely relates to the concept of communication climate. The term *communication climate* is used to describe "the quality of personal relationships in organizations."[2] More specifically, an organization's communication climate is shaped by "the perceptions employees have of the quality of relationships and communication in the organization and the degree of involvement and influence."[3] How coworkers interact with each other shapes the communication climate in positive or negative ways.

Using the metaphor of weather—factors like temperature, precipitation, wind, humidity—is a useful means for conceptualizing the concept of communication climate or environment. The key here is to use our knowledge of the weather as a means for understanding and characterizing personal relationships. Just like the weather can range from clear and sunny, to partly cloudy, to overcast and dreary, to drizzly and damp, to stormy, all the way to hurricane and tornado, so too can the overall communication climate or atmosphere in an organization range from very positive to very negative. More specifically, the relationships we have with coworkers can be warm and friendly, cold and distant, calm and pleas-

> I work in the Customer Service Department and our busiest time of year is known as "Fall Bake." Fall Bake is from September to December and is a time when a majority of people celebrate the upcoming holidays with family and friends by baking. While other departments have people off on vacation, most of my department works long, busy days. This past year, as my department was busy serving customers, one of the co-CEOs walked around the department and sincerely thanked each person for working so hard. To have a person of his position take time out of his schedule to let me know I am appreciated means a lot to me as an employee.
>
> Julie Hale Abbott
> Sales and Marketing
> Systems Coordinator
> J. M. Smucker Company, Cleveland

ant, or stormy and hostile. Research suggests that a positive communication climate is marked by qualities like supportiveness, participative decision-making, trust-confidence-credibility, openness and candor, and high goals that are communicated clearly to members.[4] All of these qualities are directly or indirectly related to the idea of civility.

What factors determine and shape the communication climate of an organization? The attitudes and communication behaviors of organizational members, to a large extent, shape and determine the climate that exists within the organization and between fellow workers in the organization. Ideally, the communication climate in an organization ought to reflect qualities like trust, openness, honesty, respect, appreciation, and a valuing of others. A negative communication climate would be characterized by the opposite qualities. In addition to the verbal and nonverbal communication strategies we have already discussed, there are specific message-construction strategies we can use to help cultivate and maintain a positive communication climate.

Many psychologists and communication scholars from the past have studied communication interactions in an effort to identify those telltale strategies that seem to be most conducive to creating a more supportive, less defensive interpersonal communication climate. Their conclusions have one thing in common: they all suggest strategies that we now know to be *civil* communication attitudes and behaviors. Several specific suggestions stand out as models for interpersonal behavior we should all adopt in the business setting.

Civil communicators create supportive communication climates by conveying positive, status-neutral expectations of others. As we begin any conversation with coworkers, we make choices about our posture, facial expression, tone, and words. Subtle differences among those choices are perceived in either positive or negative ways by others. Whether you convey positive or negative expectations, you will get what you expect, so isn't it better to establish the positive expectations? For example, a coworker stops by the office to chat while you are in the midst of a project at the computer. If you take your fingers off the keyboard and turn toward the visitor, you will be perceived as being interested in what the person has come to say and being willing to take the time to listen to it. By contrast, if you keep your hands at the keyboard and only turn your head to acknowledge the visitor, you will be interpreted as being uninterested in a conversation at this time. Any ensuing conversation will be flavored by that perceived expectation.

This principle is especially important when the conversation is between persons of different status—a boss and an employee, for instance. Civil and skilled superiors do not depend on their rank or status in the organizational hierarchy to do their work. Through their communication behavior, successful bosses and supervisors build relationships with coworkers that value "subordinates" and appreciate them as equals. This was noted in the comments of one of the managers within a *Fortune* "100 Best Companies to Work For," who stated that his superiors at the main office regularly invite not just him, but any other employee he would like to invite to attend their monthly management training seminars. By doing so, management is being status-neutral in offering advancement opportunities to their employees. That is civil!

Civil communicators use acknowledgment and affirmation of others to enhance supportive climates. By small verbal and nonverbal gestures we can affirm the value of others and ought to do so. Such things as remembering a person's name and addressing him or her personally makes that person feel important and, therefore, more willing to interact cooperatively with you. When engaged in conversation, do you use verbal affirmations like "I see," "Really?" "Interesting!" and "Okay" to emphasize that you're listening? If you do, you are contributing to a supportive communication climate because those little comments convey to the other that you are following the conversation and signal to the other when clarification or summation is necessary. Thus, they serve psychologically as the strokes that build self-esteem.

One small technique that provides affirmation is focusing on "we" rather than "I" when talking about a problem-solving approach. Employees who feel controlled, pushed, or dictated to tend to resist that control by pushing back and resenting the other's dictates. If we value coworkers and own each others' problems and work collaboratively to solve them, we can enhance civility and a positive communication climate.

Civil communicators create supportive communication climates by focusing on ideas, not personalities.

This one is hard, isn't it? It is so easy to get caught up in judging the person with whom you are speaking instead of truly listening to his or her ideas. When we work in any organization for a length of time, we develop likes and dislikes for our coworkers. That's normal. But those negative perceptions can begin to dominate our thinking to the extent that we can't even listen fairly to what certain people say, and that is something that we need to change. If the person with whom you are speaking feels evaluated and judged, he or she will tend to react defensively. As civil communicators, we can separate the message from the messenger; we can value and appreciate the sender and provide specific and constructive feedback about the message.

The overall climate for productive communication will be enhanced when we can mentally put aside our negative attitudes about persons and focus on the ideas they are bringing to the conversation. The guy who jilted your sister just may have a good idea for solving the shipping problem. The woman whose makeup is too garish just may know the person who can get you access to the data you need. We will be better off to respect the positive possibilities of every interaction than to dismiss some because of who the messenger happens to be.

Civil communicators create supportive climates by following others' trains of thought to their end before jumping on their own. Research in civil listening has identified the tendency to interject one's own experiences into a conversation as one of the most common, and destructive, communication behaviors. A recently overheard conversation is a typical example of this kind of behavior. It went something like this:

M: "Well, my husband had his final cancer treatment yesterday."

K: "That's good. Where did he go for that?"

M: "Over at the cancer center on 12th Street."

K: "Oh, really. My brother-in-law lives right up the street from there. He loves that neighborhood."

M: "Yes, if you have to go there, at least it's pretty."

K: "Yes, he's lived there for about ten years now, ever since the divorce."

As you can see, K has essentially hijacked the interpersonal conversation here. M opened with a statement that could have elicited supportive comments and expressions of concern, but instead dissolved into an exchange about geography that is of value only to K, who apparently prefers to hear her own voice, no matter what. We create a more supportive climate by keeping our ears attuned to the other's channel, not our own. Ask specific follow-up questions, encourage the conversationalist with direct eye contact and nods, and wait to add your own experience until specifically invited.

Messages of indifference or neutrality tend to devalue the sender and the relationship between sender and receiver. Civil communicators strive to convey their genuine concern for the person and the person's message. Empathy toward our colleagues helps to facilitate civil relationships interpersonally, which will translate into an overall culture of supportiveness within the whole organization.

Civil communicators contribute to long-term supportive encounters by following through with ideas raised in each exchange. This suggestion is especially important in supervisor-employee conversations. In the spirit of respecting the potential contributions of every member of the work unit, supervisors should show some evidence that they are seriously considering the ideas suggested by their personnel. This action can be easily communicated by use of emails, thank you notes, or bulletin-board notes. To see a posted memo saying something to the effect that Joe in accounting suggested we switch delivery services, and management would like to get comments from others on that idea contributes significantly to a positive work environment. It is not just a compliment to Joe, but an indication that all employees will be listened to and their ideas treated with respect. The result is a supportive climate in which people will feel free to speak, which will lead to better decision-making all around.

The follow-through should reflect a provisional response, as in the example of Joe. The supervisor is not committing to a complete understanding of Joe's suggestion or an endorsement of it at this point. Such tentativeness shows respect for the possibility of misunderstanding. A wise person once said, "It's not what you know that can hurt you, it's what you know that ain't so." Civil communicators are tentative rather than dogmatic, being open to all alternative ideas and interpretations. If we adopt this attitude and use messages shaped by tentativeness, we can contribute to a positive and civil organizational communication climate.

All of these suggestions for supportive communication can be manifested in the organizational charts that are typical in most corporations. Such diagrams are provided for new employees to establish and clarify the company's preferred reporting channels. The best ones reflect the positive, affirming, egalitarian, idea-centered, and action-based relationships we have described here.

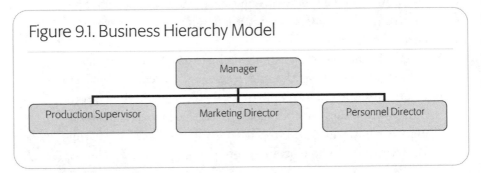

Figure 9.1. Business Hierarchy Model

Striving for Equality within the Hierarchy

One inescapable fact of organizational life is that there always have been and will likely always be bosses and workers, superiors and subordinates, and the powerful and the less powerful. "In hierarchically structured organizations, differences in members' status and power are simply a fact of life."[5] However, this axiom of organizational life does not mean that status differences need to be emphasized and highlighted.

Different people do different things in organizations and play different roles within the organization, but ultimately someone is held responsible for the work of the organization. Everyone from the custodian to the CEO is important to the success of the organization. Experts have commented that "More important that an MBA [is] an understanding of the importance of assistants as sources of intelligence and know how."[6] The simple but critical lesson expressed here, and one that anyone who has spent any time in an organization understands, is that while you may have rank and status in the formal organizational hierarchy, those "below" you in the hierarchy make your work possible. As civil communicators we should value, respect, and appreciate coworkers regardless of formal status and rank.

If managers or superiors go out of their way to emphasize status differences, the quality of personal and organizational relationships will suffer. Status differences between superiors and subordinates can be maintained without superiors emphasizing the formal organizational inequalities. If superiors insist on formal manners of address and/or titles, they are accentuating status differences and emphasizing inequalities. Effective managers and bosses can supervise without "pulling rank." If managers, through civil and effective communication strategies, build upon commonalities rather than differences, the quality of personal and organizational relationships can be improved. Research suggests that the best supervisors are those who are communication-minded, willing and empathetic listeners, and sensitive to the feelings of others, those who ask and persuade rather than tell and demand, and those who openly pass along information to subordinates.[7] The advice for managers and bosses is to "create an environment for your subordinates that you, if you were a subordinate, would like to work within every

day for the next thirty years."[8] Absent from these conclusions and advice is any emphasis on the use of status differences by supervisors to manage effectively. Relationships of civility, mutual respect, and acknowledgment of status difference can be cultivated without subordinates needing to make supervisors feel superior or superiors needing to make subordinates feel inferior.

Messages Shape the Communication Climate

The messages we exchange with coworkers in business and professional organizations, to a large extent, shape the communication climate that will develop in the organization. Negative messages tend to foster a negative communication climate; positive messages tend to cultivate a positive communication climate. Our attitude toward the construction of messages, what we are trying to do through the messages we send, becomes important. If we adopt a participative attitude toward interpersonal communication, the opportunities for cultivating a positive communication climate and quality relationships between and among coworkers will be enhanced. Adopting a participative attitude toward the verbal and nonverbal communication strategies we have explained makes all organizational members responsible for cultivating a civil environment. We'll briefly explain this attitude of participation,[9] or what is also termed rhetorical sensitivity,[10] before illustrating how it works to shape a civil communication climate and civil interpersonal relationships.

Adopting a Participative Attitude

In any given day, we all make hundreds if not thousands of choices. We have the freedom to choose how we will think, how we will behave, and how we will interact with the people around us. We can choose to take coworkers, relationships, and situations into account as we interact, or we can try to "go it alone." Given the amount of time we will all spend in organizational life, committing to take people, relationships, and situations into account as we interact is a smart choice. If we ask questions like Who am I talking to? What's our relationship? What does this situation require?, we are demonstrating an attitude of participation.

When we adopt a participative attitude toward communication, the *we* becomes important, not the *you* or *I*. Our relationship becomes important. The unique features of the situation become important. Taking these features into account will require more time, effort, and thought on your part, but the payoffs in terms of creating a civil communication climate within the organization are worth the investment.

As we participate in civil and respectful relationships with coworkers and seek to construct messages that will build positive relationships and communication climates, two basic questions become important: What is to be said? How is it to be said?[11] In other words, what is the content of the message you want to send and what is the best way for you to craft or construct the message? As you answer each of these questions, you will need to make choices. If you adopt a participative attitude, your choices will take into account who you're talking to, your relationship, and the situation. If you choose not to adopt a participative attitude, you don't care who you're talking to, the relationship will not be an important factor, and the situation will not be relevant.

Key to understanding and thereby adopting a participative attitude is your willingness to adapt your messages to the unique people, relationships, and circumstances that are presented. Here is where the concept of rhetorical sensitivity fits in. This notion of sensitivity is built on the ancient communication or rhetorical principle of audience adaptation: the more you know about your audience, the more you can adapt; the more you adapt to your audience, the more successful you will be. Notice that we have not suggested that you change the content of your message, rather that you be willing to find the best way of constructing a message that takes into account people (coworkers), relationships (superior-subordinate, peer, and so on), and situations (conflict, decision-making, casual, and so on). The civil interpersonal communicator constructs the verbal and nonverbal elements of the message in such a way as to deliver the content of the message in a way that respects the audience, the relationship between speaker and audience, and the situation at hand.

Adopting a participative or rhetorically sensitive attitude helps to guide the ways in which we construct messages. If you review the lessons we suggested for the civil use of language at work and the guidelines for the use of nonverbal behaviors in the workplace, you'll find that they are entirely consistent with a participative and rhetorically sensitive attitude. For example, we suggested that sometimes silence is your best choice, that you use words that are respectful of the specific listener, that you respect the reality of the situation by choosing temperate, not inflammatory words, that you respect the uniqueness of all individuals, and that you use clean language all the time on the job. We suggested that you can manage strategically many elements of the nonverbal message system to convey civility to individuals and throughout the organization. Employing these strategies and lessons in combination with an attitude of participation and rhetorical sensitivity will help you to cultivate civil interpersonal relationships with coworkers. They also help you to participate—to do your part in cultivating and maintaining a civil and positive communication climate within your organization.

Listening as an Interpersonal Skill

The preceding sections have emphasized the sending of messages that will help to create, cultivate, and maintain a civil and positive communication climate within organizations. Equally if not more important to the communication process and establishing a positive communication climate is the reception of messages. If we are listened to, we feel that our ideas have value, that we have value and are appreciated. Therefore, we need to turn your attention from the sending of civil messages to the civil reception of messages; we need to focus on civil listening skills.

There are many ironies with regard to the study, practice, and art of listening. For example, most communication textbooks—including this one—spend more time explaining how to send messages than how to effectively receive messages. The irony is that research in and out of organizations suggests that we spend significantly more of our communication time listening to or receiving messages than we spend sending messages. For example, workers in organizations reported the following percentage breakdown of their communication time: 32.7 percent listening, 25.8 percent speaking, 22.6 percent writing, and 18.8 percent reading.[12] These numbers certainly suggest that listening is an important if not dominant skill in organizational settings. As impressive as these numbers are in suggesting the importance of listening, additional research found that the average college student reported spending even more of their communication time listening, somewhere between 42 and 53 percent.[13] Clearly, listening is the most used and perhaps least developed of our communication skills, whether in the classroom or in the organization.

While we know that listening skills are at least as important—if not more so—than other communication skills (speaking, writing, and reading), very little or no educational and instructional time has been spent to develop these skills when compared to the other communication skills. The irony here is that our educational experiences from elementary through high school devoted considerable more time to developing our speaking, reading, and writing skills than to developing our most used communication skill, listening. This instructional disparity is possibly explained by the fact that many people incorrectly assume that listening is a passive or natural activity not requiring formal instruction. There are ears on the sides of my head; I can hear, therefore I can also listen. However, we know that listening is not the passive process of the speaker simply pouring information into the ears; listening requires conscious effort and thought on the part of the receiver. While we may passively *hear* things in the environment around us, we must actively and consciously *listen* in order to effectively receive messages. The distinction between hearing and listening is an important one. Hearing is the physiological process, while listening is a cognitive and psychological process.

Finally, while listening can be approached as a very complex and complicated behavior, the fundamentals of effective listening are really quite simple. However, while the fundamentals of listening may be simple, listening is not easy. Effectively listening to messages requires at least as much physical energy and mental effort as effectively sending messages. The irony here is that while we generally know how we *should* listen, we generally don't do what we know we should do.

Given these ironies, it is important for the civil communicator to understand what is involved in the process of listening, some of the common problems and barriers to listening, and some concrete suggestions for effective listening in order to create and cultivate civil relationships in business and professional organizations. Focusing on developing your listening skills and abilities will place you among the best of American organizations, since research suggests that 60 percent of Fortune 500 companies provide listening training and instruction to their workers.[14]

The Process of Listening

There are five steps to the process of listening: hearing, attending, assigning meaning, remembering, and responding. **Hearing** is simply the ability of the ears and the physical, neurological, and cognitive mechanisms of hearing to sense and process sound. This is the passive stage of the listening process. **Attending** is where conscious thought and effort are required to tune into and focus on one message at the expense of all the messages that exist around us at any given point in time. This stage is similar to tuning your radio or television to a particular station, channel, or program. Given the volume of potential messages that surround us, we choose to focus on some and ignore others. **Assigning meaning** is the step in which the receiver must decode the message he or she has received. This stage requires the listener to assign meaning or significance to the words being used, the structure of those words, and the context in which they are being used. We must understand the message before the process of listening can continue. If these first three steps are successful, the listener can **remember** or store the message, in either short- or long-term memory. If you have ever been caught asking, "What did you say?" just as you are recalling the message the sender has conveyed, you have experienced the movement of a message from short- to longer-term memory. **Responding** is the final step in the listening process, in which the listener responds or replies to the sender. This response can also be termed feedback from the receiver to the sender.

At a very basic level, the civil communicator understands the difference between simply hearing someone and consciously attending to and listening to someone's message. Civility requires us to pay conscious attention to and focus our energies on a particular sender and his or her message. Once they attend to a particular message, civil communicators must carefully think about and interpret the message, which again requires conscious effort and thought. Remembering messages can be difficult; some messages are important enough to make it to long-term memory, while others are quickly lost and forgotten. If we are focused on the sender and carefully assigning meaning and understanding the message, the remembering step is easier. Finally, the civil and effective communicator provides a response to the sender that confirms receipt of the content or ideas in the message and confirms, values, and appreciates the sender and the relationship that exists with the sender. Here is where we come full circle, back to the sending of civil messages. Civil and effective listening is clearly more than passively allowing the sender to pour messages into our head.

Barriers to Effective Listening and the Civil Solution.

We suggested that listening is simple, but not easy. As you read about the problems and barriers we experience as we listen, think about all the listening attitudes and behaviors you have that prevent you from listening effectively. Many of these problems and barriers are related to the concept of noise or interference that is part of the communication model. Since no such list will be all-inclusive, feel free to add your own experiences to those of others.

1 **Physical distractions**: Rooms can be too hot or cold, chairs can be uncomfortable, lights can buzz, and there can be noise and/or annoying odors from adjoining areas.

 Manage the environment: The civil listener actively manages the physical aspects of the communication environment in order to reduce noise and interference, thereby increasing the opportunities for effective communication. They close the door and make the speaker as comfortable physically as possible. They let the answering system take a call during important conversations. They turn off the radio, TV, or cell phone and focus attention on the speaker. They use nonverbal behavior that will put the speaker at ease.

2 **Preoccupations:** The big test or project coming up, a sick child, a major decision to make, a good or bad relationship, or anticipating a vacation can distract the listener.

   Manage your attention: Civil listeners recognize their preoccupations and temporarily put them aside as they focus on what the sender is saying. When they catch themselves daydreaming or their minds wandering, they return mentally to the sender. They make mental time for the speaker and her or his message, then return to their own concerns.

3 **Message over- or underload:** Too much information (too many emails and voicemails) and you can't process or respond to it all; too little information and you have time to daydream.

   Manage the information load: Skilled listeners try to optimize the flow of information—neither too much nor too little. They take in as much as they can, but they realize and are aware of their limitations. If they are receiving too much information, they ask the speaker to slow down or repeat. When there is too little information, they focus on what they have and process it carefully. They stay focused on the speaker and the message.

4 **Gender/ethnic/cultural differences:** Men/women aren't as smart/skilled/competent as men/women, she/he looks different, he/she talks "funny," that delivery style is really distracting.

   Be aware of bias: Civil listeners recognize and are aware of their own biases and prejudices. Rather than pretending they don't exist, they actively take them into account. They seek out differences and recognize that people have different styles of speaking, accents, and mannerisms. They focus on the content of the message rather than the source or how the message is delivered.

5 **Overcoming ego:** What I have to say is much more important that what she or he is saying.

   Check the ego: Civil listeners suspend their egos and assume there will be importance to what the speaker has to say, and actively search for new insights and perspectives from the speaker. They value the speaker and the speaker's message at least as much as their own ideas and opinions.

6 **Planning your response:** I've heard this all before; how can I make my case?

Hear them out: Civil listeners realize that if they are planning a reply or rebuttal while the speaker is talking, they will miss something the speaker has to say—including new ideas and arguments. They give the speaker the benefit of the doubt—they hear him or her out before they actually or mentally respond. They realize they just might learn something new—and are willing and eager to take that chance.

7 **Arguing with the speaker:** She/he needs to read more; she/he doesn't understand; they don't know what they are talking about, what a stupid argument/comment.

One at a time: Civil listeners accept that they must take turns. Both parties can't speak at the same time (even if the listener's part of the conversation is only in his or her head). Civil listeners are patient, they focus on the speaker and make sure they understand the point the speaker is making; they think about that point, and only then do they respond. They think about questions to ask to confirm their understanding.

8 **Faking attention:** I'm looking at the speaker, nodding my head, but my mind is at home, planning my weekend, or working on that important proposal.

Give your complete attention: Civil listeners are present both mentally and physically with the speaker. They are considerate enough of the speaker and the relationship to fully participate in the conversation. Their attention is genuine. If they find their mind wandering, they redirect and refocus their attention on the speaker, the message, and the relationship.

9 **I'm just not smart enough:** The material is dry, complicated, technical, not my specialty, statistical.

Stretch your mind: Civil listeners realize that not everything is interesting, exciting, and intrinsically stimulating. Sometimes they will need to stretch their minds for the pay-off of a new insight, understanding, or mastery of a new skill from a speaker. They are willing to gamble and take the risk that if they *pay* attention to the speaker, there will likely be a *pay-off* from that message and to the relationship between speaker and listener.

10 **Just give me the facts:** I need the details, not your explanation/analysis/opinion; I can't worry about the big picture. **Focus on the forest:** Civil listeners understand that the trees (facts, figures, and details) are important, but the forest (the overall idea, concept, plan) is usually more important. Civil listeners put the facts and details from the speaker together into a broader understanding of what the speaker is saying. They are tolerant of the time it takes to reach such an understanding. They are flexible in managing the details and seeing the big picture.

We began this section with the overall suggestion that you "close your mouth and open your ears." Listening takes time, attention, effort, and patience; it is hard work. Listening requires the same—if not more—effort in the communication process than the sending of messages. Listening requires that we manage our minds and focus our attention on the speaker, the message, and the relationship that exists. The civil listener is willing to expend the energy to keep these three parts in focus because she or he values and appreciates the speaker and relationship, and wants to listen to the message. Effective listening is part attitude and part behavior, a willingness to listen and use specific skills and techniques for listening. Civil listeners are willing to do the hard work required to listen effectively. Research tells us that the average worker listens with only about 25 percent efficiency.[15] Imagine the personal and organizational possibilities if that remaining 75 percent of our capacity could be tapped to the benefit of our relationships and the organization's climate. Civil communicators exploit this unused capacity to both personal and organizational benefit.

Little Things Can Make Big Differences

A civil communication climate in the workplace is a combination and accumulation of many little things that taken together create a respectful organizational environment. Likewise, positive relationships between coworkers are created and cultivated over time through many interactions marked by civil exchanges. Erving Goffman refers to these little things as rituals, suggesting that "in contemporary society, what remains are brief rituals one individual performs for and to another, attesting to civility and good will on the performer's part and to the recipient's possession of a small patrimony of sacredness."[16] It is important that organizational members remember that small acts of civility and respect can have a cumulative effect and make big differences in shaping the organization's climate and positive personal relationships. Here we will suggest several of these rituals that can make a positive difference for civility in organizations.

Smile

Assuming this suggestion requires explanation, keep in mind that one of the first things we see when we meet another person is their face—and the first thing they notice about us is our face. Dress them with a smile. It is the civil thing to do. While scientists have argued inconclusively over whether smiling requires the use of fewer muscles than frowning, folk and conventional wisdom suggests that smiling takes less effort—yet another reason to smile.

Greet Coworkers and Clients

The simple civil act of taking the time to greet coworkers and clients before getting down to business is important. Saying "good morning" to coworkers as you enter the workplace contributes to a positive communication climate and work environment. When you greet coworkers and clients, it is almost incumbent on them to reply—there seems to be a norm of reciprocity that takes over. If you greet, your greeting will likely be returned, opening up the possibility for conversation.

Engage in Small-Talk

We tend to think of small-talk as being unimportant—a nicety but not a necessity. We should think of small-talk as making way for "big talk" or the important conversation. If we ask or are asked "How are you?" it opens up the opportunity for conversation. Granted, you may want or need to be measured in how you respond to this query, but small-talk opens the possibility for building and cultivating relationships with coworkers and clients alike. Investing this time in relationship building can pay positive dividends in the form of a more pleasant work environment. There is even specific guidance available to cultivate this skill.[17]

Say Please, Thank You, You're Welcome, and Excuse Me or Pardon Me

Saying "please" is respectful of the other person and less demanding. Saying "thank you" demonstrates that you are grateful for what someone has done for you. Saying "you're welcome" literally tells the other person that you welcome them and what they have done You're welcome can also mean you are available to do the task again; the task was freely give. Asking to be excused or pardoned reflects a mannerly and respectful view of the other person. Each of these small exchanges tells the other person that you respect him or her, you appreciate what he or she has done, and you value whatever brief moment you have shared.

> At my first job, my peers gave me regular feedback on the work I was doing and paid attention to my personal development—in other words, they knew the importance of valuing each individual. I'm not saying that I, or anyone else, needs to be told constantly that we're special, but that feedback from coworkers opens a line of communication that benefits everyone involved. I learned from them and they learned from me. Our department was made better as a result.
>
> Ryan J. Anthony
> Media Specialist
> Vocollect, Pittsburgh

Praise Publicly and Often, Criticize Privately, Constructively, and Only When Necessary.

If you feel that the performance of work of coworkers is worthy of praise, don't be afraid to take the initiative and provide the praise. This is true even if you are not the boss. Doing so tells your colleagues that you are paying attention, you recognize the work they are doing, and you value and appreciate their contribution. Praising publicly spreads the recognition of a job well done among other members of the organization. In doing so, it helps to create an environment in which the accomplishments and successes of all organizational members are valued and celebrated.

Being criticized in public within an organization is the adult equivalent of getting yelled at in front of the whole class for making a mistake on your fifth-grade spelling test. It felt awful then and continues to make its victims feel demeaned, devalued, and unappreciated. Civil does not mean a lack of criticism; rather, civil criticism takes place in private. Further, it is clear and specific, something the person being criticized can do something about; it is delivered using a calm tone of voice; it takes the relationship between the parties and the situation into account, and it allows time for a response by the person being criticized.

In a similar way, creating civil and positive relationships and organizational environments also requires the sharing of praise and the equal sharing of blame. When things go well, everyone is there to share the praise and glory. It is curious how when things go wrong, no one seems to be around. Being willing to share (notice the use of the word *share* versus *take*) the good and the bad is important.

Yield the Right-of-Way

Spend a few minutes watching colleagues enter a building—or students entering a classroom. Observe the "rules of the road" or the flow of traffic. Regardless of gender, one civil thing to do is open and hold the door for others—if possible. Doing so gives the person receiving the favor the opportunity to say "thank you" and the person giving the favor the opportunity to say "you're welcome."

Avoid Gossip

We have likely all participated in and been the topic (victim) of gossip at some point in our lives. Unfortunately, gossip does not end at the office or organizational door. If the estimates are correct, we spend a considerable amount of our on-the-job communication time talking about non-job-related topics. Civility suggests that we choose to talk about ideas, events, and things, not about people. While the temptation might be strong—and you made your fellow gossiper promise not to tell anyone else—experts and experience tell us that what we say can (and likely will) come back to haunt us.[18] Civil relationships can't be built on gossip or in an environment that tolerates gossip. The best advice is worth repeating: talk about things, not your coworkers.

Be Inclusive

The simple act of inviting a new coworker to join you and others for lunch or coffee is an act of civility and positive relationship building. But it does not have to be a newcomer to the organization that you include in your group. We naturally develop circles of friends and coworkers on the job. Take the opportunity to expand your circle of friends and coworkers. Find ways to connect groups that normally don't connect. There may be pay-offs in terms of both social relationship building as well as task or work relationships. Networking throughout the organization can have positive personal and organizational benefits and will contribute to the overall positive and civil climate of the organization.

Respect Public and Private Spaces

If you made the mess, clean up the mess. If you took the last cup of coffee, make the new pot. If the copier needs paper, fill it. In our combined fifty years of experience in the academy, we have noticed an inverse relationship between formal education and practical cleaning, barista, and paper-loading skills. These tasks are generally not within the position descriptions of administrative assistants, who have real work to do.

In the age of the cubicle, respecting the limited space of coworkers is a particularly civil thing to do. Business consultants make the following recommendations for cubicle civility: keep phone and other conversations at a low volume, avoid "prairie-dogging" (popping your head over the cubicle), avoid introducing strong odors from food, perfume, and flowers, use headphones to listen to music, and respect others' privacy by treating adjacent cubicles as enclosed offices.[19] In addition, if a door is closed, knock. If coworkers are talking, wait to be invited into the conversation. Think about and be aware of how you can use and help maintain the physical space of the organization in a civil fashion.

Practice the Golden Rule

If you desire respect, give respect. If you want to be treated well, treat others—including your boss—well. The basic idea here is that we tend to get what we give, or what some would express as "what goes around, comes around." A variation on the Golden Rule is to reverse it, suggesting, "Do unto others as they would have you do unto them."[20] Such a twist suggests that we put ourselves into the other person's proverbial shoes and see things from his or her perspective in terms of recognition, respect, and needs. Doing so values and appreciates the uniqueness of coworkers.

Summary

Given the amount of time we can expect to spend in organizational life, it is important to carefully consider how our communication behavior will influence our organizational life. There are two fundamental lessons you should take away from this chapter. First, the choices we make about how we communicate with our coworkers will influence the quality of the relationships we have with them and the overall quality of the environment in which we work. Second, making civil communication choices will require more time and effort on our part, but the investment made will pay positive dividends in improving our relationships with coworkers and improving the overall quality of work life. We can choose to create a positive communication climate and use message strategies that will contribute to that end. We can choose to fully participate in organizational relationships by valuing people and adapting our communication behaviors to cultivate positive relationships with superiors and subordinates. We can strive to improve the ways in which we listen and respond to colleagues to demonstrate the value of and our appreciation of them and their work. We can choose to practice the little rituals that will mark us as civil interpersonal communicators.

NOTES

1 Terrence Deal and Allen Kennedy, *Corporate Cultures: The Rites and Rituals of Corporate Life* (Reading, MA: Addison-Wesley, 1982), 86.

2 Ronald Adler and Jeanne Elmhorst, *Communicating at Work: Principles and Practices for Business and the Professions*, 8th ed. (Boston: McGraw-Hill, 2005), 137.

3 Gerald Goldhaber, *Organizational Communication*, 5th ed. (Dubuque, IA: William C. Brown, 1990), 67.

4 W. Charles Redding, *Communication within the Organization: An Interpretive Review of Theory and Research* (New York: Industrial Communication Council, 1972).

5 Tom Daniels and Barry Spiker, *Perspectives on Organizational Communication*, 3rd ed. (Dubuque, IA: William C. Brown, 1994), 142.

6. Ibid.

7 Original research in Redding, summarized in Daniels and Spiker, 203.

8 Ted Allen and Scott Omelianuk, *Esquire's Things a Man Should Know about Handshakes, White Lies and Which Fork Goes Where: Easy Business Etiquette for Complicated Times* (New York: Hearst, 2001), 107.

9 Stanley Deetz and Sheryl Stevenson, *Managing Interpersonal Communication* (New York: Harper and Row, 1986), 20–41.

10 Roderick Hart and Donald Burks, "Rhetorical Sensitivity and Social Interaction," *Speech Monographs* 43 (1972): 75–91; Roderick Hart, Ronald Carlson, and William Eadie, [OK?] "Attitudes toward Communication and the Assessment of Rhetorical Sensitivity," *Communication Monographs* 47 (1980): 1–22.

11 Ibid.

12 J. D. Weinrauch and J. R. Swanda, "Examining the Significance of Listening: An Exploratory Study of [OK?]Contemporary Management," *Journal of Business Communication* 13 (1975): 25–32.

13 Larry Barker and Rene Edwards, "An Investigation of Proportional Time Spent in Various Communicating Activities by College Students," *Journal of Applied Communication Research* 8 (1980): 101–109.

14 Andrew Wolvin and Charles Coakley, "A Survey of the Status of Listening Training in Some Fortune 500 Corporations," *Communication Education* 40 (1991): 152–164.

15 Ralph Nichols, "Listening Is a 10-Part Skill," *Nation's Business* 75 (1987): 40.

16 Erving Goffman, *Relations in Public: Microstudies of the Public Order* (New York: Basic Books, 1971), 63.

17 See, for example, Debra Fine, *The Fine Art of Small Talk: How to Start a Conversation, Keep It Going, Build Networking Skill—and Leave a Positive Impression!* (New York: Hyperion, 2005); Don Gabor, *How to Start a Conversation and Make Friends: Revised and Updated* (New York: Fireside, 2001); Alan Garner, *Conversationally Speaking: Tested New Ways to Increase Your Personal and Social Effectiveness* (Boston: McGraw-Hill, 1997).

18 C. Kanchier, "Are You an Effective Communicator?" *USA Today* Career Network, July 9, 2002.

19 Seth Lewis, "Cubicle Courtesy Can Do Much to Defuse Office Conflict," Knight-Ridder Tribune Business News, Washington, October 11, 2004, p. 1 (available at: http://proquest.umi.com/pqdweb?index=0&did=710647611&SrchMode =1&sid=1&Fmt=3&VInst=PROD&VType=PQD&RQT=309&VName=PQD&T S=1153419198&clientId=9874).

20 Tom Rath and Donald Clifton, *How Full Is Your Bucket? Positive Strategies for Work and Life* (New York: Gallup, 2004).

10

Civility and the Interview

Your appointment for the job interview is scheduled for 8:00, first thing in the morning. You really want this job. The clothes are laid out and pressed, you have a fresh copy of your resume and portfolio in your new briefcase, and you have set both alarm clocks so you won't oversleep—a trick you learned from those 8:00 classes. You ace the interview, make it through the second plant-visit interview, and land the job. Now it is six months later and time for your first performance appraisal interview with your boss. You think it's been a good six months and hope your boss agrees. In all the interactions you've had with coworkers during the past months, work-related and otherwise, they seem to like you, and peers and supervisors alike have complimented your work. Unfortunately, your expectations were not fulfilled—oh, well, they say there are lots of jobs out there.

If interpersonal communication is the most common communication context in the business and professional world, then the interview is probably the most common type of task-related and planned form of interpersonal communication in organizations. Interestingly, it is the interview that helps you to get a job and do your work on the job, it provides a forum for evaluating your work, and—whether voluntarily or otherwise—will likely end your relationship with an organization. This being the case, understanding how to handle yourself in a variety of types of interview situations will be important to your success in the organization. While basic interpersonal communication skills are obviously the foundation for a successful interview, sharpening your civil communication skills can provide you with that additional competitive edge in a variety of interview situations.

As the scenario above illustrates, there are a variety of types of interviews that you will encounter on the job, including at least the following: hiring or selection, information sharing and gathering, persuasive, problem-solving, performance appraisal, and exit or termination. As you encounter each type, the civil verbal and nonverbal choices you make will likely determine your success in the immediate situation as well as over the course of your life with various organizations. In order to make the civil choices, you'll first need to know some of the unique characteristics of interviews as well as how to measure your success at interviewing.

The Interview: A Special Type of Interpersonal Communication

Before you can make informed choices as to how you should behave in an interview, you should understand the unique nature of interviews. Experts have identified the following characteristics as defining interviews: they are dyadic and relational, have a predetermined and serious purpose, require interchanging behaviors, and involve the asking and answering of questions.[1] While we generally think of an interview as a one-on-one situation, in some interviews there may be more than two people on each side of the exchange. Interviews are dyadic in that they involve two different parties, but they are not necessarily limited to two people. Interviews are relational, suggesting that a connection or relationship begins once the interaction starts. You are either creating a new relationship or building on an existing relationship. In either case, respecting the nature of that relationship is vitally important. We conduct interviews in order to accomplish a goal: to get a job or hire the best candidate, gather or distribute information, counsel or be counseled by a coworker, or evaluate or have our performance evaluated. Finally, we exchange information through the use of a question-answer format. To interview well, we need to master the skillful asking and informed answering of a variety of types of questions. If you understand these distinguishing features that characterize the interview, you can also use them as a means of measuring your success at interviewing.

Measures of Effectiveness

When we casually chat and carry on a conversation with coworkers over lunch, the only measure of success we really need is whether or not one or ideally both parties enjoyed the conversation. As a special type of interpersonal communication or conversation, interviews have more demanding and specific measures of success.

For example, a job interview is not a total success if you succeed in getting the job but get off on the wrong foot with the organization because of a rude or insensitive comment you made during the interview. Your mistakes during the interview will likely follow you into the organization. If you are the corporate recruiter charged with screening potential employees, the job interview can't be counted as a complete success if in your attempt to be rigorous in your questioning you offend an applicant who in turn proceeds to bad-mouth your organization to anyone who will listen. A performance appraisal interview, if not done well, can damage an otherwise positive relationship between superior and subordinate. Repairing the damage caused by ineffective performance appraisal interviews can take considerable time and effort. Coworkers may refuse your requests for information and assistance if you are not respectful of their time and your relationship. In each of these examples, the short-term goal cannot be accomplished at the expense of the longer-term relationship.

The point here is that while interviews are goal-oriented, interviews also begin, build, and maintain relationships, and civil verbal and non-verbal communication behavior will build positive relationships. While goal accomplishment may be an indication of success in the short term, relationship building through civil behavior is a more important long-term measure of successful interviews. This holds true regardless of the type of interview involved. Because the job interview begins an applicant's relationship with an organization and the organization's relationship with the applicant, civility and respect from each party are important in shaping the relationship. Similarly, performance appraisal interviews ideally provide employees with valuable career development feedback as well as cultivate and develop the human resources of the organization. Civility and respect ought to characterize the ongoing growth of the employee-organization relationship. Eventually, people leave organizations. How employees choose to leave organizations or how organizations ask employees to leave can be done with civility and respect regardless of whether the decision to depart is unilateral or mutual. In short, the interview is not successful if it accomplishes only the short-term goal of information exchange and doesn't cultivate the longer-term goal of positive relational development.

We'll examine how civil verbal and nonverbal communication behaviors can positively build personal and organizational relationships in each of the above interview situations. Before we cover these specific interviewing situations in detail, we'll suggest some general guidelines that apply to all interview situations.

The Fundamentals of Civil Interviewing

Request and Thank People for Their Time

Requesting an appointment or scheduling time for an interview with a coworker is a valuing and respectful thing to do. Trading on a good relationship by habitually interrupting coworkers damages their productivity as well as your relationship. Simply taking the time to ask coworkers for the best time to interview them to gather the information you need and then thanking them and expressing your appreciation for their time and expertise—in person or via a quick email message—are acts of civil interviewing. Avoid a phone call, which would likely be yet another interruption resulting in a loss of productivity. Researchers suggest that once interrupted, it can take workers up to twenty-five minutes to return to their original task.[2] Being civil, then, is respectful of both organizational time and productivity.

Know What You Want to Accomplish

Regardless of the type of interview or whether you're playing the role of interviewee (the person answering the questions) or the role of interviewer (the person asking the questions), establish your purpose in conducting the interview and plan well in advance. This requires a careful consideration of the language you'll use to request the information you need. Being vague and ambiguous simply consumes time as you try to clarify your inquiry. Focusing on a clear purpose invests the time of both parties well and respects their time. For example, if you are applying for a position and you know you're not qualified or that a potential candidate is not qualified, respect each other's time by not wasting it. Before you seek information from a coworker, think carefully about what you need to know as well as the best verbal choices to make in phrasing the questions to ask to solicit the information you need. Such prior consideration values the time and expertise of coworkers.

Plan and Prepare in Advance

If you are the interviewer, prepare your agenda of topics for the interview and think about the right questions to ask to solicit the information required. If possible, submit the questions to the interviewee to allow him or her time to prepare. Not only is such an approach efficient, but it is respectful. Both interviewee and interviewer should know about the different types of questions and questioning strategies and how to answer both easy and difficult questions.

While we usually don't think of conversations as having much struc-

Table 10.1: Understand and Follow the Structure of Interviews

Question Type	Sample Wording	Best Response Strategy
Open	"What is your opinion of ... ?"	Concise, honest answer
Closed	"Do you have a driver's license?"	Yes/no—don't belabor the point
Leading	"You are willing to work weekends, aren't you?"	Careful phrasing to be responsive without trapping yourself
Mirror	"You say you prefer Macs?"	Elaborate on your initial answer to a closed question.
Hypothetical	"What would you do if ... ?"	Couch response in the uncertainty of knowing about any hypothetical.

ture and organization, they normally have something resembling an introduction, body, and conclusion—more simply, a beginning, middle, and end. Allow a brief time for small-talk, that rapport-building time that prepares each party for the "working" part of the interview, in which you execute your agenda and ask or respond to the questions. It is the responsibility of the interviewer to keep the interview structured and organized by clarifying the purpose, having an agenda of topics and questions prepared, and providing a summary or conclusion at the end. The types of questions typically used in interviews are outlined in table 10.1. Experts also advise that "talk time" between interviewer and interviewee be divided roughly 70/30 percent, with the interviewee getting the 70 and the interviewer getting the 30 percent.[3] After all, it is the interviewee who should be providing the bulk of the information. The interviewer who fails to understand the structure of interviews, or is disorganized and rambles, also fails to respect his or her coworker, potential job candidate, or employee seeking feedback during a performance appraisal. You value the time and relationship you have with your coworkers if you take responsibility for carefully organizing and structuring the interview in order to cultivate your relationship as you accomplish your goal.

Following these four fundamentals of civil interviewing not only will allow you to accomplish your short-term purpose but will also enable you to cultivate and develop civil coworker relationships. While they provide a solid foundation for all interviews, there are unique consider-ations to be made in job interviews, performance appraisals, and exit interviews.

Finding the Right Fit: Civility and the Employment Interview

Success in the job interview can be measured in two ways. The obvious measure of success from the applicant's point of view would be whether or not the interview garnered a job offer or at least a second interview with the organization. From the organization's perspective, the simple meas-ure of success would be filling the vacant position. But then there is this idea of "fit." Here we return to the idea of relationships. Will you fit into the organization and thrive? Has the organization found the right person who can not only do the job but fits into the existing organization?

Given the importance of finding the right position and finding the right employees, the issue of fit is worth your careful consideration. This second measure of success, the idea of fit, revolves around the relation-ships that are created and the civil communication skills used to create those relationships. From both the applicant's and the employer's per-spectives, creating and managing impressions is key to conveying and receiving the right image in order to determine if the relationship or fit between applicant and organization is right. Creating and managing these impressions and cultivating these relationships require that both parties (applicant and employer) play their roles well and with civility and respect for each other. We'll look at several guidelines for playing each role well, starting with the role of applicant.

Prior Preparation Prevents Poor Performance

While these words of advice hold true for almost any business and professional communication situation, they are particularly true for job applicants. Notice the word *performance*. One of the best ways to think about the job interview is through a theatrical metaphor, suggesting that all the world is a stage and we're just actors on that stage. You are auditioning for a part—the position for which you are applying. You come prepared, complete with costume and makeup—you have carefully considered the impression you want to create. You have studied your character and rehearsed your lines—you know the organization, what is expected of an interviewee, the types of questions you will be asked, and the responses you plan to give.

Managers at Southwest Airlines, for example, quite literally approach the job interview as an audition.[4] Your "audition" with Southwest begins when you request an application—managers ask receptionists to note the good and bad aspects of the initial conversation—and continues if you are flown in for an interview, as gate and flight attendants observe your behavior. The audition can culminate in candidates making short speeches about themselves in front of other candidates. According to a Southwest recruiter, "We want to see how they interact with people when they think they're not being evaluated." This audition approach has kept turnover low and customer satisfaction high. This is Southwest's approach to the issue of fit and should focus your attention squarely on sharpening your interpersonal, relational, and civility skills. How you treat others is important.

A caveat to this orientation is important. Before you become too theatrical, we need to be perfectly clear that we are in no way suggesting that you not be honest and genuine. The best actors and actresses "get into character" as they live, breathe, and become the part. In no way are we suggesting that lying or being disingenuous be any part of your job interview. Practical concerns—you can be fired for lying—and our belief that civility is the right and most effective approach have shaped our advice.

Preparing Two Important Documents

Establishing and cultivating an employment relationship begins with the two most important documents you'll ever craft, your cover or application letter and your resume. There is a wealth of information and advice available in books, on the Internet, and through your campus career development center on the basics of application letters and resumes. Infusing these documents with civility and respect through the verbal choices you make in preparing them can set yours apart from the reams of paper human resource managers receive in response to job openings.

Begin cultivating your relationship with potential employers, making their job easier by respecting their time with a succinct, purposeful letter. Be sure that you **get to the point** by stating the position for which you are applying; **tailor your letter** to the unique requirements of the position; **use specific examples** from your educational and work experience to sell yourself to the organization, and **paint a picture of yourself** that they can't forget. Your language choices can accomplish these goals with civility. Getting to the point is respectful of the reader's time. Paying attention to the content and format of your resume allows the reader to quickly scan it for the information desired. Tailoring your application letter to the specific position conveys that you have done your homework and that you are genuinely interested in the position. Including language that conveys specific and concrete examples in both your letter and resume allows the employer to develop a clearer picture of your qualifications. Using vivid adjectives that paint a picture of your qualities and characteristics allows you to communicate the image you desire. For instance, it is better to state the specific computer programs with which you are familiar than to say you are "skilled in computer usage." These four simple suggestions demonstrate respect for the reader and interest in the organization. They initiate your audition process with the organization. They convey an impression of you—one that you get to control. They begin to cultivate a positive and civil relationship with the organization. They allow you to create and convey the best possible image to someone whom you have yet to meet.

The most important thing to remember about application letters and resumes is that you have complete control over the contents of each. You are the one providing the employers with the image you would like them to have of your interest in the position, your qualifications, and your personality. Long, rambling, and vague application letters attached to disorganized and cluttered resumes fail to acknowledge, respect, and value the time of the intended reader, and generally will quickly find their way into the circular file.

Looking the Part

If the cover letter and resume get you the audition (interview), your "theatrical" preparation should proceed to costume considerations. Following the impression you chose to create in the letter and resume you construct, how you choose to "costume" yourself will continue to cultivate and create an image and impression in the mind of the interviewer—before you have the opportunity to actually exchange your first words. Earlier, in the chapter on nonverbal communication, we explained the curious transformation that often occurs as soon-to-be college graduates approach the job market. Since they are taking on a new and different role, their wardrobes begin to change. Adapting to the organizational dress code demonstrates a degree of deference and respect for the organization. You will also literally feel different if you are dressed differently, which will help you in playing the role of interviewee with skill. Finally, how you manage your image can create a favorable impression in the mind of the interviewer or recruiter.

Most experts recommend that gentlemen being interviewed for professional positions should plan to wear dress slacks and a neat sport shirt at the very least and may need the full suit-and-tie ensemble. Ladies may choose similar attire or a modest, tailored dress. Comparably conservative makeup and jewelry would also be wise choices for the ladies.

Constructing the Script; or, You Know the Questions, Practice the Answers

Most initial job interviews follow a fairly predictable script, which can work to your advantage as an applicant. Knowing this gives you the opportunity for considerable rehearsal and can therefore improve your performance. Following the initial small-talk phase, one of the most common opening questions you are likely to be asked is: "Tell me about yourself and explain why you have applied for this position." Your response to this question is what many call "the two-minute drill" because it gives you several minutes at the beginning of the interview to introduce yourself and begin to sell the skills and abilities you have to offer. The civil response to this question would begin by thanking the interviewer for the opportunity to interview and proceed to explain why you have applied and how your education and work experience have prepared you for the position. This of course assumes you have done your homework on the position and the organization. Completing this homework and preparing a concise and detailed response to this question respect the time of the interviewer and allow you the opportunity to shine.

A quick search of the Internet using the key words "common interview questions" will provide you with not only a wealth of information on common questions but advice and examples on how to prepare your answers.[5] While we are not suggesting that you prepare "canned" answers to these common questions, knowing the kinds of questions you will likely be asked and having the opportunity to think about your responses in advance helps to build confidence and can also help you to frame your responses in the best possible way as you begin to cultivate a relationship with the organization.

Be prepared to answer common questions such as "Why did you choose your major?" or "What extracurricular activities were most beneficial to you?" But also be prepared to remain composed and professional when asked creative, unexpected questions such as "Who in the world would you most like to have dinner with?" The interviewer is judging not just your answer, but how you deal with the unexpected nature of the question.

Some questions are simply forbidden because they violate the federal laws about equality in employment opportunities. Questions should relate to job-related qualifications, or what are called bona fide occupational qualifications. Nonetheless, you may encounter an interviewer who steps over the bounds and asks about your religion, marital status, or parenting plans. If that happens, you are fully justified in refusing to answer. But do so politely. Do not scold or get angry with the interviewer. Simply say that there are other questions much more pertinent to your suitability for this job and steer the conversation back to your work-relevant skills and characteristics.

Know Your Dining Etiquette

It is not unusual for job applicants to be invited to lunch or dinner, especially during a second or third "call-back" interview. There are extensive resources you might want to check about the details of handling multiforked, linen-napkined business lunches. Here are a few basic principles to get you started.

When All Is Said, There Are Still Things to Be Done

If you grew up with parents who insisted that you write thank-you notes when you received birthday or holiday presents, you should be

Do's
- Sit straight at the table; no leaning forward or backward.
- Napkin should be placed on the lap to catch crumbs or drips while eating food; after the meal, it should be placed neatly on the table, not in a pile.
- Wait to begin eating until everyone at your table has been served.
- Eat slowly and quietly.
- Cut one piece of food, eat it, then cut another, and repeat.
- Chew small bites of food and swallow with the mouth closed.
- When finished with the meal, place the fork and knife diagonally crossed on the plate.
- Express appreciation for the meal.
- Wait for others to finish the meal before leaving the table.
- Eat rolls or bread by tearing off small bite-size pieces and buttering only the piece you are preparing to eat.
- Engage in table conversation that is pleasant but entirely free of controversial subjects.
- If food spills off your plate, you may pick it up with a piece of your silverware and place it on the edge of your plate.

Don'ts
- Do not slurp or gulp.
- Do not put bones or any other morsels on the tablecloth.
- Do not speak with your mouth full.
- Do not reach across your dining companions.
- Do not ask for a doggy bag when you are a guest.
- Do not season your food before you have tasted it.
- Do not order the most expensive item or the least expensive.

able to anticipate our next suggestion. Thanking an interviewer for the time and opportunity to meet is an act of civility. In addition, it provides you with the opportunity to get your name before the eyes of the interviewer one last time, clarify any lingering misunderstandings following the interview, and reinforce your interest in the position and the organization. Staffing and etiquette experts advise short personal handwritten notes expressing your sincere thanks.[6] The brief time you invest in this simple act of civility might be what sets your interview apart from the dozens a recruiter might complete in the course of searching for a new hire. Attention to these types of civil considerations and details helps to cultivate civil and positive personal and organizational relationships.

Increasingly, organizations are recognizing the importance of treating job candidates well. It is easy to assume that once the interview has concluded, the organization can take a "don't call us, we'll call you" attitude of disregard. If principles of civility suggest that applicants follow up and cultivate relationships, organizations should follow up with applicants as well. A recent survey found that 80 percent of respondents had experienced bad organizational treatment, including being told after an interview that another candidate already had the job but they were required to carry out more interviews anyway and having phone calls and emails ignored when they tried to inquire as to the status of their application.[7] Civility and practical considerations suggest that potential employers pay more attention to cultivating a positive relationship. Experts suggest that disgruntled job seekers are more than willing to share their negative experiences with colleagues and friends, potentially damaging the organization's reputation and making future recruiting more difficult.[8] Assuming the job interview has gone well and the position is offered and accepted, your working relationship with an organization will require further cultivation and maintenance.

Tell Me How I'm Doing:
The Performance Appraisal Interview

It is perfectly natural for all of us to want to know how we are doing at our job. The performance appraisal interview can be a forum for management and workers to share their perspectives on employee performance. In some organizations this is an informal, irregular, and haphazard process; in others it is very formal, regularly scheduled (quarterly, semiannually, or annually), and carefully thought out. The key is for the performance appraisal interview to provide employees with high-quality feedback on their strengths and weaknesses so that they can continue to improve and grow with the organization. In this sense, performance appraisals tend to be rather one-sided, with management largely reporting rather than exchanging information.[9] There are a variety of resources available that provide detailed explanations of performance appraisal interviews,[10] but we'll focus our attention here on how the appraiser and the appraised can approach this interview with verbal and nonverbal civility and therefore shape a positive outcome for both.

Make the Process Transparent; Take It Seriously

The performance appraisal process works best if everyone knows and understands what to expect. Managers should schedule such meetings, clearly explain the format that will be used, and brief employees as to what to expect. An attitude of "let's get this over with" on the part of a boss or employee diminishes the process and devalues rather than cultivates the relationship that exists. If done well, bosses cultivate workers, their skills and abilities, and relationships; employees are provided with opportunities to grow, see their value to the organization, and want to remain a part of the organization.

Criticize in Private; Praise in Public

It is worth mentioning this suggestion again, because the results of not following this advice can have damaging and lingering consequences. A civil and skilled manager would never criticize an employee in front of the employee's peers. Doing so obviously damages the manager-employee relationship but also does nothing to cultivate a positive communication climate within the organization. On the other hand, praising in public communicates that your manager values your accomplishments by wanting to share them with the rest of the organization.

Use Language That Is Concrete and Behavioral

The easy way to provide praise and criticism is to either say "great work" or "that stinks." The obvious question is what about the work was great, or what about the work stinks? Without taking the time and effort to describe what about an employee's work is great, or what—specifically—stinks about the work, management has provided no useful feedback either positive or negative. For example, explaining that the way a particular report was prepared in terms of the detail, research, and writing style gives concrete examples of what "great" means. Explaining that not establishing eye contact with a customer, sighing, and tapping your foot impatiently provides an employee with specific things to change.

A manager of one of the *Fortune* "100 Best Companies to Work For" reports that the appraisal of his local operation specifically includes an evaluation of the wording used to give employees praise or criticism. Reliance on concrete and respectful wording not only helped the employees but also resulted in benefits for the managers.

Keep a Calm and Even Tone of Voice

Raised voices tend to encourage raised voices in response, leading to a potential escalation in tension, which neither provides useful feedback nor cultivates civil relationships and organizational climates. The civil appraiser can deliver the message, both the positive and the negative, in a calm and even-toned fashion that will likely be more readily accepted by the person being appraised. They can separate the person and their relationship from the work. They calmly explain the strengths and weaknesses of the work without damaging their relationship by raising their voice.

Listen Calmly before Responding

While no one likes the negative (the criticism), controlling your nonverbal responses as you listen to the entire message is important. The moment you roll your eyes ("he's all wrong"), sigh in annoyance ("that's not true"), and cross your arms in defense ("but let me explain"), the appraisal process deteriorates. Turn taking is fundamental for the civil exchange of perspectives. Listen carefully, understand the message, perhaps ask for clarification, and take a moment to think before you respond. The civil employee will acknowledge the criticism, and calmly request the opportunity to respond and explain. Doing so allows the conversation to continue, additional details and information to be shared, and positive relationships to be cultivated. As was true for the appraiser, these advantages depend on the interviewee keeping a calm and even tone of voice. Following these suggestions will help to ensure that the performance appraisal interview provides constructive and useful feedback that will cultivate the employee and the employee-employer relationship.

No Hard Feelings: The Exit Interview

There was a time when once you were hired by an organization, you could anticipate a lifetime of employment with the same organization. While this may have been true for your parents and grandparents, it will likely not be true for you. For example, younger baby boomers held an average of ten jobs in their first twenty years of employment before settling into more long-term positions, while experts estimate that some high-tech employees change jobs almost annually.[11] Clearly, lifetime employment with the same company and the same people will likely be a thing of the past.

How employees and companies handle turnover in organizations becomes an important issue. Exiting the organization civilly and gracefully, whether it is voluntary or otherwise, depends on the skilled communication behavior of the employee and the employer. These interviews are usually referred to as exit or termination interviews. The employee is leaving the organization, but the employee and/or employer may not want to "terminate"—as in end—the relationship so much as change the relationship. The employee who is let go as a company downsizes may become a valuable future candidate when the economy is booming. An ambitious employee looking to take on a more challenging position with a different company may need recommendations to secure the new position. The point here, as we have been emphasizing, is to shape a long-term positive relationship even as short-term practical considerations are taken into account by practicing civility. This being the case, we have two guidelines for the civil departure of the employee from the company and for the employer to ease the exiting of an employee from the company.

Be Honest and Be Open

If you plan to voluntarily leave an organization, the civil way to depart is to provide your company with as much notice as possible. Assuming that you have cultivated a positive relationship with the organization, this should not be difficult. Traditionally, two weeks' notice has been the standard. Likewise, if a company plans to let an employee go, providing as much notice as possible is the humane and civil thing to do. If economic conditions are forcing a company to cut employment, it is likely that the rumor mill already has the information. Here again, if a positive relationship and open and honest communication climate have been cultivated between management and labor, this relationship can be used to ease the transition. Perhaps one of the most uncivil tactics that has been used by companies is literally to pack up an employee's office and escort him or her from the building. Such behavior has obvious devastating consequences for the employee and damages the public reputation of the organization and the quality of employee relations. An even worse case occurred recently in England when an employee was sent a text message stating that her services were no longer needed!

You will likely encounter situations either as employee or employer in which a previous positive relationship does not exist and cannot be used to ease employment changes in a company. Sometimes people quit jobs; sometimes companies need to fire employees. In such cases, deal with the situation quickly and calmly. State your reasons for leaving and exit the situation as gracefully as possible. If you are faced with the task of firing someone, do it in private; state the company's reasons for the termination, and conclude the interview. Such interviews should not be negotiation sessions, and allowing for extended discussion does little to make a bad situation any better.

Make It a Learning Opportunity

Employees become invested in organizations, and organizations invest considerably in their employees. Each has much to learn from the other, even when they part company. If you are leaving a company, your exit interview could be turned into a final performance appraisal opportunity in which your contributions and achievements in the organization can be reviewed and celebrated. Take the opportunity to ask for feedback on your performance and for guidance as you develop in your career. Doing so recognizes the work you have done and also the relationships that you have built in your time with the company, which you may need or want to draw upon to further your career goals.

If you are conducting an exit interview for your company, make it into an opportunity to learn how the organization can change and improve.[12] Asking for an employee's reasons for leaving and listening carefully and civilly to his or her response can provide useful insights that may help in retaining other employees or improving working conditions that had not come to your attention. Complimenting employees who leave, thanking them for their contributions, and wishing them well cost the company nothing but can secure positive relationships that may be valuable in the future. Human resource professionals advise that in cyclical supply-and-demand labor markets, the unsuccessful candidate or exiting employee today may be a top prospect in the future[13] Change is never easy for employees or companies, but change seems to be one of the few constants of organizational life. You can choose and civilly shape how you will experience employment and organizational changes.

Summary

You will participate in hundreds of interviews over the course of your career with several different employers in order to accomplish a variety of goals. Armed with some fundamental background information on the unique nature of interviews, you are prepared to handle these situations with competence. Infusing the fundamentals with a sense of civility and respect not only will go a long way to accomplishing the immediate goal of the interview but will also allow you to cultivate positive long-term relationships that will linger and be of value throughout your career.

NOTES

1 Charles Stewart and William B. Cash, *Interviewing: Principles and Practices*, 11th ed. (New York: McGraw-Hill, 2006), 1–4.

2 Gloria Mark, Victor Gonzalez, and Justin Harris, "No Task Left Behind? Examining the Nature of Fragmented Work," Proceedings of the SIGCHI Conference on Human Factors in Computing Systems: Association for Computing Machinery, 2005, 321–330 (available at: http://portal.acm.org/citation.cfm?id=1054972.1055017; accessed August 9, 2006).

3 Ronald Adler and Jeanne Elmhorst, *Communicating at Work: Principles and Practices for Business and the Professions*, 8th ed. (Boston: McGraw-Hill, 2005), 174.

4 Paul Kaihla, "Best-Kept Secrets of the World's Best Companies," *Business 2.0* and CNN Money.com, April 2006 (available at: http://money.cnn.com/magazines/business2/business2_archive/2006/04/01/8372806/index.htm; accessed August 9, 2006).

5 See, for example, Monster.com (available at: http://interview.monster.com/articles/ common%5Fquestions1/), or Careerbuilder.com (available at: http://www.cnn.com/2005/US/Careers/12/09/six.questions/index.html?section=cnn_la test), or check any college or university career development center; for example, http://pserie.psu.edu/student/cdc/interviewing.htm#questions.

6 See, for example, http://www.npr.org/templates/story/story.php?storyId=5503675 and http://www.emilypost.com/.

7 Rebecca Theim, "Why More Job Hunters Cry Foul," *Christian Science Monitor*, January 22, 2002 (available at: http://www.csmonitor.com/2002/0122/p20s01-wmwo.html).

8 Ibid.

9 H. L. Goodall and S. Goodall, *Communicating in Professional Contexts*, 2nd ed. (Belmont, CA: Thomson Wadsworth, 2006), 206.

10 See, for example, Charles Stewart and William Cash, "The Performance Interview," in *Interviewing: Principles and Practices*, 11th ed. (New York: McGraw-Hill, 2006), 237–268; Ronald Adler and Jeanne Elmhorst, "The Performance Appraisal Interview," in *Communicating at Work: Principles and Practices for Business and the Professions*, 8th ed. (Boston: McGraw-Hill, 2005), 231–236; Phillip Clampitt, "Performance Feedback," in *Communicating for Managerial Effectiveness*, 2nd ed. (Thousand Oaks, CA: Sage, 2001), 123–145.

11 See, for example, the Bureau of Labor Statistics (available at: http://www.bls.gov/nls/nlsfaqs.htm#anch5), and http://news.com.com/2100–1017– 241914.html.

12 Cheryl Hamilton and Cordell Parker, *Communicating for Results: A Guide for Business and the Professions*, 6th ed. (Belmont, CA: Thomson Wadsworth, 2001), 212.

13 Theim, op cit.

11

Teams, Teamwork,

and Civil Communication

The story is told of the person who dies, arrives at the gates of heaven, and along with other new arrivals is greeted by St. Peter. Everyone is eager to enter, but wondering if he or she is worthy. As each person is screened, St. Peter welcomes those who have lived a good, decent, and civil life. Those not invited into heaven are instructed to divide up into groups.

Stories like this are common when the topic of groups in most any context comes up. Some of you may enjoy the challenges, opportunities, and benefits of working in groups or teams; some of you have had bad experiences with groups and teams and dread all future encounters; still others may be ambivalent. Regardless of which category best describes you, working in groups and teams will be an inevitable and significant part of your organizational life.[1]

In this chapter, we will focus on the particular type of small group known as a team. The specific communication context of a *team* refers to those situations in which several employees are working together, either on an ongoing, regular basis or on a single, limited project. The distinguishing characteristic of team membership can be best understood by envisioning a team of horses pulling a wagon—the individual members are linked together to accomplish a goal cooperatively, capitalizing on one another's strengths and offsetting one another's weaknesses.

While you won't have the choice of whether to participate in teams, you can make choices about how you will participate. If these choices are informed by civil attitudes and civil communication behaviors, the experience will be more positive and rewarding.

To understand teams in the business and professional world requires that you know the types, characteristics, and developmental stages of teams you will encounter; how teamwork can be improved through civility; and some background in the fundamentals of leadership and followership. Throughout our discussion of these three major topics, we'll keep the focus on the use of civil verbal and nonverbal strategies for experiencing the success and rewards of teams. Before addressing these topics, we need to clarify some terminology.

All Teams Are Groups, but Not All Groups Are Teams

Anyone who has ever been a member of a winning sports team understands that the team is different at the end of the season than it was at the beginning. The civic, religious, and community organizations for which you volunteer and with which you participate in activities are different now than they were when you joined. Even your family is different now than it was years ago. In each of these examples of groups, the number of people may stay the same, but relationships develop over time that take a collection of people who happen to be at the same place at the same time and transform then into something we call a team. The catalyst has been communication. Specifically, team members have developed an ability to convey and interpret messages exchanged among themselves that has changed their fundamental nature from a collection of individuals into a single unit. On a recreational basketball team, for instance, one of the players had slowed considerably over the years but still had a perfect shot from the top of the key. The others knew to just look for him; if he was in his spot, they signaled the ball handler to pass the ball to "Slow Al" and they would get their two points.

When you get the right combination of players, coaches, skills and abilities, motivation and desire, liking and affection, common goals and vision, and maybe a bit of luck, everything comes together and a group of individuals becomes a winning team. The athletic team may win the championship on the court, while at work the project team may create a successful new product, find the right strategy for selling the product to the target audience, solve a vexing production problem, or increase sales. Everyone on the team knew the goal, contributed at least 100 percent to the challenge, enjoyed each other's company, took responsibility for leadership, caught a couple of breaks, and can now celebrate their collective success—take their victory lap, accept the trophy, bask in the glory of the moment. They even look forward to the next chal-

lenge. If you have experienced these types of winning moments, you understand the difference between a simple group of people and a successful winning team in and out of organizations.

Before we take the sports analogy too far, we need to recognize that teams also lose. Even unsuccessful teams are different from the collection of individuals they were at the outset. We have all known or maybe been a part of a team (in or out of organizations) whose win-loss record was terrible but who—as a team—had a great season together. The keys here are working together and the relationships that made it a great season, win or lose. Interpersonal success is still worth celebrating.

There are two important distinguishing factors that separate successful teams from less-successful teams. One factor is the nature of the relationships that develop among the members; the second is how these relationships are shaped and cultivated by the civil communication behavior of the members.

Relationships among members of a successful team should be characterized by mutual respect, a degree of affection and liking, a measure of cohesiveness to "stick" the members together, and a cooperative attitude that recognizes that a give and take will be necessary in order for the team to succeed. The best team members value the skills and talents of each member. They don't necessarily need to be best friends, but over time they come to appreciate the unique character and talents of each member. The team will draw upon these individual talents and skills to contribute to the effectiveness of the team.

Over time, the team comes to want to spend time together—both doing the work of the organization as well as simply enjoying each other's company in more social settings. Members realize that they are not and cannot always be right, that reasonable compromises from all members will be necessary for the team to succeed. Members also realize that their competition should be external to the group rather than within the group—the team versus the competition, not member versus member. Teams are that unusual combination of differently talented individuals who, when gathered together in interaction over time, come to collectively complement each others' strengths and weaknesses in the achievement of their team goals.

These valuable qualities and characteristics will develop only if the members of a team communicate in a civil and effective manner. Members must tell each other that they value each others' skills and talents. They must be willing to defer to and draw upon the expertise of other members, knowing that no one member has all the answers. "Since Joe has such a strong background in the financial situation, maybe the rest of us should focus our attention on the marketing

> Each of us fulfills a different role in the process and we have to work as a close-knit team to keep the process moving smoothly. Because this work environment is closed, we interact with each other constantly and are often aware of each individual's situation, both personal and professional. In order for everyone in our culturally diverse team to be motivated to give 100 percent effort 100 percent of the time, we all need to approach each other with courtesy, consideration and respect. We need to value each other's skills and expertise.
>
> Risa Glick
> Quality Assurance Test Manager
> Northrop Grumman Corporation,
> Sterling, VA

plan." When the inevitable interpersonal or personality conflicts emerge, civil verbal and nonverbal communication can keep the focus on the shared goal and vision of the team. "Let's not lose track of the fact that we are making good progress toward our goal even if we have some minor disagreements." Teams also spend time together *not* doing work, sharing experiences and constructing and recounting stories that celebrate the progress of the team. "Do you remember when we started on this task force, we didn't even know each others' names and now we're ahead in the company bowling standings—amazing." Team members encourage and value a spirited debate, but they have learned to state their position and listen to those of others. "I think I made a strong case for going with supplier X, but maybe Ann has a good point about their reliability being a problem."

In short, teams and team members get the work done, but through their civil verbal and nonverbal communication they also cultivate and develop lasting relationships that will extend beyond the immediate project and help to build a positive communication climate within the organization.

Teams: Types, Characteristics, and Developmental Stages

To make the best of your team experiences in organizations, you should know something of the types of groups you'll encounter, the characteristics of successful teams, how they tend to develop, and what they can do for the organization.

Types of Organizational Teams

In the course of your business and professional career you will encounter a variety of different types of teams. Some will be formally established and sanctioned by the organization and be directly related to accomplishing the work of the organization. Others will be of a more informal variety and may be only marginally associated with the work of the organization. These groups exist for more social, civic, or recreational purposes. Sometimes this distinction is referred to as task and social groups, with the task being those formally established by the organization and the social being more marginally associated with the organization.

Ongoing formal groups and teams in organizations might be called teams, of course, but may also be identified as departments (accounting, human resources, and so on), squads, units, or shifts. In addition, project teams may be established for a specific assignment and dissolve once that task is accomplished. Whether ongoing or ad hoc, formal task teams in organizations generally have a functional role to play in accomplishing the overall goals of the organization.

Informal teams might also be called "corporate camaraderie-building" teams that don't necessarily do the work of the organization but serve a necessary social function for members of the organization. For example, there are company-sponsored and -organized athletic teams—bowling, softball, volleyball—and some complete with uniforms bearing the company logo. While a winning sports team may not make the company any profit, it may go a long way to boosting employee and corporate morale. Many companies also have volunteer civic teams that participate in fund-raising walks or United Way Days of Caring events, or build houses for Habitat for Humanity. For example, members of a local investment company volunteered to prepare personal care kits for injured members of the military. These teams may have the formal sanction of the company, and company time and resources might be used in organizing such teams. There are also employee-organized "camaraderie-building" groups like the members of a work group who meet regularly to relax over cold drinks, fish together on the weekends, or participate in other hobbies and activities.

It is important to realize that both formal and informal teams are important to the success of the organization because they contribute to the welfare of the individuals in those organizations and help to build a positive communication climate in the organization. Obviously the formal task-oriented teams exist to help the company make money through the work they produce. However, the informal and more socially oriented teams exist to develop and support the social, recreational, and civic needs of organizational members and the community. These teams provide an important way for organizational members to interact with each other, develop and cultivate interpersonal relationships, and network outside of their traditional organizational units and roles. Indirectly, these teams—because they involve members of the company in the community—contribute to a positive corporate image as well as supply vitally needed support for various human, social, and volunteer service agencies in the community. Most important, they make the organization more civil and civic minded.

Your organizational experience with teams will involve some that allow for your voluntary participation and others to which you will be assigned. Formal task-related groups and teams will tend to be assigned, while informal social groups tend to be voluntary. When your boss "asks" or invites you to serve on a particular task force, project team, or ad hoc committee, you likely don't have the option of declining the offer. When the chance to join the more "camaraderie-building" teams comes along, you should treat it as an opportunity to expand your network of relationships within the organization as you benefit from the social and/or community involvement opportunities they provide. In either case, you should approach the formation of new teams with an attitude of openness and a willingness to fully commit and participate in the work of the team.

A final type of team you should expect to be a part of your organizational life would be virtual teams—those that exist and work via computer-mediated means. As technology has become a dominant part of organizational life, we no longer need to meet face-to-face but rather can meet using email, discussion groups, chat rooms, instant messaging systems, and commercial products like Net-Meeting.[2] These types of teams require special communication skills and civility requirements that will be described later.

Creating a Manageable Team

The number of members on your team will influence not only how relationships will develop over time but the productivity of the team. We know that teams must have three or more members, but the interesting question is: What is the ideal size? In Chapter 2, we explained how the number of team members influences the number of relationships that must be accounted for by members of the team. The greater the size of the team, the more two-person relationships there are that must be established, cultivated, and maintained in order for the group to complete its work (see table 11.1)

Conventional wisdom suggests that the ideal size for a group is seven members, plus or minus two—somewhere between five and nine members. The importance of the number seven can possibly be traced to its

Table 11.1 Interpersonal Connections Within Teams

$$\frac{N(N-1)}{2} = \text{Number of 2-person relationships}$$

$$N = \text{Number of group members}$$

importance in our information-processing ability.[3] Keep in mind that even with groups of seven numbers—for example, our phone number—we tend to divide the sequence into two parts. You probably do the same thing with identification numbers like your student ID or your Social Security number—we "chunk up" the series.

If you substitute members of your team for digits in a series of numbers that you're trying to remember, you will realize some clear implications for civil communication and your team's effectiveness. First, as the number of team members increases so does the number of two-person relationships you'll need to keep in mind. Increasing membership from five to seven to nine members geometrically increases the number of relationships from ten to twenty-one to thirty-six. From a civility point of view, we want to treat each person and each relationship as unique and special. This becomes difficult as the size of the team increases. In effect, at a certain point we begin to combine or lump people together and begin to address our comments and contributions to "small audiences" within the team rather than talking team member to team member. Civility would suggest that the team be as small as possible to allow for higher-quality interaction. There is some evidence to suggest that as the size of your team increases, member satisfaction tends to decrease— yet another reason to keep the size manageable.[4] As you strive to keep the size of your team manageable, you will also have to consider how size or membership influences effectiveness.

Teams need to have sufficient human resources available to address the task at hand. The more complicated and involved the task, the more minds and members will be needed to accomplish the task. The key here is to balance the need for quality and civil interaction with having the available human resources to accomplish the task. The "principle of the least-sized group" establishes this balance by suggesting that teams be as small as possible but that they have all the expertise and diversity required to effectively complete the task.[5] Just as sports teams need players with different skills and talents, the teams in organizations need the expertise to accomplish the work. Following this principle, civil verbal and nonverbal behaviors can be used to shape positive relationships among members of a group while also allowing for the group to accomplish its task effectively. A brief cautionary note: it is best that decision-making groups not have even numbers of members to avoid the problems of tie votes or split decisions.

Developmental Stages: Know What to Expect and Get Started Right

Our company's initiatives are broken down into smaller projects that are led by project managers who in turn lead teams of employees. Project and product management work to set concrete goals so that the rest of the team is always aware of where they are headed. Team meetings are regularly held and steps taken to ensure that each worker has what he or she needs to accomplish his or her part of the task. Setbacks are a part of any project and most employees know this, so if someone hits a roadblock in development, the entire team adjusts to compensate for it. No fingers are pointed, but rather, the team works together to find out how this setback can be avoided next time. The group of professionals my company has put together seems to know that if you make a mistake, it is best to own up to it and learn from it.

Ryan J. Anthony
Media Specialist
Vocollect, Pittsburgh

Regardless of the type of team, you can expect each new team to develop in a fairly predictable way as its members establish relationships and begin to address their goals or accomplish their work. Members of new teams can anticipate four stages or phases in their development that are characterized by different types and styles of communication behavior. These stages include orientation, conflict, emergence, and reinforcement.[6] As your team begins its work, you will need to orient yourselves to each other and the task at hand. Civil communication skills can ease this process when members take the time at least to greet and briefly get to know each other. Exchanging names and background information and engaging in small talk can make you and your new team feel more at ease before you get down to work. Communication at this stage is polite, tentative, and cautious as members figure out how they can and should behave with colleagues. Once you begin to feel more comfortable with each other and begin to orient yourselves to the task at hand, be sure to review and clarify the work you are assigned to complete. Make sure everyone is on the same page.

Conflict will inevitably occur as differing perspectives on a task are exchanged. Again, this exchange should be kept civil by having members state their points of view, actively listening to the contributions of others, and encouraging participation from all members. If you help to keep the focus of conversation on issues and information rather than personalities, your team will be more productive. Once all perspectives are exchanged, things will start to come together and conflicts will be resolved—you will be emerging from the conflict.

If your team has done its work well, you will want to celebrate and reinforce the decision, solution, or conclusion you have reached. In this phase, taking time to acknowledge, value, and reward the contributions and participation of each member will help to conclude the team's work on a positive and civil note. "We did a great job! Can't wait to see what management will say." If the team is of the standing variety, subsequent meetings will require less orientation time because civil working relationships have already been established, allowing the group to spend more time completing its work. Your use of civil communication skills will build relationships that will make future team efforts more successful.

Teamwork with Civility

Teams are particularly useful for accomplishing a variety of tasks within business and professional organizations. Specifically, teams can be used to generate ideas and information, make decisions, solve problems, and resolve conflicts. While it is true that you will perform each of these organizational functions individually, when you work in teams these tasks will be accomplished more efficiently and effectively. Using civil verbal and nonverbal communication, in particular, will make your team an especially dynamic workforce within your company.

Maximize the Assets, Minimize the Liabilities

We have all heard the expression that two heads are better than one. When you count the number of heads on your team, in theory, you have a powerful productivity tool for the company. Experts suggest that this is generally true—with a few manageable exceptions.[7] Your team can generate more information and knowledge than you can working alone because teams allow for the division of labor among members—this is the two heads are better than one idea. More heads and members can also tackle a problem or decision with greater diversity, yielding better results. The very activity of a team discussing, arguing, and exchanging ideas on a topic can increase members' comprehension and understanding of the issues. Teams can draw upon the age-old democratic principle that when people make decisions, they will be more likely to support the implementation of those decisions. Finally, and perhaps most important, teams generally produce better-quality decisions and solutions than individuals.[8] If your company needs quality information, values diversity, requires that employees to have a clear understanding of the issues, and wants acceptable results, teams can deliver.

There are a few liabilities of teamwork that will require your management. Since we were in elementary school, we have all experienced peer pressure and the desire or need to go along with what a group says or wants. We have also all been in a team situation in which a strong individual came to dominate and perhaps lead the team astray. You have also likely been on a team in which at least one member was more interested in the social life of the group than in contributing to its productivity.

Civil communication skills can help to manage these potential liabilities. If you respectfully and tactfully play the role of the devil's advocate, you can challenge the team to look objectively at all the information. "I think we might not be looking at all the alternatives. Before we make a final decision, let's go back and review the facts." For example, the Toro Company (the lawn mower people) employs "contra teams" to be the official voice of corporate dissent before making major decisions. The CEO of Toro recognizes that "nay-saying in corporate American isn't popular," but "the contra team is a way to create negative views that are in the shareholders' best interest and the company's best interest."[9] Managing domineering team members—especially if they outrank you—can be tricky and challenging, but skillfully stating, "While Ed makes some good points, I'd like to hear what the rest of you think before we more forward" can encourage and make it "safe" for otherwise quiet members to get involved in the discussion. Tactfully reminding "socializing" members, "We really need to stay on task and get the work done before we take a break" can redirect the focus of the team to the work at hand. Managing these liabilities requires you to be aware of their potential to hurt the team and your willingness to step in and help manage the situation.

If you have ever served on a jury, you understand that groups are generally more willing to take risks than individuals—"I didn't convict the defendant, *we* did." Risk taking is a characteristic that can be an asset or liability within the team. This diffusion of responsibility is a positive so long as members of the group have carefully and objectively examined all the available facts and information. Doing so helps to avoid a phenomenon known as "groupthink," in which the team ceases to examine information critically, becomes of one mind, and insulates itself from new information.[10] The classic movie *Twelve Angry Men* illustrates persuasively that one skeptical and inquiring juror (played by Henry Fonda) can civilly and effectively prevent the other eleven from taking too much risk and wrongly convicting an innocent defendant. (It is a film worth your time.) The same logic applies to the teams of which you will be a part. You may need to be that skeptical and inquiring mind that keeps the team objective and focused.

In a similar vein, there is the issue of time; in organizations, time is money. If you want the assets teams can provide, you and your company must be willing to invest time and money; a quality decision or solution means investing the time of the members of a group or team. In the following chapter, we'll suggest how team meetings can productively invest their available time.

Anticipate and Manage Conflict

Disagreement or conflict, risk, and time can be either assets or liabilities depending on how they are managed by you and the members of your team. Conflict is productive if it allows members to see new and useful insights but is destructive if it becomes personal. You should encourage spirited and civil argument so long as the "heat" provides light and does not escalate and consume the team. The CEO of Proctor & Gamble scrapped endless preplanned and scripted meetings and briefings in favor of "no-holds-barred debates" to improve the quality of products and profit for the company. Debate is clearly focused on "where to play" (the market) and "how to win" (strategy and tactics).[11] The conflict should always be focused on issues and information rather than people and personalities.

Whenever a group of people gather to discuss a topic of significance, there will almost always be the potential for conflict. As we all learned in physics, where there is movement there is friction. Where there is friction, there is heat. Obviously the teams and organizations that you will be involved with need to grow, develop, and change—that's the movement part of the physics lesson. The key is to anticipate and expect that you will likely encounter conflicts and to be prepared with the tools and civil communication skills necessary to manage them. These tools and skills channel the heat created by conflict in positive and productive ways to address the substantive issues involved and also build rather than destroy relationships among people in organizations. We'll briefly explain how to manage interpersonal conflict and also more group-oriented conflicts.

Managing conflict generally involves balancing the needs, goals, and desires of at least two parties—whether the parties be individuals or groups. The balancing comes as you weigh your concerns for what you want with your concerns for what the other party wants. The result of this balancing is that several different styles or approaches can be taken, including: avoiding (ignoring the conflict), accommodating (giving in), competing (getting what you want), compromising (both sides give in), and collaborating (finding a way that both sides can win).[12] While each style can be useful, compromise and collaboration are generally preferred because they balance the needs of the parties in order to arrive at an acceptable resolution.

If the conflict is between two individuals, a useful approach to follow is to manage it assertively, in other words in a way that respects the concerns of both parties. The process involves planning, then executing a strategy using the following steps:

Planning:

1 Identify the goal you are seeking.
2 Choose the best time to speak.
3 Rehearse what you'll say.

Executing:

4 Identify the specific problem behavior.
5 Explain your problem with the behavior.

6 Make a specific request.

7 Describe the consequences of the desired change.[13]

An example will help to illustrate the process. You want a member of your team who you feel has been slacking off to do their fair share of the research on the project. They want to do as little as possible to skate by. Your goal is to equalize the workload among all members. Trying to talk to the team member in question during meetings has just resulted in arguments and hard feelings, so you invite him to have coffee on neutral territory. Before you meet, you think carefully about what you're going to say and how you're going to phrase things. As you execute the strategy, you know what you want to accomplish, have chosen a good time and place for the discussion, and thought about actual verbal and nonverbal aspects of the message you'll deliver.

"The team is falling behind on the marketing part of the project. I know you're busy with other projects, but the team really needs your input on this phase of this project in order to make our deadline. The team is getting frustrated with our lack of progress and we're stressing about the deadline. By next week, we need you to have a draft of the marketing segment for the team to review. If we can get this draft, all of us will be able to help you refine and polish the final version."

The key is to deliver the message with a calm and steady voice, be specific as to the nature of the problem, how it is affecting you or the group, make a specific and reasonable request so the other person knows what he should do, and suggest either positive or negative consequences. While it may seem odd to plan and rehearse for conflict management, keep in mind that effective communication rarely happens in the heat of the moment. With careful thought to balance the concerns of both parties, the issues can be managed and positive relationships can be maintained. Managing interpersonal conflicts assertively doesn't always work, but it does allow you to provide a specific alternative in order to manage the situation that respects both parties.

A similar approach is suggested by the members of the Harvard Negotiation Project for managing conflicts within or between teams.[14] Working with conflicts from the personal to the international, these researchers suggest a four-step negotiation method "to produce wise outcomes efficiently and amicably":

1 Separate the people from the problem—attack the problem, not people.
2 Focus on interests, not positions—what do the parties need and/or want, individually and mutually?
3 Generate possibilities before deciding what to do—what are our options?
4 Objectively select the best alternative—which option mutually satisfies the most needs?[15]

The hardest step may be the first, to overcome our natural emotions and try to focus calmly and objectively on what we want or need from the situation—*not* on how we can or will get what we want or need. Focusing the attention of team members on the interests or what the parties in conflict need from the situation comes next. Here teams discuss the ends they seek rather than the means to achieving those ends. Once this occurs, the possibilities and alternatives can be discussed using techniques like brainstorming. The final step involves critically and objectively evaluating the potential of each alternative for meeting the needs, goals, or ends of the parties.

The key to your team using this method is to move away from taking, holding, and arguing for a particular position and to focus rather on first understanding what you want or need from the situation. If your team can arrive at agreement on mutual goals, needs, and ends, the means to achieving those goals and satisfying those needs becomes easier.

Leadership, Followership, and Civility

Leadership is probably one of the most studied and extensively researched topics in the field of small-group communication—and also probably one of the least understood. There are a variety of theories, perspectives, and schools of thought that have been suggested to further our understanding of leadership.[16] There are theories that assume that good leaders are born to be leaders; some suggest that leadership skills can be taught and learned, and still others argue that good leaders emerge out of the circumstances and situations that happen to come along. Some work from the assumption that all teams need a single designated or elected leader in order to be effective, while others argue that the task of leadership ought to be shared by all members of the team.

All of these approaches are valuable in different ways as they direct our attention to different issues and possibilities. Since each approach has implications for civility, we will briefly describe several and explain their relationship to civil communication and the goal of cultivating civil relationships in business and professional organizations.

One of the earliest perspectives used to study leadership was called the trait approach, which suggests that we are born with certain traits or characteristics that allow others to perceive us as a leader. These traits include physical characteristics like height and appearance, and personality and social characteristics like being outgoing, intelligent, and open-minded. One of the traits important to effective leadership would certainly be an attitude and practice of civility.

Alternative perspectives suggest that anyone can be trained to use certain behaviors that can help to lead the team and develop a certain style of leadership. These approaches focus on the functions or behaviors that members perform that will lead the team, including those that are task oriented and those that are socially or maintenance oriented. Sometimes these two categories are referred to as a concern for production and a concern for people.[17] Leaders can become very autocratic and task oriented and accomplish the work—at the expense of positive member relationships; leaders can also become very socially oriented or laissez-faire and cultivate positive team-member relationships—while neglecting the work. Since most group members tend to resent a heavy-handed authoritarian approach and become frustrated with the lack of progress toward a goal resulting from the laissez-faire approach, good leaders should try to balance their behaviors and try to maximize their concern for the work with the cultivation of relationships—what is termed a democratic or team style of leadership. If you seek to be a civil leader, your communication behaviors should fall into this last category: you assist the members of your team in accomplishing the task while at the same time carefully attending to the development of positive relationships.

There are also approaches that combine the best of the functional approach with a careful consideration of the situation or circumstances requiring a leader. These situational or contingency approaches try to take into account things like leader-follower relationships and skills, matching the style of leadership with the situation and followers needing to be lead.[18] For example, if your team includes unskilled and apathetic members, you will need to be a more task-oriented leader and focus your behaviors on explaining how and why the task is to be done. If the members of your team are highly skilled and motivated, they may require little task guidance on how to do the job and need only encouragement and reinforcement. These approaches require you and the members of your team to be skilled at assessing the needs of the team and be capable and flexible enough to provide the style of leadership that matches the members or followers.

Civility becomes especially important if you are trying to provide leadership to a relatively unskilled or unmotivated group. In such an instance, you must clearly and respectfully train and motivate members to accomplish the task.

Then there are leadership approaches that suggest that teams don't need a single or designated leader and assume that team members are willing and able to lead themselves.[19] These approaches are referred to as self-managed or self-directed groups or teams. Using such an approach in organizations assumes that members of the group are technically skilled, familiar with the tools of the trade, and, perhaps most important, have well-developed interpersonal communication skills. In order for self-managed teams to work, members must be willing to take responsibility not only for their own behavior but also for the work of the team. In addition, lacking a designated leader, they must have sufficient interpersonal skills that they can individually and collectively manage and cultivate positive relationships among the members of the group. For example, the night shift at a clinical laboratory consists of an intake clerk and several technicians. There is no manager, per se, in the facility at that hour. The technicians are trusted to know not only how to do their jobs but also to be perceptive enough and willing enough to offer help if another team member's work is backing up. That is self-directed leadership.

Followership has received less scholarly attention than leadership. Just from the sampling of theories we have described, there is considerable leadership guidance, but the simple truth is that most of us will spend more time following than leading. Clearly, many of the traits and communication skills that will make you an effective leader can also make you an effective follower. Perhaps no single factor is more important to effective followership—being a member of the team—than your ability and willingness to take responsibility and dedicate yourself to completing the work of the group and the cultivation of positive relationships among the members of your team.

The rub here is that we have all been members of teams in which at least one member is a social loafer—for whatever reason, he or she doesn't contribute to the work of the team.[20] In this case, you can spend your time trying to get the team member involved, or you and the other members of the group can pick up the slack and complete the project. While you should do some of the former (civilly encourage and actively seek participation from all members), you can't force people to participate. Students will often complain that a group member isn't pulling his or her weight, requesting that the instructor "make them." If your group has cultivated positive relationships as the work proceeds, members should *want* to contribute. The goal, however, is to get the job done. Career consultants advise that the respect you earn by picking up the slack of others and seeing the task through to completion will be worth the investment of your time.[21] Keep in mind that the team members who do commit 100 percent to the work of the team know and will remember those who participate and those who don't. Your investment in time toward completing the work of your team will pay off in the future as it will cultivate the types of long-term relationships that will help to advance your career.

Summary

Teamwork requires that you know about the nature of teams, the ways they formally and informally do the work of the organization, key characteristics related to the size, development, and success of teams, and some insight as how to lead teams as well as be a contributing follower to your team. Teamwork can multiply the effectiveness of individual players and be quite personally and organizationally rewarding. Keeping your focus on civility and how civil communication skills can cultivate and nurture relationships among the members of your teams will make them more successful.

NOTES

1 Dennis Devine, Laura Clayton, Jennifer Phillips, Benjamin Dunford, and Sarah Melner, 1999, "Teams in Organizations: Prevalence, Characteristics, and Effectiveness," *Small Group Research* 30 (1999): 678–711.

2 For a description, see http://www.microsoft.com/windows/netmeeting/.

3 Gerald Miller, "The Magical Number Seven, Plus or Minus Two: Some Limits on Our Capacity for Processing Information," Psychological Review 63 (1956): 81–97.

4 For a more complete discussion of how size influences groups, see J. Dan Rothwell, *In Mixed Company: Small Group Communication*, 3rd ed. (Fort Worth, TX: Harcourt Brace, 1998), 46–52.

5 Herbert Thelen, *Dynamics of Groups at Work* (Chicago: University of Chicago Press, 1954), 187.

6 B. Aubrey Fisher, "Decision Emergence: Phases in Group Decision Making," *Speech Monographs* 37 (1970): 53–66.s

7 Norman Maier, "Assets and Liabilities in Group Problem Solving," *Psychological Review* 74 (1967): 239–249 (available at: http://proquest.umi.com/pqdweb?index= 0&sid=4&srchmode=1&vinst=PROD&fmt=4&startpage=-1&clientid= 9874&vname=PQD&RQT=309&did=389279191&scaling=FULL&ts=1155824510 &vtype=PQD&rqt=309&TS=1155824520&clientId=9874&cc=1&TS=115582452 0).

8 See, for example, Larry Michaelson, Warren Watson, and Robert Black, "A Realistic Test of Individual versus Group Consensus Decision Making," *Journal of Applied Psychology* 74 (1989): 834–839.

9 Paul Kaihla, "Best-Kept Secrets of the World's Best Companies," *Business 2.0* and CNN Money.com, April 2006 (available at: http://money.cnn.com/magazines/ business2/business2_archive/2006/04/01/8372806/index.htm; accessed August 17, 2006).

10 Irving Janis, *Victims of Groupthink* (New York: Houghton Mifflin, 1972).

11 Kaihla, op cit.

12 Joyce Hocker and William Wilmot, *Interpersonal Conflict*, 2nd ed. (Dubuque, IA: William C. Brown, 1985), 40.

13 Ronald Adler and Jeanne Elmhorst, *Communicating at Work: Principles and Practices for Business and the Professions*, 8th ed. (Boston: McGraw-Hill, 2005), 151–154.

14 Roger Fisher and William Ury, *Getting to Yes: Negotiating Agreement without Giving In* (New York: Penguin, 1981).

15 Ibid., 11.

16 See the following for concise overviews: Katherine Adams and Gloria Galanes, *Communicating in Groups: Applications and Skills*, 6th ed. (Boston: McGraw-Hill, 2006), 251–261.

17 See, for example, Robert Blake and Jane Mouton, *The Managerial Grid III: The Key to Leadership Excellence* (Houston, TX: Gulf Publishing, 1985).

18 See, for example, Hersey and Blanchard's Life-Cycle Theory in Paul Hersey and Kenneth Blanchard, *Management of Organizational Behavior*, 4th ed. (Englewood Cliffs, NJ: Prentice-Hall, 1982).

19 See, for example, Richard Wellins, William Byham, and Jeanne Wilson, *Empowering Teams: Creating Self-Directed Work Groups That Improve Quality, Productivity, and Participation* (San Francisco, CA: Jossey-Bass, 1991).

20 Rothwell, 83–85.

21 Marjorie Brody and Pamela Holland, "Don't Be a Casualty of These Career-Killers," CareerJournal.com, Wall Street Journal Executive Career Site (available at: http://www.careerjournal.com/columnists/perspective/20011105-fmp.html).

Managing Meetings

with Civility

There were eight people seated at the conference table representing eight different business, educational, and social service organizations. Several of the representatives had not met before this meeting and were left on their own to introduce themselves. The purpose of the meeting was to plan a series of events for a nonprofit youth organization. The decision had been made to hold the meeting over the lunch hour to accommodate varying schedules, so plates of food littered the conference table and people briefly left the room to refill plates or to get another cup of coffee or a cold drink. Also on the table were no fewer than ten cell phones and other personal communication devices, which "rang" no fewer than six times during the course of an hour-long meeting—and their owners answered them without leaving the conference room. Those who knew each other spent the majority of the meeting time "catching up" and casually chatting, while those new to the group munched on salad and introduced themselves to the people on either side of them. As the announced ending time for the meeting quickly approached, there was a flurry of discussion as the participants frantically tried to finish their work; one by one, people excused themselves, saying, "I'm sorry, but I've got to get back to work."

In theory, this meeting was a part of the work of each representative at the table. In practice, because of the way the meeting was handled, the comment that "I've got to get back to work" is telling. Clearly the meeting was intended to accomplish work, but as you can probably discern from the description, little of substance was accomplished— except as participants were on their way out the door. This chapter will focus on managing meetings with civility, a skill those who call meetings should master and all those who attend will appreciate.

The need for these skills is demonstrated by research by human resource managers who found that unproductive meetings are a costly drain on businesses and that there is a lack of training in meeting management. [1] Such training is not particularly difficult but does require careful planning and preparation, discipline and a willingness to manage the conversation, and some knowledge of the tools and methods of the meeting trade. We'll conclude this chapter with a list of meeting do's and don'ts that will help to insure meeting civility and productivity.

Four Steps to Civil Meeting Planning and Management

Most communication transactions require planning and preparation to be effective and successful. Meetings are no exception. Careful planning and preparation on your part can ensure that the time (and money) and talents of your team members are invested wisely to arrive at a quality conclusion. There are four steps that should guide the planning and management of any meeting. Following these basic steps, we'll explain some special tools you can employ depending on the type of task your team needs to accomplish.

1   **To Meet or Not to Meet: The Most Important Question.** There may be times when the decision of whether or not to meet is dictated by organizational policies and legal considerations. There are ritual and ceremonial-type meetings in organ-

izations that are mandated by legal rather than functional considerations. For example, most publicly traded companies are required to hold annual shareholder meetings at which the official state of the company is reported. Many social service organizations hold annual appreciation meetings to recognize member and organizational accomplishments. These are not the types of meetings that often consume the time and money of organizations and their members. Our focus will be on what might be termed functional meetings—in other words, meetings that are designed to accomplish a specific goal like the exchange of information, making a decision, or solving a problem.

Your decision of whether to call a meeting or choose an alternative method for communicating with your team ought to be made based on how a meeting would allow you to capitalize on the assets of the team while minimizing the liabilities associated with teamwork. Among the questions that should guide your decision are the following: Do you need to generate new ideas and information? Does the task require a diversity of opinion and perspective? Is there a high likelihood for misunderstanding and confusion? Do members need access to each other to complete the task? Will buy-in and acceptance of a decision be necessary to implement the decision? The answers to these questions should guide your decision to call a meeting or use other means to accomplish a particular task. If your task is simply to disseminate information, send an email or memo to team members rather than invest and possibly waste the time of team members in a meeting. If you have already made a decision, don't call a meeting asking for input and alternatives. If the task is straightforward, the potential for confusion is low, and team members really don't need to talk with each other, don't waste their collective time. If, after careful consideration, you make the decision to call a meeting, your planning should continue as your formulate your game plan or agenda.

2 **Establish the Agenda.** If the main ideas of a speech provide the structure of the speech, then establishing an agenda provides the structure for a meeting. An agenda can be viewed as a "to do" list of items that require some type of action by your team, a list of discussion topics requiring input by members, or a com-

bination of these two. Simply, an agenda contains the work the meeting is designed to accomplish. An agenda should include at least the following: the time (starting and ending), location, and list of team members attending; necessary background information (make sure everyone is on the same page); and items or topics for discussion, in the order in which they will be addressed. Preparing and disseminating an agenda forces you to think carefully about the tasks you want the team to complete. Indicating a starting and ending time is obviously important, but it also sets expectations for the work to be completed and allows team members to plan the rest of their workday. If team members know the items to be discussed and who will be in attendance, they can, at least, begin to prepare mentally for the meeting.

The arrangement of items on an agenda may seem an incidental consideration, but it can have practical and strategic consequences. Experts suggest arranging agenda items in the form of a bell-shaped curve, with easy items at the beginning and end of the meeting and more difficult items in the middle.[2] The idea is to start with easier items that require little energy and time to complete in order to get team members warmed up, tackle the difficult work that requires considerable energy and time in the middle (at the top of the bell-shaped curve), and conclude with easier tasks. This bell-shaped agenda structure considers the relationship between how much time and energy an item will require and where the item should be placed on the agenda. It is also important that the team leader keep an eye on the time and pace the meeting such that the entire agenda is covered. This leads to the potential for using agendas in a manipulative fashion—which we are not necessarily advocating. If there is information, a decision, or a problem that you simply do not want to discuss or deal with, scheduling this item toward the end of the agenda or meeting can ensure that the item won't be covered. "Gee, look at the time. Guess we won't have a chance to talk about salary and bonus issues." If you are ever confronted by such a strategic decision, you can simply request that the item be placed first on the agenda for the team's next meeting. If you must solicit items for an agenda, there is likely not a compelling reason to call a meeting. With the decision made that a meeting is necessary and armed with a carefully prepared agenda, your next task is to manage the meeting and the interaction that will take place.

3   **Manage the Meeting and the Members.** If you called the meeting and prepared the agenda, your next responsibilities are to manage the structure of the meeting (introduction, body, and conclusion) and the interaction that will take place (encouraging and balancing participation). The introduction to a meeting should welcome and introduce team members, if needed, explain the purpose, goals and objectives, and background information, and clearly lay out what is required of the team—the agenda items to be addressed. Tactfully reminding the team of time constraints can encourage the efficient use of time. "We all need to keep our eyes on the time so we get through our agenda." Once the leader gets the meeting going, the body of the meeting—the interaction and conversation—will require management; it needs to be kept on track and focused. Here is where your agenda becomes important by providing an initial structure, but team members are likely to stray and require redirection. If tact and civility fail, the use of what are called relevancy challenges[3]—simply challenging a team member to explain how his or her comments are relevant to the item being discussed—can be a useful technique to keep meetings on track. Depending on the formality of the meeting, a record of the proceedings in the form of meeting minutes should be kept. As each item on the agenda is addressed, the action taken should be reflected in the minutes.

Depending on the team involved, you may need to encourage fair and equal participation from all members of the team. The skillful use of questions is perhaps the best way to encourage participation, especially from the more reticent and quiet members of the team. Questions can be directed to the team as a whole to get things started or to particular members who might have insight or who are not actively participating. Leaders and members can also use questions to deflect attention away from themselves back to the team or from the more talkative members of the team toward those who are less participative. The key is for all team members to use questions and answers as a means to solicit the necessary information to cover the agenda items.

There will likely be times when talkative team members will need to be silenced to ensure full and balanced participation. "We've heard from Bob and Ellen; I think we need to hear from Bill—what do you think? Can you give us the sales perspective?"

An interesting technique to equalize and distribute participation and focus the attention of your team members on each contribution is the use of a "talking stick."[4] This Native American custom was used to ensure a just and impartial hearing by suggesting that the person who literally held the talking stick had the right to speak. After one team member's contribution, the stick was then passed to the next speaker. While a physical stick may not be necessary, the concept is a useful one for both speakers and listeners.

4 **Know When and How to Quit.** If you scheduled the meeting from 1:00 to 2:00, around 1:45 you should be preparing to wrap things up. If you have skillfully managed your team's time, you will likely have made good progress toward completing the agenda. Most communication transactions require a sense of closure and completion—a conclusion. As with the conclusion to a good speech, a meeting should be concluded with a brief review of what agenda items have been covered and the action taken and/or what is left to be covered, followed by an expression of appreciation for the time and talents of the team members. If your team concluded its work—covered the agenda—members should review, reinforce, and possibly celebrate your progress.

As with most work, the task is not complete till the paperwork is done. For meetings, this paperwork involves the preparation of minutes. Minutes are a summary of the actions taken with regard to agenda items (what the team did) and should not become a transcript of the meeting (who said

what to whom). These records are useful if questions or issues arise in the future as to what the team decided during a particular meeting. The preparation of minutes becomes easier if a careful and complete agenda guided the work of the team.

If the agenda was not covered and tasks were not completed, the time, place, and new agenda for the next meeting should be established. This should be based on the remaining agenda items or future tasks to be completed. Before the meeting breaks up, it is a good idea to "task out" the remaining work—who will do what before the next team meeting? Using the last few minutes of one meeting to plan for the next meeting helps to ensure some continuity to the work of the team. Team leaders who follow these four steps can maximize the advantages and minimize the disadvantages of meetings.

Choose the Right Tool for the Task

Depending on the goals of the meeting—to generate ideas and information, make decisions, or solve problems—specialized methods or tools may need to be employed in order to accomplish the task. The right tools make any task easier, provided that you know how to use the tools properly. In order for your teams to accomplish the tasks of generating ideas and information, make decisions, solve problems, and resolve conflicts, you will need a set of tools and some guidance as to how to use the tools with skill and civility.

If Your Team Needs Ideas, Brainstorm

If you work in any field that requires creativity (for example, integrated marketing, sales, product design and development, or engineering), you and your team will be faced with the task of generating new ideas and approaches. Brainstorming is the right tool for the job. Developed by an advertising executive who was constantly challenged to come up with new ways to pitch products, brainstorming is premised on the idea that your creative and inventive mind should be allowed to function before your critical and evaluative mind makes a final decision.[5]

Brainstorming usually involves following four rules: (1) adverse criticism should be avoided—negativity and criticism stifle creativity; (2) "freewheel"—encourage wild, speculative, and imaginative thinking; (3) seek quantity over quality—the more ideas, the greater the probability for good ideas; and (4) "hitchhike" on the ideas of others—ideas can be mathematically added to, subtracted from, and divided to create even more possibilities. After these rules are explained and understood, the team is presented with a specific task and appoints a moderator, who gently enforces the rules, and a recorder, who keeps track of the resulting ideas. The team then generates as many possibilities as they can, while the moderator facilitates the interaction and the recorder compiles the results. Brainstorming sessions usually happen quickly, with bursts of energy and ideas punctuated by lulls and silence, followed by another burst of ideas. When team members "run out of ideas," then and only then should the critical and evaluative faculties of their minds come into play.

Effective facilitation and civil communication skills are required to make brainstorming sessions productive. Initially, the rules and the specific task need to be clearly explained. If you are the moderator, respectfully **remind members of the rules**—especially if members begin to criticize each others' ideas prematurely. "Let's wait to evaluate till later." "Can we combine those two thoughts?" **Actively encourage participation** from all members by calling on people by name. "Sara, anything you'd like to add?" **Manage the interaction** so that everyone is heard and everyone can hear and follow the ideas. "Make sure you get Joe's idea down on paper. Fred, now tell us more." **Keep the energy level high** with verbal and non-verbal encouragement. "You folks are doing great, what else can you come up with?" Once the energy subsides, have the recorder review the team's work and ask for clarification of the ideas. When you have all the possibilities down on paper, your team can begin to examine and evaluate the results critically and decide on the best course of action or choose the best alternative. Additional tools like Nominal Group Technique,[6] which limits the free-for-all interaction associated with brainstorming, and the Phillips 66 Technique,[7] which allows large groups to brainstorm, can also be used to generate ideas and information.

Decision-Making: Use the Right Method to Choose an Effective Alternative

If brainstorming generates possibilities, decision-making tools and techniques can help to organize the critical and evaluative work of your team. Decision-making involves choosing the right alternative from the available possibilities—simple enough. The key is for your team to know what constitutes an effective decision and then to select the decision-making tool or method that will yield an effective decision.

A particularly useful way to measure an effective decision is to examine the relationship between the technical quality of an alternative and the degree to which it will be accepted by those who will be affected by the decision.[8] Stated as a simple equation:

Effective decision = Quality x Acceptance

If you plug some numbers into this equation, you'll see the logic and the importance of carefully considering this relationship. For example, if your team has generated an alternative that is technically of high quality (95 percent correct) but that team members won't accept or help implement (50 percent), the result is an effectiveness "score" of 48 percent. If your team looks at another alternative that is less technically correct (90 percent) but that they find more acceptable (90 percent), the result is an effectiveness score of 81 percent. The point here is not to get lost in the numbers but to realize that the acceptance of a decision by team members is a critically important variable in effective decision-making and should therefore guide the methods used to make decisions in organizations. This suggests that the methods used in making a decision should be guided by how it will cultivate relationships and be accepted *and* whether it is technically correct.

Especially in the business and professional setting, civility concerns ought to guide your selection of the best decision-making method because each method has implications for relationships and for the acceptance of the decision by those who will be affected by the choices made. There are at least six different tools or methods that can be used to choose among alternatives, including:

1   Consensus—all members agree on the best alternative, at least in principle.
2   Majority vote—51 percent or more of the members agree.

3 Minority vote—those with rank or a coalition agree on a course of action.

4 Authority with consultation—the boss seeks the advice of workers before deciding.

5 Authority without consultation—the boss makes a choice without seeking input from others.

6 Expert—the most knowledgeable member chooses the best alternative.

Each of these methods can be used to choose among the available alternative courses of action, but you and your team must realize that each also has implications for civility.

Consensus is generally regarded as the best method for making decisions because all members are in agreement on the alternative—at least in principle. However, it takes time and civil communication skills on the part of you and your fellow team members to arrive at a consensus decision. Remember that time equals money; if you seek quality, you must invest time. Consensus requires that team members examine all the possibilities, vigorously argue points of view, be tolerant and carefully listen to others, and be willing to compromise. Consensus is respectful and values of the opinions of all members and therefore contributes to the civility of the organization and results in high-quality decision-making.

Voting, whether it results in the will of the majority or the tyranny of the minority, clearly has potential as well as problems. While it might be "the democratic way," voting can potentially leave a disgruntled and sometimes vocal minority in its wake, which might make decision implementation difficult. If consensus is not possible or time constraints are present, voting is a reasonable and effective method. Following any such votes, you and your team should take care to include members of the minority opinion in the implementation of the decision and to try to rebuild damaged relationships.

Given the hierarchical nature of organizations, authority decision-making with or without consultation will always be a possibility. As a smart and civil-minded team member or manager, you should exercise your authority arbitrarily only when decisions are of minor consequence or when time pressures simply don't allow for the use of more inclusive and therefore civil alternatives that incorporate input from other team members. A caution for savvy team leaders who do seek consultation before making decisions is to either use the input received or clearly explain why you choose to disregard the counsel received. If team members or your subordinates are repeatedly asked for input and routinely see it ignored, they will cease to provide it in the future.

Authoritarian styles of decision-making have the potential to damage relationships and will likely encounter resistance when it comes time to implement decisions. Expert decision-making can be effective if in fact everyone agrees on who the expert might be and if that individual in fact is an expert.

It is important to return to the relationship between quality and acceptance in the choice of decision-making methods. If your goal and that of your team is to cultivate and maintain civil and positive relationships, it is important to use decision-making methods that will not only accomplish the goal of choosing the best alternative course of action but also build civil relationships. Keep in mind that an important part of effective decision-making is whether or not those affected by the decision will in fact support and help in the implementation of the decision. Therefore, methods that involve the widest possible participation by those affected by the decision will cultivate civility within the team and the organization in both the short and long term. If you want your team on board and will need their help to implement a decision, involve them in the process.

Problem Solving: Follow a Systematic Pattern

When you and your team are faced with a problem, your natural inclination will be to seek a solution. However, if you prematurely jump to a discussion of solutions without fully exploring the nature of the problem, you'll likely not really solve the problem and may in fact create new problems.

Effective problem solving requires the use of a systematic and logical pattern of thinking that will allow you to understand clearly the nature of the problem, critically investigate all the available solutions, arrive at the best solution, implement the solution, and monitor how it is working. There are a wide variety of problem-solving techniques available, most of which draw their logic and approach from the work of the philosopher John Dewey, who looked to the scientific method as a way to organize problem solving.[9] A systematic or what Dewey called a reflective thinking approach to problem solving should include the following steps:

1 Clearly state and agree upon the definition of the problem.
2 Analyze and gather all the necessary background information.
3 Establish guidelines or criteria an acceptable solution must meet.
4 Generate possible solutions to the problem.
5 Evaluate each alternative against the guidelines and criteria.
6 Implement the solution.
7 Follow up to make sure the solution has resolved the problem.

Following Dewey's logic, when the mind is confronted by a problem it tends to think through that problem in a logical and reflective way. Using these steps will provide your team with two clear advantages: first, they will provide an agenda to keep you on track, and second, because of their inherent logic, they will allow you to systematically rather than haphazardly arrive at a quality solution. Your team's civil communication skills should guide your progress through these steps.

You and your team gather to address the following issue: Production and productivity in your company is down. Your team has been assembled to meet and get things back on track. Is it an engineering problem, a sales and marketing problem, a shipping problem, a quality-control problem, a personnel problem, a slump in the economy? How your team defines the problem will influence the solution you arrive at in the end. Therefore, it is critically important that you spend meeting time carefully and clearly arriving at a definition of the problem on which everyone can agree (consensus)—and that is supported by the facts. "Let's be clear on what we think the problem is and make sure we hear from everyone before we proceed." "Let's not get ahead of ourselves. Before we jump to solutions, let's make sure we know what the problem is."

This definition will then allow you to gather all the available information and facts that will be necessary in solving the problem. Here is where your team's ability to divide their labor becomes important. "Since we have expertise from several different departments, let's all go back and take some time to talk to our departments to gather more information." As you gather your research, the goal or ideal solution should become clear, which in turn will shape the guidelines and criteria you will use for its selection. The standard or stock criteria usually include things like practicality, workability, desirability, and feasibility. The specifics will depend on the situation. Brainstorming all the possibilities your team can think of builds a list of alternatives, which you will then systematically compare to the criteria.

Especially if your team involves representatives from various departments, be sure the team manages the brainstorming meeting with skill. "We need to hear from all departments." "We haven't heard from line-production workers. We need their input to tackle this issue." As the best solution emerges—based on the criteria—you can turn your collective attention to implementation and follow-up issues. The decision-making tools and methods described earlier will need to be used here to arrive at the best alternative that balances the technical quality with the acceptability of the alternative. "We need buy-in from the marketing folks if this new approach is going to work. How can we make sure that happens?"

Your team's work isn't done until you have implemented the solution and determined if your solution did in fact solve the problem— did you get things back on track without creating new problems? If so, the team can reinforce its work and celebrate the relationships that have been built that can be drawn upon in the future.

It should be clear that problem solving may involve several different meetings over a period of time. Such meetings will draw upon your team's knowledge at managing the development of the team, generating ideas using brainstorming skills, and ultimately decision-making skills to arrive at a final solution. The quality of the final solution will depend on the civil, disciplined, and logical application of an agenda that will guide your work.

Point of Order: What about Parliamentary Procedure?

Depending on the formality of the organization and the nature of the meeting, the use of parliamentary procedure may be required. As the name suggests, parliamentary procedure was originally developed to manage the work of legislative and deliberative bodies. Henry Roberts was a Civil War-era military officer who found himself wanting in the skills necessary to manage meetings. Over time, he compiled *Robert's Rules of Order*, perhaps the gold standard in parliamentary procedure—now in its tenth edition and available in several versions from complete to brief.[10] There are several basic principles of parliamentary procedure that deserve mention: the will of the majority rules, the rights of the minority are protected, members are to be treated equally, and freedom of discussion should be the norm.[11] The most important thing to remember about the use of parliamentary procedure is the simpler the better; the fewer rules and cumbersome procedures employed, the better; less is good.

If you need a formal means of managing a meeting or if the use of parliamentary procedure is mandated to be used in formal meetings in your organization, there are a number of compilations and brief guides available online or in any library that will provide enough information to get you started without overwhelming you with mind-numbing details. From a civility perspective, the most important thing to remember would be to follow the principles without getting bogged down in the details of motions, voting, and how to address the chair. Parliamentary procedure is simply a means for respecting the will of the majority, respecting and allowing the voice of the minority to be heard, and conducting the business of a team so that the free exchange of ideas is ensured. Civil and effective managers and communicators need to know and be able to use the proper tools of the meeting trade.

Civil Meeting Do's and Don'ts

1 **Turn Them Off.** If it is important enough to gather and "spend" the time of team members, it ought to command the full and undivided attention of members. Unless the transplant team might be calling; your wife is in labor; a multimillion-dollar deal is in the balance; or the end of the world is imminent, turn off all personal communication devices or, at the very least, switch them to silent-vibrate mode. Researchers found that the vast majority of workers (87 percent) are irritated by ringing phones in meetings and 80 percent feel it is unacceptable to answer them during meetings.[12] T-Mobile in the United Kingdom, which commissioned the research, advocates raising mobile etiquette standards so the technology enhances rather than impinges on work life.

2 **Take Turns.** The simple lesson we all should have learned in kindergarten applies to team meetings: one person at a time speaks. If you want the full and undivided attention of your team members, grant them your full and silent attention.

3 **Welcome Newcomers.** Established teams require little by way of introduction and background information. Imagine sitting around a conference table where everyone is on a first-name basis except you. You can't address people by name; you're not sure of all the issues, and you're afraid of saying the wrong thing—so you say nothing. If the rest of the team fails to notice, you should take the initiative and ask for introductions and a bit of background. While it may seem extreme, certain types of meetings benefit from name tags or name cards to facilitate the discussion.

4 **Be Judicious with Food and Drink.** If you want team members to attend, promise to feed them. However, if you feed them you should anticipate that the meeting will take more time and possibly become messy. Obviously there is a difference between offering coffee, coffee and pastries, a Continental breakfast, and a full meal. If time is an important consideration, keep things simple.

5 **No Sidebar Conversations.** Talk during a meeting should be directed toward the task of the group. Sidebar conversations are distracting to the team and decrease the productivity of the meeting. If you are carrying on a side conversation, you and your partner are missing the meeting and will likely need to be caught up at a later time—which wastes time and therefore money.

6 **Pay Attention.** Sounds simple, but if you choose to shuffle your papers, prepare for your next appointment, or read unrelated correspondence, your behavior is rude and will likely result in you missing important information and conversation. If the behavior of one or a few are distracting the many, as the leader of a meeting it is your responsibility to gently remind colleagues of their manners and obligations to respect the time of others.

7 **Prepare an Agenda, Distribute It, and Follow It.** Yes, we repeat ourselves, because it is that important. Planning and developing an agenda helps to determine if in fact a meeting is necessary, who should be asked to attend, and what issues are to be

addressed. If it is distributed well in advance of the scheduled meeting, participants have time to prepare, which makes actual meeting time together more productive. Following the agenda and using what one marketing company calls a "taskmaster" to keep everyone on topic also improve meeting productivity.[13]

8   **Take a Stand—Literally.** While it may not work for some meetings and situations, literally requiring meeting participants to stand during meetings seems to decrease the length of meetings and increases the productivity of the meeting because participants tend to be a bit uncomfortable, and therefore collectively invest their time in being productive. UPS, the package delivery company, uses a variation on this idea called "the Three-Minute Huddle."[14] At the beginning of the shift, office managers and driver supervisors routinely gather workers for a 180-second meeting for company announcements, updates, bulletins, and traffic information. These meetings always end with a safety tip. These huddles are an extreme form of meeting management and brevity.

9   **Watch Your Watch.** In our monochromic business and organizational culture, time and money are inextricably linked. Not only should you think carefully about investing time and money in meetings and managing the meeting time well, but you should also carefully consider when to schedule meetings. Generally, mornings are good (but not too early), while immediately before and after lunch as well as late afternoons tend not to be good, and Friday afternoons and days before holidays tend not to be good.[15] Granted, it is often a chore simply to find a time when five to seven coworkers can meet, but if you can consider these timing factors attendance and civility may increase.

10   **Translation, Please.** Depending on the composition of your team (whether you are from the same or different departments within the organization), you may experience significant problems in translation. The simple fact is that team members from accounting, engineering, marketing, human resources, and sales literally talk differently, at times almost speaking different languages. If you are leading such a multilingual meeting, be sure to ask that unique terminology, jargon, and acronyms be translated and explained. Assume that misunderstanding is likely

rather than that everyone understands. Even if you are not leading the meeting, don't be afraid to ask for translation of unfamiliar language. Chances are that others around the conference table will thank you for taking the initiative.

Summary

Meetings are a frequent and necessary part of business and professional life. Over the course of our organizational lives, we will all attend and chair hundreds of meetings consuming countless hours of time and dollars. The key question should be whether or not the hours and dollars were wisely invested. Meetings can be effective, efficient, and civil if the leader is well prepared and follows some straightforward advice in terms of planning for the meeting with care, using the proper tools to accomplish the job, and remembering to conduct the meeting with skill and civility.

NOTES

1 Stephanie Armour, "Some Companies Aim to Tame Meetings," *USA Today.com*, July 5, 2006 (available at: http://www.usatoday.com/money/companies/management/2006–07–05-meeting-usat_x.htm; accessed July 6, 2006).

2 John Tropman, *Effective Meetings: Improving Group Decision-Making* (Newbury Park, CA: Sage, 1980), 68.

3 Ronald Adler and Jeanne Elmhorst, *Communicating at Work: Principles and Practices for Business and the Professions*, 8th ed. (Boston: McGraw-Hill, 2005), 303.

4 Carol Locust, "The Talking Stick," Native American Research and Training Center, August 30, 2006 (available at: http://www.acaciart.com/stories/archive6.html).

5 Alex Osborn, *Applied Imagination: Principles and Procedures of Creative Thinking* (New York: Scribner's, 1959).

6 See Andre Delbecq, Andrew Van de Ven, and David Gustafson, *Group Techniques for Program Planning: A Guide to Nominal Group and Delphi Processes* (Glenview, IL: Scott, Foresman, 1975); or Gay Lumsden and Donald Lumsden, *Communicating in Groups and Teams: Sharing Leadership*, 4th ed. (Belmont, CA: Thomson Wadsworth, 2004), 180–182.

7 See J. D. Phillips, "Report on Discussion 66," *Adult Education Journal* 7 (1948): 181–182; or Lumsden and Lumsden, 344.

8 Norman Maier, "Improving Decisions in an Organization," in *Problem Solving Discussions and Conferences: Leadership Methods and Skills* (New York: McGraw-Hill, 1963), 1–19, reprinted in Stewart Tubbs, *A Systems Approach to Small Group Interaction*, 3rd ed. (New York: Random House, 1988), 350–362.

9 John Dewey, *How We Think* (New York: Heath, 1910).

10 See the official website for Robert's Rules of Order at http://www.robertsrules.com/ for more information.

11 Ray Keesey, *Modern Parliamentary Procedure* (Boston: Houghton Mifflin, 1974), 11–15.

12 Dan Thomas, "Bad Manners with Mobiles Winds up Work Colleagues," *Personnel Today.com*, September 22, 2005 (available at: http://www.personneltoday.com/ Articles/Article.aspx?liArticleID=31698&PrinterFriendly=true; accessed June 13, 2006).

13 Armour, op cit.

14 Paul Kaihla, "Best-Kept Secrets of the World's Best Companies," *Business 2.0* and CNN Money.com, April 2006 (available at: http://money.cnn.com/magazines/business2/business2_archive/2006/04/01/8372806/index.htm; accessed August 9, 2006).

15 Ted Allen and Scott Omelianuk, *Esquire's Things a Man Should Know about Handshakes, White Lies and Which Fork Goes Where: Easy Business Etiquette for Complicated Times* (New York: Hearst, 2001), 131.

13

Civil Communication

in the Electronic Context

In our earlier description of various communication contexts, we noted that the key factor distinguishing one context from another was the number of people involved. One person speaking with just one or two others is interpersonal communication, and one person speaking without interruption to more than twenty-five persons is public address. Sounds like a simple distinction. However, the line blurs in the world of mediated communication— that in which the message is carried electronically. When Larry King has a heart-to-heart, intimate conversation with Elizabeth Taylor or Vice President Cheney, it looks very much like interpersonal communication. But when you factor in that this conversation is being observed by several million at-home listeners, it muddies the waters. Likewise, your cell phone conversation conducted in the stands at Yankee Stadium and your email message using the office computer have more "listeners" than you intended. Do guidelines for interpersonal communication apply here or should the participants be following recommendations for public speaking?

Most communication scholars observing the evolution of electronic communication have agreed that it actually is best to think of this as a completely unique context, one that our "founding father," Aristotle, had no way of envisioning. It is the blending of the interpersonal and the public—some might say the misguided confusion of the two—that makes the electronic context distinct. Technological capacities are expanding and diversifying faster than most can keep track of, so it is a communication science still in the making. As soon as we mastered communication via email, along came "texting" and, right on its heels, webcasting, and on and on and on. But it is the continuing mix of the interpersonal and the public that remains the hallmark of the electronic context.

Cell phone use is the best way to illustrate the schizophrenic character of electronically mediated communication. The beauty of the cell phone is its portability, of course. You can make a call at any hour of the day from just about any place. Say the boss sends you to the office supplies store to pick up a new photo printer. Once at the store, you discover that printers come with more options than those you and the boss had discussed. No problem— you can just pull out your trusty cell phone and, standing there in the printer aisle at the store, you can call the boss, who is dashing down the hall at work to a meeting, and check which options  are actually needed for your purposes. On the surface, this appears to be an interpersonal conversation between just the two of you. However, the portability that makes the cell phone so handy also means that this call has taken place within a public, not a private, environment. Your conversation has been easily heard by every other shopper in that section of the office supplies store and by every person your boss passed in the hallway at the office. This is the mixed context typical of all electronically mediated communication—in a class by itself!

The class includes several different specific electronic media: radio, television, email, cell phones, pagers, land-line telephones, and the Internet. Since the first two are media not typically used in the business setting, we will omit them from consideration here. Each of the other forms has been in continuous use in business for long enough that a particular "etiquette" or civility standard has been developed for each. It is quite clear from the experience of frequent users that civil use of electronic media can be a boon to business while the risk of rampant electronic rudeness remains a minefield to be carefully traversed.

Email and E-etiquette

We will consider first the ubiquitous email. Although in common use only for about fifteen years, it has already become such a fixture in the workplace that most cannot imagine conducting business without it. We can access our messages from multiple sites, including those lacking a wired connection to our home base. It really is amazing—amazingly wonderful and amazingly tricky.

Like any means of communication, email requires the user to make wise choices among numerous options. The user who chooses the best circumstances under which to use this medium and then chooses wisely the content, wording, style, and execution of the message will get the desired results, whereas a bad choice of any of the above can result in unintended offense, confusion, and errors of fact or judgment. Just ask any of the number of individuals who have been fired from their jobs because of the contents of an email they sent.

Let's look at the issue of the right circumstances for email to begin with. While the medium is handy for trying to accomplish a variety of goals, it is really best for

> Civility plays an important role in emailing because although emails don't "speak," they are certainly read as having an implied tone. I am just as careful in my word choice in emails as I am when speaking with someone directly. Emails allow us more time for word choice, but they also allow the reader more time for digestion and dissection because they can be reread and reinterpreted any number of times.
>
> Risa Glick
> Quality Assurance Test Manager
> Northrop Grumman Corporation
> Sterling, VA

only three circumstances. First, it is the ideal medium for contacting individuals who are unreachable by the more personal medium of the telephone. Often, you will have colleagues who are traveling in remote areas or who can't be interrupted for periods of time. Sending an email is the perfect solution as long as the receiver is a person who regularly checks the "in box." Similarly, you would be wise to use email to confirm a message that has been left via some other avenue. Leaving a voicemail message or sending something by post is always a little unreliable, so a confirming email is an appropriate way to increase the odds that the person will receive your message. The final circumstance for which emailing is appropriate is contacting multiple persons simultaneously. The email format allows you to send exactly the same message to scores of individuals with very little effort.

That final circumstance provides a good segue into the question of the types of content for which email would be a wise choice. Since the message can be sent to so many people at once *and* can be seen by your supervisor should he or she wish to know how you are using the company's Internet service and time, email is appropriate only for certain kinds of content. Keep in mind that the email message can be read and reread, carries an implied tone, and typically encourages little complex thought. With that as background, the following guidelines should be observed when considering what to say in an email and whether email is even the best medium for the message you need to address.

Use email to request or provide brief pieces of objective, unequivocal information

It is a great way to exchange basic data about projects, itineraries, and so on. You need to check which form to use for requesting a travel reimbursement. Don't interrupt the staff assistant's busy day by calling or stepping into the office, just send the question via email to be read at the assistant's convenience. You need to confirm with your colleagues the exact specifications for a design on which you are collaborating. Send your information via email so that the others can have it on record and access it at the time needed. In instances such as these, the information being exchanged is unarguable fact that can easily be put in a brief written message. Its impact will not suffer by being stored electronically for days or weeks, and it is a brief enough message that the receivers are likely to read it in its entirety when first received.

All of these advantages of factual exchange email argue against using it for more complicated or arguable content. Trying to explain instructions, for instance, that include more than four or five steps is not suited to an email message, since the receiver typically just glances at messages and sets aside those that look like they might take more time for careful comprehension. If too complicated, the receiver may never come back to it at all. Similarly, trying to have an argument via email is a doomed effort from the start, since it forces the receiver to process all of the sender's points before having the opportunity to respond to any one of them. Essentially, then, email is for "fill-in-the-blank" questions, not essays or multiple choice. Sending a colleague an email message asking for advice on a complicated issue—for example, "Should I invite Harry to join our team or do you think he is too limited in his perspective? If we don't choose Harry, who would be better? Do you think we have the money for a wider search? How will Mr. Bigshot take all of this?" Argh! Email was simply a bad choice for such a message. It frustrates the receiver, disrespects his or her time, and increases the likelihood of reaching a bad decision. Instead, use it just to exchange basic facts.

Use email to address nonsensitive issues

The issue here pertains to the emails you would send from your business computer, owned by your employer. Given that employers have the legal right to check the content of employee email at any time, it is prudent to minimize personal emails and to stick to "G-rated" content no matter who the intended recipient is. All of us make occasional use of the office computer for personal matters from corresponding with family members to checking the times for movie showings. Employers are aware of this occasional use and are generally tolerant of it. Extreme reliance on the office computer for sensitive, personal correspondence is inappropriate, however. You should not be sending messages revealing the depths of your passion to anybody on the office computer. You should not be discussing your child's behavioral problems on the office computer. You should not use the office computer to discuss anyone's personal problems unless there is an absolute urgency of time and accessibility. The "you should not" list could go on for some length, but you get the idea.

Instead, use email when the content is clearly denotative, legal, and able to be addressed with polite language free of multiple or suggestive meanings. Send messages to colleagues about the work in which you are mutually involved, not about their health or economic problems. That is a proper and appropriate use of the employer-owned email service that helps to advance the corporate goals by maintaining a professional relationship among the employees.

Use email to praise an employee or coworker "publicly"

Since electronic media have the power to convey interpersonally toned messages to a mass audience, they provide a fine medium for dispensing praise. The oft-cited business maxim "Praise in public, reprimand in private" is sound and civil advice that is quite applicable to the electronic context. A staff member has received an award, completed a degree, won a grant, secured a major contract—all of these are great achievements that should be publicly acknowledged. Using email to send a message to all employees on the list-serv is the quickest and surest way to make sure that everyone is aware of the staffer's achievement. In addition, it effectively connotes the supervisor's appreciation and pride in this staff member's work, which creates a positive, civil image of the supervisor, which, in turn, contributes to overall employee satisfaction and productivity. It is a link in the chain of civil communication.

Use email to share insights, not to incite

The practice of "flaming" is a capability of the computer age that has no productive benefit in the workplace. This refers to sending messages whose sole purpose is to anger the recipient. Some might try to cover such intentions with excuses like "I just wanted to get his attention" or "I was just so mad I had to say something." But no excuse is good enough in this situation because email is just not well suited to accomplishing such goals.

Choose email because its nature meets your needs, not just because it's handy. If you need to get someone's attention, a phone call or a neon sticky note will work much better than email. If someone has done or said something that makes you so angry that you could scream, choose a setting in which you actually can scream—go outside and yell to the heavens or confront that person when the two of you are in a private enough situation to allow for screaming. Trying to vent your anger electronically is totally counterproductive and tends to take time away from the receiver's productivity as well as yours. Remember too that the profanity used in person will eventually be forgotten, whereas that used in a flaming email may be preserved to fester for months or years to come.

Observe the same content cautions for or attachments as you do for the email itself

Concerns about the appropriateness of content and language are even more important for documents attached to your email because they are likely to remain stored in the receiver's system longer than the message itself. No matter how quickly the receiver punches the discard or trash button on an email, the attachment is not affected. It will remain in the attachments file until it is specifically removed.

Use clear, original wording in the subject line of an email

The subject line is essentially the title of your email message. As such, it is a filter used by the receiver to decide whether or not to open and/or read your message. The title should give a clear "hint" as to content without using any features or words that might be off-putting.

If, for example, you received an email about this book, it might come with one of the following subject lines: "Civility in Business," "Troester-Mester book," "Must Read," or "FW: civility book." Your inclination to open the message would probably vary among those four different titles. Most people are less inclined to open forwarded messages than they are originals, so heading number four would likely be least motivating to you. If you know Troester and Mester personally, you might be more inclined to open the header with our names. If you don't know us, but have a great interest in business civility, header number one would be more motivating. As for the "Must Read" title, that is so vague that it probably would not motivate anybody but a true bibliophile. So choose a subject line that is most likely to motivate the particular person(s) to whom you are sending the message.

Choose a pleasant, legible font for all emails

One of the advantages of personal computers over the ancient typewriters is their ability to print in varied fonts and colors. That is a significant benefit, since font changes carry implications of meaning. In this list you are reading now, we have chosen to use one font for the main text and a different one for the specific tips being explained. This differentiates the relative importance and relationships among the ideas and words.

The same thing holds true for fonts used for email—changes from the norm are interpreted as carrying meaning in and of themselves. If the entire message is written in a single font, no individual part of it is perceived to be more important than any other part. So if you want to call attention to a particular piece of information, such as a change in a meeting time, type it in bold or in a more vibrant color or a significantly different font style. Type only the emphasized segments that way so the distinction of import will be clearly conveyed.

Whether using the same font for the whole message or including some highlighted pieces, stick to at least medium size and a color that contrasts sufficiently with the white background for legibility. The pale turquoise may be cute, but it gives the reader eyestrain and certainly does not come across as having been written by a professional.

Loud vibrant color used for an entire message conveys to the reader that the writer is shouting. Consequently, it is a great idea to use that style for an exciting, positive announcement. For any other purposes, it should be avoided because it will likely be perceived as an angry shout, not an uplifting one. The standards and goals of civil workplace communication would be violated in that instance.

Choose the appropriate "send" option

This is the final step in your communication via email, and it is the step that seems often to turn disastrous. You do have several choices for sending. The message can be sent as a reply to an individual person who sent you a message; it can be sent as a reply to that person plus all the others that the originating message was sent to; it can be sent as a new message to a single individual; it can be sent as a new message to a predetermined list of linked recipients; it can be sent to one person with copies sent to others unknown to the primary recipient; it can be sent to one person with copies sent to others made known to the primary recipient. Each of these options may be appropriate under different circumstances.

If you want the message to be essentially interpersonal, not public, just send it to one person, either as a new message or as a reply to a message from that person. Be especially careful if you choose the "Reply" button to make sure that your reply is going only to the single originator and not to the entire list of recipients of that original message.

If you choose to send the message to a larger group of individuals, you are casting it as a one-to-many, public message instead of interpersonal. That may necessitate going back over the content of the message to make sure that language used would not be open to many different interpretations and that the substance is uncomplicatedly factual.

Finally, before clicking on the "Send" button, make sure that it is going to only that individual or individuals for whom it is specifically intended. The claim of sending a hurtful message "by accident" stands up about as well in the court of public opinion as a sloppy driver's claim of not seeing a stop sign.

All of the above tips about email usage in the workplace are based on a respect for the technology and its users. Too often, we find ourselves tempted to use new technology just because we can. It is convenient and efficient and fun. But email, in particular, can also be very problematic and easily misused. Communication choices guided by the listed recommendations will be more likely to accomplish your goals efficiently and contribute to workplace harmony.

Cell Phones and Pagers

Portable communication devices used to refer just to pens and pencils but no more. Wireless communication has made even the most sophisticated technology virtually completely portable. Recently, a group of coworkers happened upon a huge rainbow arching beautifully over our campus. One in the group happened to be the college's marketing director, who lamented not having a camera. "No problem," replied a colleague, who pulled out his cell phone, aimed it at the rainbow, and took a picture. He then turned to the marketing person, asked for her email address, and, with the tap of a thumb, sent the rainbow photo to her email, where she would later retrieve it for use in college publicity. That type of scenario is essentially commonplace in our new digital age and illustrates the remarkable communication capabilities now available.

Within most businesses and industries, it is fairly common for certain categories of employees to be issued cell phones or pagers to guarantee that they are reachable at any time. This would include individuals in human resources, security, maintenance, and health services, especially. Many others choose to use cell phones and pagers because they want to remain accessible even though their jobs frequently take them away from their desks. In addition, of course, literally millions of people use personal cell phones and have those with them at work. Given the deserved reputation of rudeness associated with many cell phone users, it is clear that some guidelines are needed for best use of the devices within the workplace.

Again, tips for using both personal and business cell phones are all grounded in the need to distinguish between interpersonal and public communication. If you are talking on the phone in a public place, it is not a private conversation. Therefore, certain rules for public communication apply.

Limit cell phone use in terms of number and duration of calls

Being in a public arena means that other people are nearby or passing by and should constitute the primary focus of your attention. You are physically in the presence of other train riders, or coworkers passing on the steps, or fellow guests at a dinner. To turn your attention from those present to those who are present only electronically at the other end of a phone call is fundamentally rude.

As you walk about your workplace or community, you pass by many people. Typical communication behavior would be to glance at the others you pass and utter some greeting to those you know. When that expected exchange cannot take place because one party is talking on a cell phone, the other feels disrespected. This is really bad for the relationship. The feeling of being ignored or disrespected is becoming more commonplace as cell phones become less visible. The person you greeted who did not respond to you may have been engrossed in a conversation on a phone that is a mere earplug or built into his or her eyeglasses, so you did not even detect that he or she was on the phone.

Therefore, it is wise to keep any public cell phone conversations as brief as possible and to avoid placing calls yourself until you are in a more private setting.

Step away from other people when you must speak on the cell phone in a public space

A recent ABC program followed the workdays of several self-employed individuals, who felt compelled to answer any calls at any time in order to be successful in their businesses. Consequently, as viewers, we observed these persons answering their cell phones while at dinner with friends in a restaurant, while in meetings with staff, and so on.[1] Not only does such behavior convey the disrespect noted in our first guideline, but it also makes it very difficult for the other people in your space to try to ignore your phone conversation and sustain their own interpersonal conversation. So there is a pragmatic complication layered onto the fundamental incivility. Both are bad for relationships and bad for business.

Instead, prevent your friends from experiencing the embarrassment of listening in unwittingly on your phone call by excusing yourself to a more private spot if you must take the call. That's the beauty of the cell phone, after all—it's portable! So answer the call briefly, excuse yourself, and walk away. Go to an empty area of the room, ask to borrow somebody's vacant office, or go outside to complete the necessary phone conversation.

Use a relatively low volume when using the cell phone in a public setting

Even if you have walked away from other people and tried to find a private spot for your conversation, it is still possible that your conversation will be heard by others unless you lower your voice. One of the authors tells of hearing a detailed cell phone discussion between an adult man and his mother about the mother's pet skunk, which was ill. This occurred in a public waiting area that had relatively private seating nooks. But the man's voice was so loud that everyone in the entire room could hear him quite clearly. Given the emerging content of the conversation, it was quite difficult for any of the inadvertent listeners to keep a straight face.

If you want the conversation to be a truly private, interpersonal exchange, you must make several adaptations to remove it from the public domain.

Turn off the phone when you will be in a setting where a public presentation or interview will occur

We are all accustomed to the announcements before concerts, speakers, movies, and so on asking everyone to please turn off their cell phones. The rationale, of course, is that the ringing phone will unnecessarily distract the listeners and the presenters. The story is told of a concert pianist whose performance was interrupted by the ring of a cell phone from somewhere in the audience. Without missing a note, the pianist called out, "If that's for me, tell them I'm busy."

The same concern for the sanctity of public communication ought to apply to any formal business setting. Coming into a meeting and setting your phone on the table does not bode well for the others' sense of your commitment to the meeting. If you must have access to the phone to catch a vital incoming call, just tuck it in your pocket and set it to vibrate instead of ring. If you don't have reason to expect any vital calls, turn off the ringer altogether when entering a meeting or presentation. Keep in mind that generations before us conducted business very successfully without answering phones in the middle of speeches and meetings.

It should go without saying that you should not have your cell phone on during an interview. But recently a groom nearly caused the shortest marriage in history when his bride heard his cell phone ring during the picture-taking following their wedding ceremony. So maybe the obvious needs to be stated. Interviews are intense communication encounters in which both parties are focusing on the other, trying to observe and interpret all aspects of verbal and nonverbal behavior. To run the risk of diminishing that intensity by allowing a cell phone to ring is completely unwarranted. Both interviewer and interviewee need to show respect for one another and for their conversation by having their phones off.

During a call, avoid the distractions of multitasking

This is a difficult temptation to avoid. Because the phone is portable, it seems natural to walk around while speaking. Before long, walking yields to paper shuffling, coffee drinking, letter signing, and even using the bathroom. Time is a precious commodity, so the temptation to do several things at once is completely understandable—but it is a terribly bad idea.

Most often, whatever you are doing while talking on the phone creates a sound that is audible to the person with whom you are speaking. Consequently, the person is aware of not having your undivided attention. This is interpreted as a sign of disrespect, whether you intend it to be or not.

Additionally, unless you are extraordinarily gifted, it is quite difficult to follow the phone conversation effectively while giving part of your attention, or several parts of your attention, to some other activity. Remember our earlier discussion of "noise" as a component of communication in this context. Telephone communication is often difficult under normal circumstances because of the limitations of voice-only messages. Any simultaneous activity that distracts your focus from that call increases the chances of missing or misinterpreting an important part of the conversation. Avoid this risk as much as possible.

The highest risk of cell phone rudeness is found in the multitasking situation referred to in passing earlier—the bathroom. Never, ever continue a cell phone conversation as you walk into a public bathroom. This is not a suggestion; this is a prohibition. The background sounds you introduce to the conversation will totally destroy your chances of a successful phone call. Enough said.

Choose a very basic ring-tone
for the cell phone you will use for business

One of the fun aspects of cell phones is the entertainment value of the ring-tones and wallpaper available. Your phone can announce an incoming call to the tune of the Dukes of Hazard's General Lee or the pealing bells of Westminster Abbey or anything in between. These options are entertaining but not in the way that should generally characterize a person's professional conduct. Everything about you contributes to your image and therefore to others' inclination to treat you with respect. Even your ring-tone contributes to that image.

Leave a professionally worded prompt for receiving voicemail messages

As college professors, we have had occasion to hear interesting message prompts on our students' phones. "Yo, leave a message" may be the tamest of the bunch. This is acceptable (not ideal, but acceptable) for the college crowd.

But once you enter the world of business, you have to think of that prompt as a first point of contact between yourself and a potential client or colleague. Your message should be cordial, clear, and inviting. State whose phone the caller has reached, say you can't answer right now, and invite the caller to leave a brief message and call-back number. There is no need to include any details about why you cannot answer right now or how long you will be unavailable. A simple prompt respects everyone's concerns about using time and still gives the caller the opportunity to convey the relative importance of this call.

This suggestion also applies to your personal cell phone. Since this phone should be turned off most of the time that you are at work, you may get quite a few messages left on your voicemail. Invite the callers to leave messages by leaving a prompt that clearly establishes that they have reached you during working hours. That way they understand that there is no need in their continuing to try to reach you by phone and they are less likely to feel disrespected by your failure to call back in short order.

Make extremely limited use of personal cell phones while at work

The reason for having a personal phone at work is essentially for emergencies. You may need to contact a distant family member who is reachable only during your work hours. The cell phone is a great asset in such circumstances. During your lunch hour, you can place the call from the privacy of your office and not abuse your employer's phone service. In most cases, the company will have a written policy about using company time or phone lines for personal purposes. You will be apprised of that policy during new employee training.

During such personal calls, again make sure to speak quietly and in a private place. Your coworkers do not need to overhear you making therapy arrangements for your troubled kin.

Respecting your colleagues' time and space by the way you use your cell phone contributes to limiting noise in your communication exchanges and thus increases the odds of successful communication. It is valuable to have these devices so we can reach one another as we travel through different areas of the workplace, but it is very important that they be used and not abused. Rude cell phone practices have caused numerous venues to ban them altogether. By following sensible guidelines, that need not happen in your workplace.

Old-Fashioned Etiquette for Old-Fashioned Electronics: The Office Phone

While cell phones have constantly grown in use and popularity, the "old-fashioned" technology of land-line phones is still a fixture in most offices. That does not mean that they are all alike, exactly. There are several significant variables in office phones that impact the communication recommendations for their use.

Do you have a private office, a shared office, or a cubicle? In each case, you probably still have a private phone line, but the degree of privacy available for your conversations will vary. Choose the content to address and the words about the content giving consideration to the relative privacy of your space.

Do you answer your own phone or does an assistant or secretary serve as gatekeeper? If the latter, it will be your responsibility to tell your assistant your preferences for how the phone should be answered and what guidelines should be followed to determine which calls should be put through to you and which should be handled by others. This person's telephone demeanor and approach will contribute to the image the caller develops of you, so it is important to establish how you want that image to sound.

Does your telephone have features like caller ID, speaker phone, and/or conference calling? Each of these features serves a beneficial purpose if used correctly. Use caller ID, for instance, just to identify, not to screen your calls. Callers seem often to have a "sixth sense" about when their calls are being screened and they do not take it well. If you use the speaker phone with several people in the room, let each identify himself or herself so that the caller will recognize the different voices as they occur during the conversation. The same practice should take place with conference calls. With video conference calls, this is less important, since everyone will actually see all the other participants on their video screen. For audio-only calls, however, being able to connect names and voices will facilitate a smooth, respectful conference.

Regardless of the combination of specific variables pertinent to your particular office phone, observing some basic principles of civility will allow the phone to be an asset to your business and not a liability.

Answer your telephone with clarity and cordiality

The best "pick-up line" is to say hello and state your name. Doing so will clarify instantly for the caller that you are the person sought. This will require, of course, that you articulate your name precisely. It is generally best to assume that the caller does not know you, so speak your name as you would to a new acquaintance who you hope will remember you the next time your paths cross. Since the caller has only the sound of your voice to go by, make it distinct. Sounds like "m" and "n," "s," and "z" can easily be confused by a muttered pronunciation. Being clear in your initial words on answering the phone conveys an implied gratitude for the call that gets the conversation off to a positive beginning.

If you are having a conversation with someone in the office and the phone rings, you have a dilemma. To answer or not to answer: that is the question. The best advice is that it depends on the nature of the person-to-person conversation in which you are engaged. Can you essentially put that conversation "on hold" long enough to determine who is calling and whether the call can be returned later? If so, politely excuse yourself from the conversation and take the call, keeping it as brief as possible. On the other hand, if the conversation is too vital to be interrupted, just let the answering machine handle the incoming call. To answer and speak abruptly is worse than not answering the call at all.

This brings us to the issue of the answering machine and the best strategy for its use. As mentioned earlier in the suggestions about cell phones, the voicemail option is very handy and saves you from interrupting meetings, giving you the freedom and flexibility to deal with a call at your convenience. The system should be used for those purposes, not as a "moat" that insulates you from perceived intruders.[2] Create a message prompt that establishes who you are and that you will return the call. Do not overload the prompt with unnecessary details about your absence or complicated instructions about calling your assistant's assistant.

Place calls that are well planned and timely

A telephone call can be thought of as a miniature speech. You use the call to convey a message to another person or persons, and you try to create the message with high odds of clarity and goal accomplishment. All of that translates to the usefulness of planning your call's organization prior to dialing the number.

Make clear to yourself the purpose for your call and think about the best way to lead into that. You probably should plan to open the call by clearly identifying yourself and your affiliation, move on to a few pleasantries, and then transition promptly to your thesis. Leaving the callee wondering about the purpose for your call creates unnecessary confusion and, in some cases, worry. Get to the point! Plan ahead also how you will end the call. Once your goal has been accomplished, you should summarize or at least thank the person for the conversation. Every good speech, after all, needs a conclusion.

Planning ahead also means choosing wisely the time at which to call. In our global economy, you may be calling people all over the world. Check the time in their time zone before placing the call. Important calls should be made as early in the callee's workday as possible. We all know how our ability to concentrate begins to diminish late in the afternoon. Respect that reality by calling at a reasonably early hour. Even though you have carefully chosen the time for your call, it still may not be convenient for the other person. It is always a good idea to inquire (after identifying yourself) whether this is a good time to chat or not.[3]

Speaking of time, be sure to return those voicemail messages! Generally, the rule of thumb is that every business message should be returned within two business days. Your message prompt said that you would call back, so that's an obligation. Unless the caller's message said that you didn't need to call back, you should return every call. Doing so establishes that you are a person of your word and that is a terrifically positive business image to create.

Communicating in the Wired Web World

While you may use the Internet for a variety of research purposes, you may also have occasion to use its interactive features, making it a communication medium, not just a repository of information. You may create your own web page, participate in discussion boards, or visit blogs to post or read messages. The continuing growth of these arenas makes it likely that more and more business purposes will be served via interactive use of the Internet.

Treat any interactive Internet function as public, not interpersonal communication

It is easy to think of discussion boards and blogs as places where you just chat with a couple of other people. We hear people speak of "meeting online" as if it were a situation comparable to meeting at a concert or at the spring dance where you chatted one-on-one with this other person. The truth of online discussions, however, is that hundreds or thousands could be reading your postings and those of the other individual you are "speaking with" on the blog. Some participants may post a message to you and/or your new friend, others may simply be "lurking" and following your seemingly interpersonal conversation. So treat the online conversation just as you would a conversation held in the middle of a busy dining hall: you are speaking to the person next to you, but dozens around your table can hear the whole thing. Choose the content and wording of your messages carefully.

Create your online postings with the realization that some who read it pose an insidious danger to you

As was mentioned earlier in our treatment of the history of civility, the criminal element includes many individuals who are quite skilled with the newest technology. Consequently, some of those "listening in" to your online conversations and discussions may be trolling the Internet looking for a potential victim or may be lurking for nefarious purposes. The online audience is considerably more diverse and more unknown than any audience in live communication. This should make it imperative that you make all of your choices regarding what to say and how to say it with considerable caution.

Analyze the source of Web postings as much as possible

A cardinal rule of all communication is that messages must be constructed relative to the specific nature of the intended audience. With web postings, as we said, it is not always easy to know who has posted a message to which you wish to respond. Without knowing anything about the individual you want to reply to, how can you determine the best words to use, issues to raise, references to incorporate, tone to adopt, and so on? Here's where your Sherlock Holmes skills need to be used. Track the source of the message as much as possible before formulating a response. If, for instance, a message is posted on a professional organization's weblog—such as the National Communication Association or the Democratic National Committee—you can trace the source through their national directories to determine if the writer is a college professor, a student, a business owner, and so on. Since some weblogs are the handiwork of imaginative twelve-year-olds as well, you can see why it is important to figure out who you are addressing before posting any of your own messages on that site.

Consider using the Web for marketing

It is quite possible that you have not realized the communicative potential of the Internet as a marketing device. Welcome to the world of "viral marketing."[4] Not necessarily the right communicative tool for every product or for any product for an endless time, marketing by asking your customers to send your product information or newsletter to their friends is a viable new option for the business communicator.

With very little investment in time or money, you can reach tech-savvy consumers with the wonders of your product within a few minutes. The cautions addressed above also apply to this electronic use, of course. But don't let the risks stop you from exploring the business potential of Internet marketing.

Summary

With the constantly expanding possibilities of electronically mediated communication, it is not possible to write anything today that will remain completely up-to-date six months from now. We will all be "speaking" with others via some yet unsold electronic equipment in the decades to come. But the general principles and recommendations addressed here will remain as touchstones for any future decisions about when and how to communicate via cyberspace.

The choice to use an electronic medium at all and the subsequent choices about how to use it should be guided by principles of respect for the relationship between sender and receiver. Whether you are talking face-to-face or face-to-keypad, you are still engaging another person or persons in message making. Respecting that other person's values, needs, and perspectives will allow you to capitalize on the technological capabilities of the new age without sacrificing its fundamental

Our corporate culture remains focused on our basic beliefs of valuing one another, employee and customer alike. Consequently, we have a detailed policy stating how employees are expected to communicate and the technological vehicle that should be used. For example, all employees are to use face-to-face communication whenever possible; if that is not possible then the telephone should be used; then voicemail; then email. We believe that civility is a must to ensure corporate growth and promoting the most personal of communication forms is the best way to achieve that civility.

Julie Hale Abbott
Sales and Marketing Systems
Coordinator
J. M. Smucker Company
Cleveland, OH

humanity.

Choose and use the electronic context wisely. Making the better choices is good for relationships and good for business.

NOTES

1 Frank Mastropolo and Joanna Breen (Producers), "That's So Rude," *20/20*, ABC News, February 3, 2006.

2 Jared Sandberg, "Out-of-Office Replies Offer Venue to Boast, Swagger and Mislead," *Wall Street Journal*, April 13, 2005.

3 Ted Allen and Scott Omelianuk, *Esquire's Things a Man Should Know about Handshakes, White Lies and Which Fork Goes Where: Easy Business Etiquette for Complicated Times* (New York: Hearst, 2001), 49.

4 "An Epidemic of Viral Marketing," *Business Week*, August 30, 2000 (available at: www.http://businessweek.com/bwdaily/dnflash/aug2000830_601html).

14

Podium Civility

Two hundred people have filed into the auditorium; the lights have dimmed, and you hear someone giving a brief sketch of your credentials and accomplishments. This can only mean one thing—you are about to give a public speech! Like many young professionals, you may have assumed (perhaps even hoped) that this day would never come, thinking that very few business professionals actually have to give public speeches. That assumption is true only for those individuals who have no aspirations of moving up within their company or profession. The Bill Gateses and Lee Iacoccas of the business world got where they are, in part, because of their success at the podium, being able to inform and influence large numbers of listeners in one setting. If that's the club you want to be in, read on.

Skillful public speakers contribute significantly to any society's accomplishment of its goals, be that society politics, education, religion, or business. Numerous public speeches, in fact, are perceived as having "changed the world."[1] Those include pivotal addresses by such historical luminaries as Oliver Cromwell, Winston Churchill, John F. Kennedy, Mother Teresa, General George Patton, and Adolf Hitler—no business leaders there. But turn to the pages of the publication *Vital Speeches of the Day* for any given year and you will find business speeches featured as prominently as those by elected public figures and social commentators. The word *vital* in the title of that magazine is worth noting. It says that these speeches are not just important but necessary life-giving events. Leaders of organizations as diverse as Eli Lilly Pharmaceuticals, State Farm Insurance, Kelly Services, the AFL-CIO, McGraw-Hill, Deloite and Touche Financial Services, Verizon, and the American Medical Association will find their speeches reprinted there. These most successful and influential of public speeches share several key characteristics from which we can all learn. Principal among those characteristics is their fundamental civility.

Civility in Public Speaking

Remember that we have conceived of civility as both an attitude and set of behaviors that are grounded in a fundamental respect for others. That may appear to be a concept easily applicable to the intimate, personal exchanges of communication among just two or three individuals, but less applicable to the more formal, less interactive setting of one person speaking uninterrupted in public address. A review of basic Aristotelian perspectives on public speaking, however, reveals a clear emphasis on speaker civility.

Consult as many explanations of the principles of public speaking as you like, and you will find consistent reliance on the speaker's responsibility to do two things: analyze the expected audience and make rhetorical choices based on the audience's nature thus discerned. Everybody agrees! Nearly three thousand years ago, Aristotle first laid down that two-step concept of preparing for public speaking, and no rhetorical scholar since has found reason to disagree. It is a process that we now can see is fundamentally civil because the speaker is basing all decisions about what to say and how to say it on a *respect* for the character, background, and sensitivities of those who will listen to the speech.

Chrysler's Lee Iacocca speaking to the National Association of Manufacturers, General Electric's Jack Welsh speaking to a shareholders' meeting, or your local director of human resources explaining the new insurance plan to your assembled coworkers have all planned their speeches by thinking first and foremost about who the listeners are. What is their reason for coming to this speech; what do they know of the speaker; what is their educational and socioeconomic status; what are their cultural frames of reference; what is their likely listening and learning style; what are their current concerns and needs? These and other questions about audience have to be answered so that the speaker's message preparation can be grounded in respect, leading to wise choices of speech structure, idea development, wording, and delivery.

Never forget the key reality of public speaking: the listeners are giving a precious commodity to the speaker—their time. All of us as speak-

ers should have a respect for that gift, realizing how important time is to everyone in this fast-paced world. Whether your listeners are "captive" or voluntary, they have still taken time that could have been used to work on a project, take a trip, visit with friends, play tennis, sleep, and so on and given that time to you, the speaker. Appreciate that and respect it and you will be a successful speaker. A recent political speech in our area drew a crowd of 2,900 people to listen to a ninety-five-minute presentation—a collective gift of 275,500 minutes! Can you imagine what else could have been accomplished in that time? The speaker wisely planned his speech with the enormity of that gift in mind and was able to relish genuine, exuberant applause at its conclusion from listeners who clearly felt that their gift had been returned in kind. This can be each of you.

Public Speaking in Business

If you are reading this book, it is because you have already completed a basic speech course of some flavor. Some emphasize public speaking, while some focus on the skills more appropriate to interpersonal communication. Regardless of the specific focus of your first course, you have already learned some of the basics about preparing and presenting public messages. Here we will focus on applying those basic concepts to the specific kinds of public speaking you might need to do as a businessperson. Whether your setting is the business world or not, the principle of choosing what to say and how to say it out of respect for your specific listeners remains our foundation.

All managers and supervisors have to do a certain amount of public speaking. The purposes vary depending on the specific industry in which you work and on your particular position within the industry. The typical forms of business speaking include: sales presentations and proposals, technical talks, motivational or inspirational speeches, information-giving updates and seminars, reports to governing boards, and release of "breaking news" pertinent to the company or its management.

Sales presentations are often handled by employees of the sales or marketing department, of course. In smaller companies, however, it is not unusual to find engineers, designers, and managers making the sales pitches to potential clients and customers. The skill with which that presentation is made can spell the difference between landing multimillion-dollar contracts and losing millions—it is a very consequential presentation for which all businesspeople will need some skills. You may find yourself talking to government leaders in China about the value of the locomotives your company proposes to build for them or pitching your company's interior design services to the upper management of May Company department stores or selling your concept for a hotel construction project to a city government. It is all sales and it all requires skillful public speaking.

Technical talks, on the other hand, are limited to those speakers with technical expertise. The engineers and scientists who have created or improved various designs need to regularly inform their professional peers and their employers about the technical aspects of that work. Such talks may occur at professional meetings such as the American Society of Metallurgical Engineers or the American Petroleum Institute or the National Home Remodelers' Association, or may take place within an individual corporation. The key distinguishing characteristic of such talks is that the audience is assumed to be as technically conversant as the speaker; there is a greater homogeneity in the audience than in other types of business presentations, making diverse adjustments to the message less necessary.

Presenting motivational or inspirational speeches may seem out of place in a text about business communication. However, the reality is that many such speeches are given by business leaders. Sometimes it is a highly successful manager who is asked to give a motivational speech to those who aspire to business success—such as when the president of Harley-Davidson was asked to speak at a convention for young entrepreneurs. In other instances, business leaders are perceived as role models in general and may be asked to speak at an Eagle Scout award ceremony or a church conference or a college or high school graduation. Finally, many upper-level managers routinely give inspirational talks to their own employees when the company is faced with special challenges or opportunities.

Informative speeches and seminars are required of many, many individuals in the business world. The staff in a company's human resources department is probably the busiest in this regard because they have to present regular updates on corporate policies to employees at all levels and locations. Many others within retail-based companies present informative speeches to specific cohorts of their customers. For instance, a store that sells household appliances may sponsor a cooking lecture; the craft store offers lectures on flower arranging or scrapbooking; and the home and garden supply store holds workshops on building your own deck or laying a brick patio. Sometimes, the store hires outside experts to present such seminars, but, more often than not, it is the store's staff itself that is expected to do the planning and speaking.

Speeches presented in the form of regular or special reports at corporate board meetings are as common as hot dogs at a picnic. It wouldn't be a board meeting without several people standing up and giving their departments' reports. While typically brief and delivered to a captive audience, the reports still need to be prepared with that same sense of respect for the listeners mentioned at the outset. In fact, these routine reports may require even more civility than other kinds of business speeches because

they are so routine. Routine can too quickly become boring and monot-
onous, causing listeners to have negative expectations going into the meeting. If you are the engineer whose department just solved a major
technical problem in one of the company's rolling mills, however, your
report needs to be captivating, not boring! Out of respect for the board's
expertise, resources, and power, the speaker has an obligation to make
every routine report uniquely arresting.

The release of "breaking news" is the kind of speaking typically
handled by a company's public relations department. For these employees, public speeches are part of their regular job requirements. These
are the individuals we see on television when a company announces
the release of an exciting new product or the acquisition of another
company, for instance. Often they have the happy opportunity to
announce major philanthropic gifts such as the recent Warren Buffet dona-
tion to the Bill and Melinda Gates Foundation. Sometimes, unfortunately,
they have the less pleasant obligation to announce company downsiz-
ing or indictments of corporate scalawags. Across this broad spectrum
of public speeches, the public relations staff's obligations remain the
same: to explain clearly the company's news in a way that respects the
interests of both the public and the corporate audiences.

What to Say: Preparing Content

The fundamental process of building a speech's content is the process
of making choices from among all the available ideas and details that could
be included. The typical business speaker is told what his or her topic
will be. The boss wants a report on last quarter's earnings; the scouts want
a speech about the value of commitment; the potential client wants to
hear about the company's new composites used in home building mate-
rials, and so on. The notion that a speaker gets to pick a topic is just not
realistic. You are assigned a general topic area. Your task, then, as the speaker
is to choose a way to narrow down that broad topic to a focus that can
be covered in the allotted time and to organize specific subpoints in a
way that makes the ideas comprehensible and interesting to the anticipated audience.

This overall task can be accomplished simply by following a sequence of steps in which you make a set of decisions based upon your understanding of the audience's interests and frames of reference. Keep in mind at each step of this process that no one wants to hear *everything* you know about the assigned topic. Be selective out of respect for your audience and you will be successful. Let's go through the steps.

1 **Identify the speech's goal.** While the topic is assigned, the goal may be not be. For a sales presentation, clearly the general goal is persuasion, but what is the specific goal? For an informative press briefing, the general goal may be informing, but, again, what is the specific goal?

   The more precisely that you can state your goal as a speaker, the easier it will be to plan the speech. Goals should be stated in terms of desired listener behavior. What do you want the listeners to do or understand as a result of having heard your speech? When the boss says to go and present the firm's ideas for school design to the greater Denver school board, ask yourself what specifically you hope to accomplish. The concept of just "presenting" an idea is a speaker-based concept. In other words, you can "present" your ideas based solely on your own interests, but that is not good public speaking. The better concept is to think of your goal in terms of getting the listeners to understand or moving the listeners to take a particular action. That is audience-based planning, and its civility makes for more successful speeches.

   Go back to the question of articulating a goal for your presentation to the school board. Your decision should be grounded in an understanding and respect for the nature of the board. Are they in a position to make a building commitment in the short term or long term? Do they need a design that will create more positive learning environments or do they just need more space for a growing population? How well informed are the board members in the area of educational architecture? Is your speech to be the sole item on the meeting agenda or are you sharing the time with routine matters of budget, curriculum, and staffing? The answers to these and related questions will guide you to a decision narrowing your goal. Take the boss's instruction to "present the firm's ideas" and change it into a narrow audience-based goal such as "for the board members to understand that our design concept meets their specific space needs in a more pedagogically sound fashion than any other plan" or "for the board members to commit to establishing a planning committee to work with our firm to refine the details of the building plan." Such a narrow goal will make your speech preparation more focused and audience-relevant, enhancing the chances of your success.

2   **Articulate your speech's thesis.** The thesis statement may be the single most important decision you make as a business speaker. The entire speech is built around that single statement. And it is your choice! The boss or the person who invited you to speak has provided the topic, but the angle that you take in developing the topic is up to you. What do you think is the overall point most appropriate for these listeners on this occasion?

Let's take the example of giving an inspirational speech at the high school graduation. Your host has asked you to speak about the importance of commitment and, given the nature of your audience, you have set the specific goal to be: "for the students to appreciate the importance of the commitments they will make in the coming few months." Now, what will your thesis be? With that goal, you could focus on several specific points, including: "Commitments are signs of maturity"; "Young adults have to commit to get fit emotionally, physically, and intellectually"; "The commitments we make in our twenties drive the success we experience in our thirties, forties, or fifties"; or even "Be committed before you *get* committed." Any one of those statements could serve as your thesis. They each fit the basic requirements of a thesis statement that you may remember from your basic speech classes because they are each single, complete sentences that provide a narrow focus and suggest a specific organizational approach for the speech. So the possible theses are equivalent in terms of their basic rhetorical character.

But what about the audience? Respect for the audience's nature should drive the choice of thesis just as it will drive every other choice you make in planning the speech. In this case, our likely audience is a couple hundred overexcited adolescents and hundreds of their family members. They have come to this event to be seen accepting the paper saying they graduated from high school. They did not come to hear the speaker. They hope, however, that the event will be fun and memorable, marking a true final highlight to their high school lives. These considerations suggest that the best thesis will be the one that can be developed in brevity, mixing a certain amount of ceremonial solemnity with a healthy dose of fun. Looking at our list of possibilities, the last one seems to fit the bill: "Be committed before you *get* committed." Write down the selected thesis on a blank piece of paper and you are well on your way to a successful graduation speech. One sentence does not a speech make, however, so what's next?

3 **Select the best overall structure for the speech.** You will recall from your basic speech courses that there are about half a dozen organizational patterns that are considered to be standard for public speeches. It is important to remember that these patterns (for example, chronological, topical, cause-effect, spatial, analogical, problem-solution) are standard only because they reflect what we understand about how listeners' brains take in and interpret messages. We choose a particular overall pattern for development of the thesis out of respect for the audience's ways of thinking.

So, at this phase of the speech preparation, look at the thesis and ask yourself which way of developing that idea will be most readily followed by the listeners. If your thesis suggests a cause-effect relationship, break it down that way, structurally. Don't impose a contrived organizational pattern on a natural order, because your listeners won't be able to follow it.

For instance, assume that you are giving a report to your board of directors about the safety problems identified at one of the company's plants. You have decided that the thesis is: "The relatively increased level of safety infractions at plant X are within a normal range for a new operation with so many entry-level employees." This thesis implies a causal connection between the inexperience of the employees and the safety problems. Your listeners will be expecting to hear about cause and effect once you have articulated that thesis. Therefore, you should plan to organize the report into two major sections, the first explaining the level and range of inexperience among employees at that plant and the second describing the specific safety issues that have resulted directly from that inexperience. It may be tempting to organize the ideas differently—say, in climactic, storytelling order. But that is not what the listeners will be expecting, and they will essentially feel offended by being asked to work to discern the causal relationships from your random tales. Instead, respect their expectations and use the organizational pattern best matching your thesis.

An additional consideration in choosing a specific organizational pattern is the need for cohesiveness or continuity. Listeners generally are not single-minded in their attention to the speaker. While you are talking about safety infractions, some of your listeners will be thinking about their child who fell off a bicycle; some will be thinking about their friend who told them about the latest safety violation and what else the friend said at the time about another employee; some will be thinking about whether that color of shirt looks good on you or not; some will be thinking about the coming lunch break; and some will be mentally "out to lunch" already. That is not because these listeners are bad listeners, but because they are human. Their minds are keeping track of a myriad of ideas at all times, and your speech is only one of them. If that speech or report is to be correctly heard and interpreted, it should be structured so that there is an obvious cohesiveness among all the ideas, allowing the listener who occasionally tunes out not to get lost on the way back in.

This concern for cohesiveness speaks again to the value of using standard organizational patterns. Listeners are accustomed to hearing things organized chronologically, spatially, topically, causally, analogically, and in the problem-solution format. If they tune out while you are on point two of your cause-effect explanation and tune back in on point four, it helps them to know that what you are saying fits somewhere in a cause-effect continuum. Choose one of those standard organizational patterns and stick to it.

Standard patterns refer to the overall structure of the major ideas of the body of the speech. Obviously, organizing the speech requires attention to a few more pieces. At this point in your planning, that blank piece of paper you started with should now have a thesis written on it and two or three major subpoints that are obviously connected via one of the standard organizational patterns. The missing pieces are the introduction and the conclusion, two brief but critical sections of the speech.

Both the introduction and the conclusion are critical because they occur at the two points when the listeners are most attentive. At the beginning of your speech, you will have listeners who are curious about what is coming and will be paying fairly open-minded attention to you. Keep in mind, however, that gift of their time. They are sitting there thinking, "This had better be good, because I've got other work to do." Similarly, at the end of the speech, they are listening closely, knowing that this is their last chance to redeem that gift of time and thinking, "What was said here that I need to remember or act on?"

A successful introduction, then, is one that captures the listeners' attention and makes them willing to listen to the rest of the message. Clearly, beginning by just stating your thesis is a really bad idea. Some creativity is needed to entice the listeners away from thoughts of their children, the office gossip, the color of your shirt, or the flavor of their lunch. Many authors would suggest to you that a good joke will accomplish that goal. And it just may, but jokes are not always the best option and there are other good alternatives. It depends on the nature of your listeners—again and again, we come back to that same criterion.

Do you know the listeners well enough to know the nature of their sense of humor? Are your listeners relatively homogeneous or extremely diverse? How well do they know you? Is your topic one that they are already curious about? Answering such questions will give you a sense of what type of introduction will work. If they already have some knowledge and curiosity about the topic, stimulating them to remember the topic's import will be a good introduction. You can do that with a real example from their frame of reference, asking them a question or two or stating a provocative quote. If they lack much knowledge and are attending this speech only because their bosses required them to do so, a little humor would be a better idea. So, first think about your listeners, then choose an introductory strategy that will respect their particular needs. The best options to choose among include: telling an anecdote, asking a rhetorical or direct question, quoting someone more famous or articulate than yourself, previewing the speech structure, or building suspense. Whichever strategy you choose, there are some guidelines that will help it to work best.

When opening with an anecdote (an interesting, detailed story that may be humorous, but not necessarily), keep it brief and relevant to the audience. Listeners will be intrigued by stories that they can relate to but bored by protracted tales of situations foreign to their experience. It would not be unreasonable to begin that safety report with the story of our young puppy who got stuck in the shrubbery on his first attempt to jump off the back deck, for instance. Many listeners have dogs and enjoy listening to stories about the humorous things they sometimes do. The story, kept to brief but colorful details, would be an attention getter. But it is also a good strategy idea because of its relevance to the thesis: "beginning employees can be expected to make mistakes that may have safety implications." It begins the speech in a way that does not point fingers at any specific managers among the listeners and shows respect for their need to spend their listening time wisely and comfortably while still setting up a clear theme for the speech.

Similarly, if you choose to ask them a question or ask them to imagine a particular scenario, make it pertinent to their actual world. Often speakers will begin by asking the listeners to close their eyes and envision themselves in a particular setting—"imagine yourself sitting in a hospital in Nepal. . . ." What ordinary person sitting in a business meeting in the United States can imagine such a scene? It is a ridiculous request that serves only to distract the listeners rather than capture their attention. Not to mention that listeners whose eyes are closed at the beginning of a speech are listeners who have just shut themselves off from any useful connection to the speaker! It is far better to ask questions or pose an imaginary scene that causes the listeners to mentally connect with you and your thesis. So instead of putting them in Nepal, ask them to remember their first year as a licensed driver or ask them if they have taken up any new hobbies lately. Such an approach will orient them to your safety thesis and help them to relate personally to the point on which you plan to focus.

Opening a speech with an articulate quote is a time-honored tradition. Dickens's opening line from *A Tale of Two Cities*, "It was the best of times, it was the worst of times,"[2] for instance, has been used to open many a business presentation. That one works well because it is brief and likely to be familiar to the listeners. Consequently, as soon as the speaker has uttered the first half of the quote, the listeners are finishing it in their own minds, thus drawing them mentally into the speaker's thesis. That introduction has perfectly and civilly accomplished the goal of any introduction. If you think a quote will work well, choose one like Dickens's that is brief and articulate. A long-winded quotation disrespects the listeners' attention span and fails to achieve the introductory goal. Equally effective is to use a quotation by a person the listeners might have reason to be curious about. Opening by saying, "To quote Dickens [or Tom Peters or Allen Greenspan or the Dixie Chicks] . . ." will attract the listeners. They know those names and wonder what you might have chosen to say about them. Respect the listeners' frames of reference in choosing an opening quote and you are more likely to get their attention.

The introductory strategy of previewing the message's structure is particularly effective for a relatively long speech to be presented to an audience that is already motivated to attend and to be attentive. The strategy simplifies their listening process and gives them a frame of reference for the material to come. For such an audience it is a very effective, purposeful strategy. If, on the other hand, your listeners are not there voluntarily, you will need a more captivating introduction than the idea preview and should choose one of the other options we have discussed. Let the listeners' attitude toward you and toward your material guide your choice.

The most unique category of introductory strategies from

which you might choose is the type that builds listener suspense. There are several specific variations of the suspense strategy, but they all have the same effect of making the listeners truly curious. For instance, a well-known professional football player became a successful motivational speaker after having gone through several years of drug abuse and incarceration. His name was so famous that when audiences heard he was going to speak, they would come, eager to hear some fascinating football stories. Knowing that was the listeners' frame of reference, he typically began his speeches with the suspense device known as an obverse iteration. With that strategy, he began by announcing that if they were here to learn about the football legends with whom he had played, they would be disappointed. He continued by listing the other football-related topics that he was *not* going to talk about. Within a short time, his listeners were really wondering what on earth he *was* going to talk about. At such a heightened level of interest is exactly where you want the listeners to be! This strategy works because it builds on a respect for the listeners' expectations.

One other important point needs to be made in that regard. If your presentation will include some "bad news" that the listeners have been expecting, include the gist of that news in the introduction.[3] To proceed in apparent ignorance of their negative expectations is perceived as the height of rudeness and will cause the listeners to dismiss your message altogether.

The final piece of the speech structure to be planned is the conclusion—the part your listeners will love the best. Realizing that you are at the end of the speech, the listeners become a little more alert, so it is a good time to remind them of your thesis. Do so with memorable brevity. A good conclusion will contain elements that stick in the listeners' minds for a while. Such "adhesiveness" could come from an interesting story, a strong quote, a reference back to your introductory idea, or a call to action. If your purpose has been informative or inspirational, the first three options will work well whereas the final option, a call to action, is best suited to a persuasive goal.

4 **Plan the development of each subordinate idea.** With the

basic speech structure planned, it is now time to think about the details. In most cases, you will be speaking about a subject with which you are extremely familiar, so there are many, many details in your storehouse of possibilities. Remembering the overriding need to respect the listeners' time and perspectives, be selective about those details.

For instance, I could explain the theories and principles of problem solving in a competitive business environment or I could tell you the story of the squirrel and the WD-40. Which would you prefer? Most listeners would be much more interested in the latter because it sounds curious and unique and would find it fairly easy to pay attention to. That is the beauty of well-chosen supporting details—they attract listeners like bees to honey.

Without further ado, let me tell you what squirrels can teach us about problem solving and how that is applicable to the business setting. We had a pole-mounted bird feeder directly outside our kitchen window and about twenty feet from a magnificent maple tree. On a nearly daily basis, we would see a fat squirrel descend from that tree and scamper across the yard and up the bird feeder pole, where he would munch on all the seeds his cheeks could hold. Wanting to preserve some of those seeds for the birds, we bought a squirrel baffle, which is slid about halfway up the feeder pole to prevent squirrels from climbing beyond that level—seemed like a good idea. The next day, we saw the squirrel jump down from the tree and make his usual trip across to the feeder. He climbed up the pole, making it only as far as the baffle and had to come back down. Not more than five minutes later, we spied him run from the tree, climb up the small shrub growing near the feeder, leap from the top of the shrub to the top of the baffle and climb up to his beloved seeds— round 1 to the squirrel! The next day, we bought a different style of baffle that seemed like it would pose a bigger challenge to the squirrel. It only took him ten minutes to figure out how to change the angle of his leap to circumvent the new baffle— round 2 to the squirrel! Having watched him for so many days, it finally dawned on us that he would find a way around any barrier and shimmy up that pole, so maybe we needed to address his shimmying ability rather than his access. It was at that point that the WD-40 solution came to mind. We sprayed the pole with the greasy oil and sat back and waited. Sure enough, along came the speedy squirrel, who leaped to the pole and did about two paw-over-paw moves before sliding back down the pole. Undaunted, he tried several more times, changing his leaping angle each time, but meeting with the same result—round 3 to the humans!

Problem solving in business is very much like this episode, a matter of two opposing forces making changes and adapting to the opponents' changes until a workable solution is derived. While that is a fairly clear principle, it is made much more memorable if developed with the squirrel story.

Stories about real people or real situations with which your listeners can identify will hold their interest and make your message more likely to accomplish its goal. Naturally, any stories told must be relevant to the thesis and should not embarrass or criticize any members of the audience. Explaining the importance of some new safety policies within the company by describing the most recent misstep by one of the actual listeners, for example, would offend not just that person but everyone seated nearby or in that person's circle of friends. The listeners' minds, therefore, would be on the degree of offense felt instead of on the safety lesson you want them to remember—by being uncivil you would have diminished listener attentiveness. Instead choose a story from another location of the company or another era, making sure it is a story with fascinating details.

In our technologically obsessed world, presentation aids are often used as a means of delivering the details. Instead of just stating a statistic, describing a situation, or listing several major points, speakers are creating slide shows using technology such as PowerPoint to present the statistic, situation, or list visually. Since some people learn better visually than aurally, that may seem like a good idea. But most business audiences are feeling oversaturated by the ubiquitous technology. A Harvard Business School guide to public speaking went so far as to refer to the "visual blight" of most PowerPoint programs.[4] Another business publication referred to the danger of a speaker being "templatized."[5]

To slide show or not to slide show: that is the twenty-first-century question.

The best answer is, of course, it depends on the audience. If, for instance, you are speaking to your staff about a new piece of equipment that they have not yet seen, a photo of the machine would be helpful and respect their need to see as well as hear your explanation. If they are quite familiar with it, don't insult them by putting a picture up on the screen. If you need the listeners to understand some complicated statistical data, respect the limits of their eyesight by putting the data in a handout rather than trying to fit too many small figures on a single slide projected during the speech. In other words, just because we have the technology available does not mean it must be used. It has become so routine and predictable that many listeners immediately tune out when the slides begin. Keep it fresh and productive by selecting only those visual images that are truly needed and respectful of your audience's existing expertise and perspectives.

If you have decided that a few PowerPoint slides will enhance the clarity and impact of your ideas, create the slides with issues of listener attention in mind. Principally, that means that each slide should be uncomplicated and brief, including very few words, if any. Bullet-point slides tend to reduce complicated issues to dangerously simplistic levels. It is better to offer the spoken explanations without the visual list of simply phrased highlights in order for the listeners to attend to your words and work to comprehend the complexity of the explanation. Additionally, avoid the slide gimmicks such as sound effects, which serve only to distract the listeners. Remember those great speeches that "changed history" mentioned earlier? None of them used PowerPoint.

By following these four steps sequentially, you will have created a well-organized and interesting speech built around the listeners. All communication scholars agree that the organization of a message is the most significant single factor in a speech's ultimate success. Careful crafting of the structure, without writing it out as a manuscript, will be time well invested.

How to Say It: Presenting the Planned Content

Have you ever heard someone described as a "born speaker"? Many people believe that some people are just naturally good at standing up in front of others to speak and some are not so good. While it is certainly is true that some individuals take to delivering speeches more comfortably than others, it does not mean that delivery cannot be learned. Anybody can learn to deliver a speech well, and everybody should.

There a few simple principles to follow that will allow you to speak with the vigor and directness that listeners demand. First and foremost, observe the principles that we have just described about preparing the content of the speech. If you are well prepared and fully familiar with the material on which your speech is based, you will experience the sense of self-confidence needed for effective delivery. Plan the ideas and know the ideas without trying to commit to exact wording of those ideas. What you are going for here is *extemporaneous* speaking, not reading from a manuscript.

Why? Again, it's all about the audience. The listeners are there on the assumption that they are going to hear from somebody who knows more about the subject than they do. You need to respect that expectation by speaking from a few brief notes that allow you to reveal your expertise and maintain relatively consistent direct contact with the listeners.

Such expert extemporaneity can be achieved simply by preparing the speech sufficiently far in advance to give yourself ample time for rehearsal. Plan the speech with some sort of outline and brief notes, then start "talking it." By that, we mean saying the speech aloud several times, preferably while walking around. Practicing that way makes the ideas, their order and detail, become more permanently affixed in your memory. You are not trying to memorize a text word-for-word, just trying to get a working familiarity with the basic flow of ideas. This method of rehearsal will encourage the fluency your listeners will be expecting while easing your own anxiety about the act of speaking.

As you rehearse and, eventually, as you present the speech, say it like you mean it. Think of the sound of ordinary conversation. It is varied and relatively vigorous. A person recounting a frustrating event, for instance, speaks somewhat rapidly with frequent pitch changes and probably with an increasing volume. That natural variety reflects the person's feelings and ought to typify the nonverbal expression of more formal presentations as well. Our voices and faces are capable of enormous variation, and a significant amount of that ought to be used in a speech. Remember that the listeners may not have been eager to hear this speech; their attention will need an occasional nudge. Your naturally vigorous voice will provide it.

Similarly, it is our nature to move physically when we speak. If you find your company's new product to be exciting, you will not be able to stand still when describing it to potential customers. Can you envision a sales director essentially saying, "This is the greatest thing since sliced bread" while standing absolutely still? It's just not going to happen! In the political arena, for example, Senator Elizabeth Dole demonstrated meaningful movement when addressing the Republican National Convention some years ago while speaking about the candidacy of her husband, Robert Dole. Because of her enthusiasm for his campaign, she broke from tradition and stepped down from the podium to give the whole speech while walking around the first few rows of listeners. With the availability of highly portable microphones, this is easy to do. More important, it provides visual confirmation to the listeners of the speaker's natural conviction about the topic. So don't fight your instincts; move around while speaking. A big part of speaking with civility is speaking with personal integrity. A moving speaker conveys that integrity.

This may seem like a very brief description of the delivery skills and choices that are best for making business presentations. The reason for its brevity is that delivery is such a personal matter that providing a prescriptive description of excellence is impossible. Jesse Jackson, Jay Leno, and Michael Eisner all have effective delivery when they speak, but they are hardly the same. Their delivery is effective because it meets the very basic standards of being vigorous, varied, and true to their individual personalities. Observing these basic principles allows them to connect with the listeners, which is the highest standard of any public speech and any attempt to communicate with civility.

Any commentary about presentation skills must include some words about words. That is, "presentation" includes choices about delivery (the nonverbal elements) as well as choices about words (the verbal elements). As we have already stated, the best extemporaneous speakers do not prepare their speeches by choosing precise wording for the entire speech, but rather choose the flow of ideas and their development, generating the actual wording in the moment of speaking.

That will work well if the speaker has a generous repertoire of words within his or her working vocabulary and is accustomed to drawing from the repertoire on a regular basis. That repertoire, of course, should include words that are varied, original, concrete, and civil.

In a public address situation, our listeners expect us to speak with a civil tongue. Any use of coarse, vulgar, or obscene terms will be perceived as an offense to their expectations, even if they themselves occasionally use such words under other circumstances. At a recent world economic conference, for instance, President Bush was clearly heard using an expletive in talking with British Prime Minister Blair about the Arab-Israeli conflict. The public was stunned, not because the word was shocking in and of itself, but rather because it was used in a formal communicative setting involving the highest level of international leaders. We are not bothered when such language is spoken by someone wearing a T-shirt and jeans and running around a neighborhood ball field, but coming out of the mouth of someone wearing a suit, starched shirt, and necktie is another story. Stunned listeners are distracted listeners, making the use of coarse language a detriment to successful communication in the public address setting.

The choices you will make in delivery and wording will be successful if they are guided by the principles of varied vigor and appropriateness to audience and situation. Wisdom in these areas comes from practice—and practice alone. You cannot get to the point of regularly speaking energetically and articulately without effort. Performance skills, in a sense, are comparable to the physical skills required for success in athletics. Everyone can appreciate that shooting foul shots in basketball requires that the feet be balanced, elbows bent, eyes on the rim, and hands poised for follow-through. But getting the ball in the basket on a regular basis requires that the shooter practice, not just know the principles. It is said that Larry Bird, one of the greatest foul shooters in NBA history, for instance, regularly took five hundred free-throw shots in daily practices from the time he was in high school until his retirement as a professional.[6] Those who simply knew the principles and had the basic skills were still good, but they were not masters. As one who strives to master public address, you will likewise need to practice being articulate and dynamic; you can't stop with just reading about it.

How to Finish It: Preparing for Questions

It is fairly typical for listeners to be granted the opportunity to ask questions immediately after the speaker has finished. Since the reality of all human communication is that errors of expression and interpretation are common, allowing the listeners to ask follow-up questions is simply respectful of the process. The listeners will perhaps want clarification of a point you have made, want more elaboration on that point, or may want to argue its validity. Whatever their goal, your goal is to provide answers that advance your own perspective while respecting their right to question or disagree. This requires some advance planning.

As you prepared the speech itself, you thought about the exact nature of the expected listeners. The same applies to planning for questions. Think ahead of time about what questions you are likely to be asked and plan your answers. Such planning will allow you to reply in a professional, clear, and articulate manner. Any leader within the energy industry today, for instance, can expect that after speaking about price increases there are going to be questions about the company's profit margin. The speaker will have anticipated the question and been able to respond briefly and fluently, revealing an intelligent sensitivity to the listeners' perspective. If the speaker is less specifically prepared, he or she is likely

Civility and government are often perceived as two diametrically opposed concepts, yet they share a common goal. The governmental bureaucracy has grown in size and complexity, posing a challenge for those who work within it as well as those who try to access its services. The bureaucracy is multifaceted, competitive for resources, tainted by political posturing, layered with security filters and gatekeepers and often serves overlapping functions. Government workers receive numerous types of training in an effort to prepare them well to deal with the citizens they serve, no matter how disgruntled those citizens can become. After all, each of us, both within and outside of government, is working toward preserving "the common good." As a government spokesperson, my speeches frequently had to find that elusive balance between civil forthrightness and national security.

On a regular basis as a military spokesperson at the Pentagon and elsewhere, I found myself in an adversarial relationship with reporters. My role was to take questions, responding when I had ready knowledge of the answer or saying "I don't know, but I will find out, sir/ma'am." No matter that some information might be difficult to obtain or risk catastrophe if shared, reporters still considered incomplete answers an attempt by the government to hide something. My answers needed to show respect for the reporters' jobs and for national security simultaneously.

(continued on next page)

(continued from previous page)

An even more challenging question-answer situation involved my interaction with ordinary citizens. On numerous occasions, I was faced with concerned citizens of the community in which I served. These encounters ranged from giving an informative presentation at an elementary school to responding to hurled epithets by protesters marching past my office. If the citizens asked embarrassing or potentially damaging questions, I had to act professionally, keeping a "civil tongue" lest I make a bad situation worse or bring shame upon the government broadly, or the military in particular.

In military operations, the podium can be another type of minefield to be traversed with careful attention to every rhetorical step.

Mel Sundin
Public Affairs Officer
United States Navy (ret.)

to answer vaguely and defensively, creating a destructive relationship with the listeners. Former Secretary of State Henry Kissinger reportedly revealed his own approach to planning for questions by opening one press conference by asking, "Does anyone have any questions for my answers?"[7] In other words, he had already given specific thought to the questions he would be asked and had planned specific answers. That is smart.

Preparing for questions should take into account that the listeners are not as well informed as you are and that, in some cases, they have their own agenda in asking the questions. As you plan, be sensitive to that while being clear about your own agenda. That energy industry official, for instance, will want to answer honestly about the company's profits, but put those numbers in the context of investments needing to be made to provide better service to the public. The questioner may have been hoping to catch the speaker admitting to some degree of corporate profiteering, but the speaker will want to deflect that effort, turning the focus back to corporate investment for future productivity.

Another tactic some listeners will use to try to advance their own agendas is to ask questions couched in hypotheticals. Again, as a speaker, be prepared for and sensitive to the concerns that drive such questions, but don't let yourself get trapped into giving an answer about a situation that hasn't actually happened. The energy official may be asked, "If gas prices increase to four dollars a gallon, will your executives return their usual bonuses?" Answering such a question in any specific terms, positively or negatively, lays the foundation for accusations of greed or poor planning later on. You cannot win. The better strategy is to prepare to refuse politely to answer some questions. The speaker can say something like "I understand the public's concern about price increases and executive compensation, but it is our hope that gas prices will not reach that point for some time." This answer is respectful of the motives behind the question but maintains the speaker's control of the agenda.

Famed political communication advisor Roger Ailes provides a good summation of our suggestions about preparing for audience questions when he asserts, "Never go to a media interview unprepared."[8] As he has recommended to corporate and political leaders alike, your preparation for public address cannot be limited to the speech itself. You must also consider the final part of your dialogue with the listeners, the questions. Know what points you want to make during the questions and what subjects you don't want to get into at all. Preparing for the questions will allow you to speak with the clarity and civility that will maintain positive relationships with your listeners and therefore increase your chances of overall communicative success.

Summary

As an aspiring business leader, you cannot avoid giving public speeches. They are part of the package in your upward mobility. Take advantage of every opportunity you have now to make speeches so that you will get comfortable with the role of speaker and the process that it takes to be successful in that role. Speaking to the local 4-H club may seem a little intimidating, but it is a starting point that will prepare you to speak later in life to the National Association of Manufacturers or a joint session of Congress. Be prepared, be wise, and be civil.

NOTES

1 *Speeches That Changed the World* (London: Smith-Davies, 2005).

2 Charles Dickens, *A Tale of Two Cities* (New York: Penguin, 2000).

3 Nick Morgan, "The Three Toughest Presentations," in *Presentations That Persuade and Motivate* (Cambridge, MA: Harvard Business School Press, 2004).

4 Judith Humphrey, "You Are the Best Visual," in *Presentations That Persuade and Motivate* (Cambridge, MA: Harvard Business School Press, 2004).

5 Brian Fugere, Chelsea Hardaway and Jon Warshawsky, *Why Business People Speak Like Idiots* (New York: Free Press, 2005), 60.

6 Larry Bird, 1989 *Drive: The Story of My Life* (New York: Bantam, 1989).

7 Cheryl Wiles, "Impromptu Speaking: The Secret Is to Prepare for Spontaneity," in *Presentations That Persuade and Motivate* (Cambridge, MA: Harvard Business School Press, 2004).

8 Roger Ailes, *You Are the Message: Getting What You Want by Being Who You Are* (New York: Doubleday, 1989), 186.

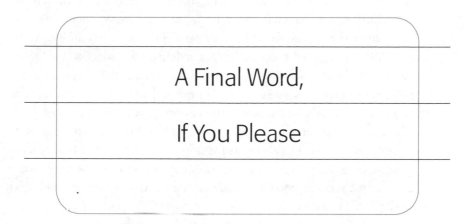

15

A Final Word,

If You Please

The word is *success*. Do you want to be a success in your chosen career? Do you want to be a part of a successful business or corporation? You probably answered "yes" to both of those questions. By now, you know that your adoption of a civil attitude toward your coworkers, supervisors, customers, and vendors will help you to achieve that desired success. You also know that a specific set of communication behaviors will convey and be perceived as conveying the respect that is at the heart of civility. Be assured that successful companies also have that civil attitude and encourage civil behavior in their employees—it is not just the opinion of your authors.

You may recall the story of the W. T. Grant Company, whose tendency to corporate incivility contributed, at least in part, to its eventual bankruptcy. Grant's was one of the first so-called upscale discount department stores, a business concept that is now a prominent part of American commerce. But they just didn't get it right.

A more successful story is found in Grant's more recent counterpart, Target Stores. Honored by *Barron's* magazine as one of the "Most Respected Companies" and enjoying revenues growing at 12 percent per year, Target is, not coincidentally, quite committed to being respectful to their employees, their shareholders, and their community.[1] With $50 billion in annual revenue, Target is definitely a success.

Certainly, we should not be so naïve as to assume that corporate commitment to civility is a guarantee for financial success, nor that there is any simple formula for success in the twenty-first-century marketplace. The situation is far too complex to be reduced to such easy answers. Business success will likely result from a combination of having at least the following components: a good product, a good sense of the target audience for the product, good financial management, good workers, and good leadership. Luck may also play a part, of course. But, as far as the success-producing factors that can be controlled, at least two of them—having good workers and good leadership—are clearly linked to the principles of civility. We see that relationship in reviewing the corporate philosophies of some of America's leading companies.

Many of the *Fortune* "100 Best Companies to Work For" stress respect for employees in their guiding principles. From manufacturing to retail to financial services and the hospitality industry, the companies sound a similar theme. Pella Windows pledges to "create an atmosphere where everyone is trusted, treated with respect and encouraged to develop to his or her full potential."[2] Starbucks employees report that their stores are successful because the product is consistently good. That simple strength results from the care taken to provide crystal-clear instructions to the workers. The result is the same cup of coffee, no matter who made it, *and* a workforce that rarely needs to be criticized because they have been treated with "respect and dignity" in the first place.[3] FedEx, which is first in job growth in the country, boasts of a philosophy centered on "a belief in the value of our employees and our commitment to treat each other with dignity and respect."[4] Aflac perhaps sums it up best in its statement of corporate culture: "The best way to succeed is to value people . . . treating employees with care, respect, dignity and fairness, creating an environment where all employees can perform at their very best."[5]

Such philosophies are not just empty words. The companies make firm commitments to carry through on these goals by evaluating potential new hires' ethical principles and providing required seminars in business ethics. At Sherwin-Williams, new employees are tested on their knowledge of business ethics, and at Edward Jones Investments, employees are regularly reminded that all their work with customers must exhibit the respect required to keep the company in compliance with federal ethics rules for the investment industry.[6]

In this context, you can see that civility is not just expected, but required.

As part of compiling the list of *Fortune*'s "100 Best Companies to Work for," employees were surveyed about their opinions of their workplace. The companies participating were all financial successes, so the magazine was looking for a perspective that goes beyond the balance sheet. If the required civility were coerced, the employees would not have evaluated the companies as they did. Clearly, in their view, the business provides them a decent pay and benefits package but also a pleasant place to work, where their opinions and needs are respected. Such attitudes translate into loyal employees and satisfied customers.

> At Smucker's, not only are ethics talked about in the interview process, but training is given involving ethics as well. Every year, all employees are expected to review the company ethics policy, sign it and submit the completed form to Human Resources.
>
> Julie Hale Abbott
> Sales and Marketing Systems
> Coordinator
> J. M. Smucker Company
> Cleveland, OH

The civility of these successful companies is also evident in their sense of corporate citizenship. Most create opportunities for their employees to volunteer as a group for community projects in addition to making significant financial contributions on the corporate level. We were talking earlier about the success of Target. Did you know that they commit 5 percent of all their pretax revenue to community charities? Through this mechanism Target has helped build a veterans' memorial, increased literacy of urban youths, and made significant contributions to environmental conservation efforts.[7] And it is not alone. Wegman's grocery stores, whose corporate philosophy states the belief that "good people working together toward a common goal can accomplish anything," gave community food banks 14 million pounds of food in 2005.[8] Another of *Fortune*'s best, Marriott Hotels, embraces a corporate commitment it calls a "Spirit to Serve" philosophy that has driven the company to part-

In 2003, Channellock implemented what has quickly become a nationally recognized employee enrichment and involvement initiative called the Falcon Program. It brings into focus those things that matter most to people beyond a paycheck every other week: recognition of efforts on and off the clock; the love of family and community; self-improvement; convenience and cost savings. The program includes five different specific rewards and incentives that help to create loyal and hardworking employees.

A blacksmith forged a standard for the appreciation of people in founding the company in 1886 and today that standard is borne on the wings of a falcon. Times may change, but the value of people respecting one another is timeless.

Randy Ferguson
Director of Communication
Channellock, Inc.
Meadville, PA

ner with Red Cross, Red Crescent, Children's Miracle Network, Habitat for Humanity, America's Second Harvest, and the United Way.[9] Such far-reaching and generous charity is an obvious outgrowth of a fundamental sense of corporate civility.

With such plentiful and exemplary corporate role models, those individuals and businesses looking for factors that will enhance their own or their corporate success need not look much further. As the retail industry has proven time and time again: all other things being equal, customers will shop at the store that treats them well. Whether the "customer" is a nation shopping for locomotives, a business shopping for an insurance partner, or a mom shopping for children's school shoes, civility matters. It is not just a nice treat if you can get it; civility is a necessity in today's business world. "As far as commercial organizations are concerned, their overriding objective is to maximize profits . . . and that commercial success depends substantially on the goodwill they have generated and can generate among their customers."[10]

As the analysts at CNN/Money point out, we are in a new era in American business. Old rules driven by shareholder values are being superseded by a focus on customer satisfaction that requires companies to hire and promote caring, passionate people.[11]

Adopt the attitude of respecting others and their ideas and practice the specific communication behaviors described here that convey that respect. The result will be success—yours on a personal level and the company's on the corporate level.

NOTES

1 Target Stores (available at: http://sites.target.com/image/corporate/aboutpdfs/ 2005_annual_report.pdf).

2 Pella Windows and Doors (available at: http://www.pella.com/careers/default.asp).

3 Starbucks Coffee Company (available at: http://starbucks.co.uk/en-GB/_About+Starbucks/Mission+Statement.htm).

4 FedEx (available at: http://home.businesswire.com/portal/site/fedex-corp/index).

5 Aflac (available at: http://www.aflac.com/us/en/careers/CorporateCulture.aspx).

6 Mark Modlo (manager, Edward Jones Investments), personal correspondence, July 2006.

7 Target Stores, op cit.

8 Wegman's Food Markets, Inc. (available at: http://www.wegmans.com/about/ pressRoom/overview.asp).

9 Marriott Hotels (available at: http://go.marriott.com/careers/Benefits.mi).

10 J. Essinger and H. Wylie, *The Seven Deadly Skills of Competing* (London: International Thomson Business Press, 1999), ix.

11 Betsy Morris, "Tearing up the Jack Welch Playbook," *CNN/Money,* July 2006 (available at: http://cnnmoney.printhtis.clickability.com/11).

Index